YORK HANDBOOKS

GENERAL EDITOR:
Professor A.N. Jeffares
(*University of Stirling*)

THE
VICTORIAN AGE
OF LITERATURE

Harry Blamires
MA (OXFORD)
*Former Head of the English Department,
King Alfred's College, Winchester*

LONGMAN
YORK PRESS

YORK PRESS
Immeuble Esseily, Place Riad Solh, Beirut.

LONGMAN GROUP UK LIMITED
Longman House, Burnt Mill, Harlow,
Essex CM20 2JE, England
and Associated Companies throughout the World.

First published 1988

ISBN 0 582 96605 1

Produced by Longman Group (FE) Ltd
Printed in Hong Kong

Contents

Preface

The first aim of this book is to sum up the achievements of the writers whose work gave the literature of the Victorian age its richness and diversity. The second aim is to set this account of Victorian literature in the context of any historical developments, political or social, religious or scientific, philosophical or aesthetic, which were especially relevant to it. Any notion of satisfying these two aims separately or sectionally would be absurd. It is when we explore the works of novelists, poets, dramatists and prose writers, and trace the connections between them, that the manners and ethos of the Victorian age, its social conditions and its movements of thought come fully alive for us today. There are some preliminary observations in the introductory section of this book about the public scene in the Victorian age, the technological developments, the social and political changes and the challenges to traditional habits and beliefs which new thinking provoked, but the substantial exploration of these issues emerges in the subsequent study of the individual writers themselves. Accounts of their lives and works are designed both to give a direct impression of what has earned them their place in literary history, and to clarify aspects of their experience and their output which notably reveal their age and reflect its attitudes.

February 1987

HARRY BLAMIRES

Part 1

Introduction: the Victorian scene

The character of the age

The word 'Victorian' carries rich associations. Among them is the notion of magnitude. The Victorian age was for Great Britain physically an age of immense power. It was the age in which the British Empire attained its maximum size and significance. Victorian novelists speak naturally of London as the world's capital and of the Houses of Parliament as the world's most powerful and prestigious legislature. Within the British Isles achievements in engineering, in the construction and development of railways and steamships, similarly impress by their vastness. And the splendour and wealth of the country houses and estates in the hands of the landed aristocracy and of newly rich industrial magnates have for us an awesomely gigantic excess.

Victoria's reign itself was of monumental duration. She came to the throne, a girl of seventeen, in 1837 and died in 1901 nearly sixty-four years later. A label given to so long a stretch of history cannot be exact in its connotation. In our own century we know what we mean by 'the thirties' or 'the sixties', but we should have to survey a period taking in the reigns of Edward VII, George V, Edward VIII, George VI and the first dozen years of the reign of Elizabeth II if we wished to look back over a period of comparable duration to the Victorian age. International upheavals and vast changes in social conditions and technology would prevent us from picturing any six or seven decades of the twentieth century as an 'Age' with a character of its own. Similarly any notion of uniformity of social conditions or material environment or of attitudes and thought over a period so long as the reign of Victoria would be absurd.

The Queen herself went through different phases in her relationship with her people. At the time of her coronation people wondered whether so outmoded an institution as the monarchy could possibly outlive her. For some, republicanism seemed to be the only possible form of government for the future. Yet by the time Victoria died the monarchy was stronger than it had been for over a hundred years. In herself she epitomised what have loosely become known as the 'Victorian' virtues. She was conscientious and hard-working, *mercy*

she had an unflinching sense of duty and a total respect for moral proprieties. She married her cousin, Prince Albert of Saxe-Coburg-Gotha, in 1840 and it was an extremely happy marriage. As a devoted wife and mother of a large family Victoria set a standard of solid homely virtues that appealed especially to the middle classes. She was not in the least an intellectual, but her common sense and her attachment to simple indoor pleasures and outdoor pursuits helped to shed glamour on a wholesome way of life admired by those too modestly placed to share the extravagances of the aristocracy and too well rewarded for their honest labours to share any of the appalling privations of the numerous poor. While not being notably gifted with vision or imagination, the Queen embodied a plain common sense which the most influential body of her subjects admired. Disraeli (1804–81) himself once said, 'If ever I want to know what the middle-classes are thinking, I always ask Her Majesty's opinion.'

Many details of Victorian social life and conditions will come to light as the reader explores the literature of the period in the following chapters. Nevertheless a word may be said in advance about that quality to which the label 'Victorian' is now so frequently applied – the reticence about sexual matters, the supposed prudery, the seemingly absurd evasion of the facts of life which 'Victorian morality' has been assumed to entail. Of course, the very strict regulation of what could properly be put into print is a separate issue from the regulation of public manners or morals. Thomas Bowdler (1754–1825) had published his ruthlessly expurgated edition of Shakespeare in 1818 and bequeathed us the verb 'to bowdlerise'. Delicacy and reticence in reference to anatomical or sexual matters predated the Victorian era as readers of Scott (1771–1832) or Jane Austen (1775–1817) will realise. It is too easily forgotten that a common middle-class practice was for the family to sit together through long dark evenings while one member read aloud to the rest. What was heard must not be embarrassing to a mixed gathering in which the youngest daughter might take her turn to read.

As for life itself, it is self-evident that husbands and wives who produced families so large as the Victorian families were not inhibited in their sexual behaviour behind the bedroom door. Whether the restraints laid especially upon young women took their character more from a sentimentalisation of feminine purity or from some hidden sense of the havoc which the unfettered feminine libido might wreak on a stable male-dominated society is a matter for the philosophers. The student of Victorian literature, however, should recognise the changing phases in the history of Victorian morality. The Queen's reign began with a seemingly conscious reaction against the moral looseness, the dissipations and debaucheries of the preceding decades. The coarseness and grossness of aristocratic manners and conduct during the Regency had been notorious. Overeating, drunkenness and sexual libertinism had been rampant among the wealthy under the Regency and in the reigns of George IV (1762–1830) and William IV (1765–1837). The pendulum of public opinion was no doubt swinging anyway when the new Queen began to set the standard of sobriety and respectability which was, superficially at least, to characterise much of her reign. There came a point, however, when her public influence was vastly reduced. Her happiness was shattered when Prince Albert died in 1861. She retired into seclusion. She virtually disappeared from the public scene. Before her bereavement she had come more and more to depend upon Albert's judgement and guidance. With his death she threw herself into a period of profound and prolonged mourning. It was said that his rooms at Windsor were preserved as they had been during his lifetime and that clothes were daily laid out for him as though he still lived. On the wedding day of Edward, the Prince of Wales (1841–1910), bride and bridegroom had to be photographed beside the bridegroom's mourning mother with her gaze fixed on the bust of the deceased father. The royal withdrawal from public life and loss of touch with society played a part indirectly in the decline in moral standards which eventually set in and led to the laxities of the 'naughty nineties'. More important no doubt was the influence of the Prince of Wales, who was denied that share in royal consultations and decision-making which would have given him a serious purpose in life. Victoria distrusted him: indeed she associated Albert's early death in part with the anxieties Edward's conduct had caused him. The Prince's recourse to a life of pleasure and dissipation certainly helped to erode moral standards in society life.

The Queen's determination to mourn for a lifetime inevitably produced a wave of unpopularity, but in her last years public esteem for her increased dramatically. She gradually resumed occasional public appearances, and when the time came for the celebration of her Diamond Jubilee in 1897 popular enthusiasm greeted the magnificent occasion with acclamation. She was loved as a lonely widow and revered as sovereign of what was now the mightiest empire the world had ever known, the empire on which the sun never set.

The coming of the railways

Of all the developments that transformed life in the Victorian age the growth of the railways is probably the most fascinating. Their construction was, of course, only one facet of a vast increase in industrial expansion. The expansion produced a new class of wealthy magnates who had made their money from constructing canals or railways, from mining coal or iron, from building steamships, from equipping factories with up-to-date machinery, and from the manufacture of textiles and other goods in the massive new mills serviced by the populace of the growing industrial cities. The novels of the age make clear that the newly rich industrialists were not readily accepted by the landed aristocracy as their equals, or even as fit to share their social life in the way that the local parson might. Nevertheless the same developments that produced the industrial barons enriched many landowners too, if only because deposits of iron or coal were discovered under their estates or because a railway company sought to buy a strip of their land essential to a planned route. In many Victorian novels the sudden loss or acquisition of wealth is crucial to the plot. Transformation of people's financial position was common enough when financiers and entrepreneurs were gambling in railway shares or competing for the possession of land which was suspected, but not proven, to lie on a likely railway route or to be rich in deposits of coal or iron ore.

The Stockton and Darlington railway was opened in 1825, and by 1850 the country was covered with a railway network which seems to us now to have been a mammoth engineering achievement. The work had been done by teams of navvies ('navigators') employed by contractors to dig the cuttings and pile up the embankments, to drill the tunnels and lay the track. They moved from one encampment to another, creating sensational problems in the rural areas they invaded. It was a rough life they led and they were coarse labourers, often from Ireland. They were preceded in their invasion of remote villages by visitants of a very different calibre, the surveyors and engineers and technical experts whose duty it was to inspect the terrain and map out the route. We see something of the effects of this invasion in Mrs Gaskell's novel, *Cousin Phillis* (1864).

In Victorian fiction of the succeeding decades a reader can trace the decline of the stage coach and also of travel by sea between England and Scotland, and the increasing use of the railways. By the time Anthony Trollope's maturer novels of the 1870s were issued the world of, say, Dickens's early novels of the 1830s was beginning to seem very remote in that, by the 1870s, totally different standards of mobility applied. Lady Eustace takes only two days to travel between London and her home in the Scottish Highlands in *The Eustace Diamonds* (1873): she chooses to break her journey and spend a night in a hotel at Carlisle. By the time we reach *The Duke's Children* (1880), the last of Trollope's Palliser novels, society people are darting about the country between country houses in the north and the south, and Lord Silverbridge takes his American bride for a honeymoon in the United States. When Queen Victoria first came to the throne it would have taken a month to cross the Atlantic by sail. The first steamship made the journey in twelve days in 1842 and a screw-propeller – a major innovation – was fitted to *The Great Britain* in 1845. It seems odd that, while steel passenger-liners were taking over the sea-routes, the Royal Navy was still equipped with wooden vessels at the start of the Crimean War in 1854. The construction of larger steamships created a demand for larger docks and deeper waters. As a result, some of the older ports, such as Bristol, and many of the smaller ports scattered round the coast began to decline. London and Liverpool grew in importance as a consequence. The old arch which gave the entrance to Euston station such magnificence is a monument to the fact that here was the doorway to the New World, for it was via Euston and Liverpool that passengers travelled to and from the United States. It was said that at the time of Queen Victoria's death ten per cent of the world's shipping came from Liverpool.

Steam travel operated only between ports and between railway stations. The need to travel between home and station meant that few journeys could be undertaken without horse-transport. The railways solved the problem of long-distance travel and emptied many trunk roads, but the gentry and the well-to-do still needed to keep or hire their coaches or cabs. London streets remained chockful with horse-drawn vehicles of every kind and often ankle-deep in manure until the motor-car came along. No doubt every market town was the same, but the demise of long-distance coach traffic cut off many hamlets where previously horses had been changed and refreshments taken. 'Deserted, lonely highway!' Thus Arthur Norway apostrophises the Great North Road in *Highways and Byways in Yorkshire*, published in 1899. He is surveying the Great North Road just south of Doncaster, re-calling what it was in the heady days of coach traffic before Doncaster became a major railway town on the main line from London to Edinburgh. The few years during which the A1 was a deserted, lonely highway mark off Victoria's age from our own with a stark clarity.

Upper-class attitudes

Rail travel catered rigidly for the class-system of Victorian society. The railway companies provided drawing-room comfort in the first-class carriages and what were virtually cattle-trucks for the third-class passengers. The hiring of a private first-class coach for a journey was common. We need only to peep inside the luxurious interior of Queen Victoria's saloon carriage on the royal train preserved in the National Railway Museum at York to glimpse why the wealthy readily took to travel by rail. Class-distinctions were also preserved *en route* from country house to railway station. E. F. Benson (1867–1940), in his book of Victorian memories *As We Were* (1930), lists among the notable eccentricities of the celebrated society figure, Lady Dorothy Nevill, the fact that she refused to have Lady Radnor's carriage ordered to take her to the station after a weekend visit to her home at Cookham. Lady Nevill felt that as a cab would also be required to transport her maid and her luggage, she might just as well join her maid in the cab and so avoid the trouble of having to look for the maid at the station. So extreme were Lady Nevill's 'eccentricities'. In such memoirs as Benson's we get a picture of society life and the attitudes it engendered which to the twentieth-century mind seem remote indeed. The massive parties at stately homes and the magnificent London dinners were presided over by indomitable hostesses who devoted great energy to the task. As many of them revelled in acquiring literary lions at their tables, their efforts impinged on the lives of writers such as Tennyson (1809–92) and Browning (1812–89), Thackeray (1811–63) and Henry James (1843–1916). A kind of cameraderie developed among the socially accepted. That the Victorians could laugh at themselves in this respect is evident from a story which went the rounds in connection with one of the most brilliant of Victorian hostesses, Lady St Helier, a story preserved by E. F. Benson. It tells how a famous explorer who had been her guest fell into the hands of a cannibal tribe in Africa. He was tied to a tree while 'a message was sent to the cannibal king that there was a juicy young English traveller ready for the royal larder'. When the hungry king arrived, with sharpened appetite, the sight of the captive took him aback. ' "Surely we met at Lady St Helier's," he exclaimed in excellent English, "I owe you a thousand apologies for the inconvenience you have suffered. You and I will dine together on the wretch who tied you up. Kill him at once. How is her ladyship?" '

No doubt one reason why the English aristocracy retained its grip so long is that its ranks were not closed to new entrants as the French nobility was. As the new industries threw up men of newly acquired wealth, the magnates felt the incentive to buy for their sons the education which would give them an entry into high society and compensate for their own failure to gain recognition. As landowners got into difficulties through their extravagance or simply through the demands on their purses made by numerous sons to place and daughters to marry off, the newly rich of the industrial world inevitably came to the rescue, marrying into the class which could no longer afford to despise them openly. The plots of many Victorian novels reflect this social development. Thus the new rich might be represented as worthy (see Disraeli's *Sybil* (1845)) or as comically absurd (see Dickens's (1812–70) *Our Mutual Friend* (1865)). Yet Dickens had himself risen from poverty to affluence by the exercise of his own skills. Indeed when Jane Carlyle, wife of the writer Thomas Carlyle (1795–1881), went to dinner with Dickens she found the lavish display 'unbecoming to a literary man'.

Social conditions and social progress

Much of the new wealth was made for employers by the toils of workers in whose working and living conditions they showed not the slightest interest. We must not exaggerate the difference between the old landowners and the new factory owners in this respect. No doubt there were plenty of well-run estates where resident landowners took a personal interest in the welfare of their tenants and retainers, but of course there were others where the landowner was as remote from his tenants as the mill-hands were from the boss whose pockets they filled. The very nature of Victorian technology, so heavily dependent on coal and steam, on chimneys belching out smoke from morning to night, guaranteed a filthy environment for the masses who kept its machinery ticking over. In the days before town-planning, mill-owners and mine-owners threw lines of cramped terrace houses across the landscape. In the big cities squalid tenements over-ridden by viaducts from which trains poured out clouds of smoke have survived, in many cases, to our own day. No one who reads Dickens can be unaware of the alleys and basements, filthy and insanitary, in which the London poor were imprisoned. The crumbling buildings, the bare furnitureless rooms, the damp, the lack even of clothes and warmth, and the appalling overcrowding were natural breeding-grounds of disease and vice. Infant mortality was high, and Victorian parents seem to have expected that they were likely to lose some of their children by death. Prostitution flourished. Drunks littered the streets. It seems scarcely surprising that they did when we read that in 1849 'off Oxford Street, Portman Square, a single court, only twenty-two feet wide, with a common sewer down the middle, housed nearly a thousand human beings in twenty-six three-storied houses. Further east it was no better, for in Wapping the courtyards were deep with filth like pig-sties, in which ragged, starving, and often naked children crawled in their search for vegetable parings and offal among the refuse.' So writes Sir Charles Petrie in *Great Beginnings in the Age of Queen Victoria*.

The conditions in the rows of back-to-back houses thrown up in the northern industrial cities were little better. The Industrial Revolution had pulled population from rural areas into towns that expanded at an enormous rate. By the early years of Victoria's reign the textile industry in particular had made vast fortunes for the manufacturers out of the misery and privations of the poor. Child-labour was tolerated to what was an intolerably inhuman extent. Droves of pauper children were handed over to the mill-owners to work in shifts and sleep in prentice-houses. In 1844 it was estimated that in some areas of Lancashire over three-quarters of the hands in the cotton mills were under eighteen and over half were women and girls. The working day could well last from 5 a.m. to 8 p.m. with brief breaks for breakfast and dinner. Saturday was a working day too.

The Victorian conscience was gradually disturbed by these inhumanities, and writers such as Dickens and Charles Kingsley (1819–75) played their part in disturbing it. The Factory Act of 1847, known as the 'Ten Hours Bill', limited the daily working hours of women and youths in the textile industry, and thereby of the men too, since female-labour and child-labour were necessary to the working process. The limitations imposed by this Act were later extended to cover other industries. Lord Shaftesbury's Mines Act of 1842 had already banned the underground employment of women and of children under ten; but it was not until 1875 that Shaftesbury managed to get a truly effective ban on the use of little boys as chimney sweeps, for the Chimney-sweepers Act of 1864, passed after the publication of Charles Kingsley's *The Water-Babies* ('1863), was not rigorously applied. In respect of public health and sanitation government action, in hindsight, seems to have been belated indeed. G. M. Trevelyan notes in his *English Social History* that 'the worst period for sanitary conditions in the industrial regions was the middle of the Nineteenth Century rather than the beginning, because so many of the new houses had then had time to become slums, since no one repaired or drained them as the years went by'. Liverpool had the greatest density of population in the country and its death-rate was correspondingly high. The city took the lead in 1846 in appointing a Medical Officer of Health who, within a year, had condemned five thousand cellars as unfit for human habitation. The Public Health Act of 1848 laid down principles without making action compulsory, and it was only slowly that the connection between such diseases as cholera and typhoid, and inadequate or non-existent sanitation was understood, and practical action taken to deliver clean water to the cities and establish adequate sewage and drainage systems. A writer who did much towards stirring the social conscience in this respect was Henry Mayhew (1812–87) who investigated the conditions of those lowest placed in London society in his survey, *London Labour and the London Poor*, which began to appear in the press in 1849 and was published in book form in four volumes in

1861–2. It is a lively and sensitively observant record of researches, rich in factual detail. It was followed by studies of criminals and prisons.

As the Victorians were gradually driven to grapple with the need for sewage systems and for clean water supply, so too they tackled the need for an educated public. When Queen Victoria came to the throne less than half the country's children had any schooling, and those who had for the most part left school by the age of ten or twelve. On the whole such schools that existed to provide primary education for the people at large were Voluntary schools run by private subscription under Church patronage. 'The National Society for the Education of the Poor' ran Church of England schools, and 'The British and Foreign Schools Society' ran undenominational schools for Dissenters; while in Ireland there was the National school system, established in 1833. It was not until 1870 that Gladstone's (1809–98) Education Bill, the work of W. E. Forster, gave substantial grants to Church schools and at the same time set up Board schools financed from local rates to fill up the gaps left by the provision of Voluntary schools. Thus primary education became universal before the end of the century.

There were some areas in which reform was particularly slow-moving. At the turn of the century only about a sixth of the population had the vote in parliamentary elections. The 1832 Reform Bill had begun the assault on the powers of the wealthy landowners, who filled the House of Commons with their nominees, by extending the franchise to 'ten-pound householders'. This represented a modest improvement. Readers of Victorian novels know how long it took to weaken the power of landowners, to have their chosen nominees 'elected' without opposition or to bribe their way to a seat. The impetus to further reform came from the Chartist movement, that is from the supporters of a People's Charter drawn up in 1838, who sought improvement in working and living conditions through parliamentary reform and demanded universal male suffrage, secret ballots and equal electoral constituencies. The Chartists presented their Charter to Parliament without success and eventually extremists gave a violent revolutionary character to the movement. There were disturbances and moderate opinion was alienated. A challenging demonstration planned in London in 1848 petered out when the government banned the procession and Wellington posted troops to guard the capital. It was twenty years later, in 1868, that a Reform Bill gave the vote to the working classes, and the secret ballot, which did most to put an end to bribery, was established in 1872.

The House of Commons continued throughout the century to include a strong body of landowners and a fair number of barristers and solicitors. The pendulum swung between the two parties, the Conservatives and the Liberals. The Prime Minister might come from either the House of Commons or the House of Lords. If he came from the Lords his main spokesman in the Commons would have an almost comparable status. The Conservative Prime Minister Benjamin Disraeli especially won the confidence of the Queen, whom he flattered with a gallantry and tact which she found irresistible. By contrast, William Ewart Gladstone, the Liberal Prime Minister, a man given neither to flattery nor to flippancy, somehow rubbed her up the wrong way for all his gravity and integrity. She complained that he talked to her as though she were a public meeting. The two rivals dominated the political scene for nearly twenty years between 1868 and 1886, and Gladstone returned to power for two years at the age of eighty-three in 1892.

The status of women

Among the major social developments of the Victorian age was the change effected in the status of women. Many women and girls worked in factories, where legislation gradually ameliorated conditions, but domestic service occupied a much larger body of women than the factories. In the large households there were many grades of domestic servant, and not all were downtrodden. Wilful cooks or stubborn coachmen could make themselves a nuisance to their masters or mistresses if special dishes were required or the carriage was called for late at night. Victorian issues of *Punch* contain plenty of jokes about the problems created by stupid or obstreperous servants. Middle-class households of modest means employed servants as a matter of course. In Harriet Martineau's (1802–76) novel *Deerbrook* (1839) encroaching poverty has to reach a very menacing stage before the ladies of the household take the desperate step of actually dismissing the last paid girl and tackling the chores themselves.

Among the wealthy the lady's maid would travel with her mistress and often became her confidante. Even dressing and undressing in an inn required assistance. The complexities of female finery at the time made preparation for a dinner or a ball a labour-intensive occupation. Here is one of the extreme contrasts that characterise the age: the sweated labour of ill-paid seamstresses was the other side of the coin to the luxurious magnificence of women's dresses, and the ever-available attentions of the ladies' maids were the other side of the coin to the perfection of toilette in those splendid entries into drawing-room or dining-room.

In considering the treatment of ladies' maids or kitchen girls we must remember that it is not primarily a question of the status of women that is at issue, for male servants such as footmen and valets were required to be no less obsequious and self-effacing. E. F.

Benson tells how the Duchess of Devonshire was one day showing two guests the countryside around her Wharfedale home. As she climbed into the carriage one of the horses shifted and the coachman checked it, but the sudden slight movement was enough to cause the Duchess to be thrown forward to her knees. 'Without a word she hit her coachman smartly over the back with her stick, and then seating herself said to her companions, "As I was just saying . . . " '

There is clearly no question of male domination and female subservience when a Duchess treats a coachman as most people would not treat a dog. Indeed the peculiar status of women in Victorian society was certainly not a matter of undervaluing the sex. On the contrary it was, in some respects, a matter of over-valuing them. The idealised heroines of Victorian fiction are worshipped by their suitors with extravagant adoration and cherished by their fathers and brothers with a devoted protectiveness. Their very wrappings, if their clothes and accoutrements can be so described, proclaim their inestimable value as things too precious to be handled with anything other than the maximum respect and delicacy. Intelligent women, however, do not want to be mere *objets d'art*, and we can trace in Victorian fiction the rebellious movement among women which sprang from acute feminine awareness of talents unemployed and led eventually to the transformation of women's status in our own century. And it is not just in the work of women novelists such as George Eliot (1819–80) and Charlotte Brontë (1816–55) that spirited womanhood stakes its claims but in portraiture such as that of Diana Warwick in Meredith's (1828–1909) *Diana of the Crossways* (1885).

One taxing problem was the limitations on the aspirations of educated women in a society where public and professional spheres were closed to them. The post of governess, or school-teacher, was just about the only conceivable occupation open to restless young women like the Brontë sisters. The nineteenth-century replacement of eighteenth-century cottage industries and individual craftsmanship by the mass-production of the city factories separated middle-class men from their womenfolk. Middle-class girls were brought up to occupy themselves in reading and sewing, painting and music, and in so doing to acquire a smattering of culture that would give them something to talk about with men. For men expected, in female company, to lay aside any interest in the graver matters of life and relax from all concern with business or politics into a mental world of drugged make-believe, which the precious things were supposed to wish to inhabit. Female dress in the days of the crinoline sacrificed utility to decorativeness. What could a woman do, so garbed? She had to be ornamental. Well-to-do girls were brought up to find a suitable husband. Marriage presented the only social ladder for aspiration to climb. 'To get ready for the marriage market a girl was trained like a race-horse. Her education consisted of showy accomplishments designed to ensnare young men.' Thus Thackeray described Miss Pinkerton's academy in *Vanity Fair* (1848).

The emotional core of many Victorian novels is the anxiety and even agony caused by the convention that imposed the maximum reticence upon women about their own feelings. Plots often revolve around the limitations and inhibitions of the female role. In the early decades of Victoria's reign the husband acquired absolute rights over the property of his wife and indeed over her person in so far as it was her duty to obey him in all things. The situation was such that by marrying a woman of some means a man might be sufficiently enriched to be able to keep a mistress in a separate establishment on what his wife had brought him. The Matrimonial Causes Act first made divorce possible in 1857. (Previously only an Act of Parliament could dissolve a marriage.) But only with the passing of the Married Woman's Property Act of 1882 did it become possible to ensure that a woman's property did not automatically become her husband's when she married.

The age and its literature

Great Britain's international status reached its peak in the Victorian age. By the time of the Queen's Diamond Jubilee in 1897, when Britain ruled a fifth of the habitable world, the celebrations took on an unparalleled splendour from the uniforms of troops drawn from every quarter of the vast empire. We should expect the literature of such an age to reflect something of the confidence of the imperial era, and indeed when novelists such as Trollope (1815–82) touch on the sphere of parliamentary debate and cabinet government, awareness of London as the paramount world power seems to be assumed. There was indeed reason for national self-satisfaction. The British Isles had not suffered during the Queen's long reign events as cataclysmic as the two world wars which have overshadowed the literature of the twentieth century. Neither the Crimean War of 1854–6 nor the Indian Mutiny of 1857–9 produced great literary repercussions such as we associate in our own century with its disasters and upheavals. Dion Boucicault (1820–90) was quick to stage a play, *Jessie Brown*, about the Relief of Lucknow in 1858, a year after the events treated, and Tom Robertson (1829–71) took his audience to a military outpost near Balaclava in his play, *Ours* (1866), within ten years of the Crimean War; but English literature is for the most part concerned with matters nearer home. Events in Ireland, especially the potato famine of 1845, which reduced the national population from eight to five millions, seem to have had a far profounder and more extensive influence on the literature produced in these islands. It was to be left to the second half of the twentieth century to produce a substantial literature of the British Raj in India.

In many respects Victorian literature very faithfully represents the age. Certainly the literature is remarkable for its magnitude, its spaciousness. When the novelist Hugh Walpole (1884–1941) called Anthony Trollope's novel *He Knew He Was Right* (1869) 'Trollope's *Timon of Athens*' he made an equation between a seven-hundred page Victorian novel and a five-act Elizabethan play. Trollope's novel displays the domestic grief caused by a man of wilful, inflexible temperament, obsessively possessive and masterful. Shakespeare's play shows a hero's lavish generosity converted by the experience of ingratitude into embittered misanthropy. Hugh Walpole's comparison between the two works equates the thoroughness, expansiveness and comprehensiveness of Trollope's fictional record with the compact intensity of Shakespeare's play. The comparison is not unnatural. Plays such as *Hamlet* and *Twelfth Night* spring to mind when there is talk of 'Elizabethan literature', while novels such as *David Copperfield* (1850) and *Vanity Fair* spring to mind when there is talk of 'Victorian literature'. A few moments spent with a pocket-calculator would inform us exactly how many *Hamlets* one would have to write in order to pen as many words as *David Copperfield* contains. The achievements of the great Victorian novelists, Dickens, George Eliot, Hardy (1840–1928), Trollope, Meredith and Thackeray, represent a body of literature overwhelming in its sheer vastness and variety. The poets, too, believed it a duty to produce works of epic dimensions, such as Tennyson's *Idylls of the King* (1889) and Browning's *The Ring and the Book* (1869).

The spirit of the Victorian age seems to be notably reflected in its literature when the output is viewed in its place in English literary history; for it is technically a literature of confidence, spaciousness and consolidation. That is to say, after the vast experimentation of the poetry of the Romantic age and the extraordinary innovations of literary presentation and imaginative range that produced Scott's Waverley Novels, Victorian poets and Victorian novelists were content to consolidate the ground gained, enriching inherited forms, lyrical and narrative, with all manner of fresh substance. It is substance derived from a detail of observation and a clarity of human penetration beyond the reach of any but the very greatest geniuses of previous ages. To reflect on the imaginative scope and human insight revealed in the great works of the major Victorian novelists and poets is firstly to be overawed by the magnitude of the achievement. The output of the period represents a vast phase of consolidation falling between the turbulent upheavals of the Romantic

Revival and the restless experimentation of the twentieth-century modernist movement. But this is only half the story. One cannot look far into Victorian literature without sensing the inner unease and dissatisfactions of minds sensitive to the challenge to traditional religion presented by the developments of science. Nor can one evade the disquiet of conscience before the spectacle of accumulating exploitation and injustice that imperialist capitalism bred.

The Victorian novel represents the full flowering of the literary form which Fielding (1707–54) launched on its course and Scott so richly diversified. The Victorian novelists still occupy an eminence from which twentieth-century novelists have been unable to dislodge them. The diversity of social levels represented in their fiction, the range of backgrounds vividly depicted, and the fullness of human portraiture brought to life, give us a feeling for the age which responds to what is dynamic as well as to what is static in its ways of life and thought. For however firm the outer framework of life, however equable or sure the novelist's surveyal of his world, the reader who enters the hearts and minds of the Victorian heroes and heroines, their relations, their friends and their enemies, can never wholly escape the intrusion, whether fully recognised, faintly recognised, or totally ignored in the text itself, of crucial social and moral problems whose solution was destined to transform their world; issues such as those of class-division, sexual behaviour, feminine subservience, parental authority, poverty and wealth, exploitation and injustice, and the validity of traditional Christian faith and practice.

Thus the massive fabric of Victorian literature, with all its marks of confident achievement, is, like the age itself, shot through with threads of unease and undermined by threats of change. There is no need to anticipate or repeat in summary here what will inevitably emerge from surveying the literature itself about the great movements of change or renewal which swept through the minds of thinking people. Such developments as the impact of Darwinism on traditional Christian belief, the impact of the Anglo-Catholic revival on the life of the Church of England, or the impact of the Pre-Raphaelite movement and the subsequent Aesthetic movement on the country's art and literature, are all best sensed and understood from within the lives and works of the writers who experienced them. It would be unthinkable to survey the significance of Tennyson or Matthew Arnold (1822–88), of Dante Gabriel Rossetti (1828–82) or William Morris (1834–96), of Newman (1801–90) or Charles Kingsley without examining the movements of thought which possessed them or which they rejected. That the Victorian age was an age of intellectual exploration as well of imaginative abundance will emerge clearly from all that follows.

Part 2

The Victorian novel \

Charles Dickens

Charles Dickens (1812–70) has a predominance among Victorian novelists because of the magnitude of his artistic achievement and because of the comprehensiveness of the picture it gives of his age. Indeed the prodigality of Dickens's output earns him a place beside those towering European geniuses who gave nineteenth-century art its spaciousness and immensity. He was born the year before Verdi and Wagner, whose works remain as prominent on the shelves of our record shops as Dickens's remain on the shelves of our bookshops. And like Verdi Dickens achieved the appeal of the popular entertainer by using the imaginative craftsmanship of the great artist. As for his place in the history of English literature, Dickens has been compared with Shakespeare for the variety and vitality of the imaginative world he created.

Dickens, like Scott before him, was heavily indebted to the great eighteenth-century novelists, especially Smollett (1721–71) and Fielding. He shared their zest for life and their urge to grasp it vividly in packed and sweeping surveys. He derived from Smollett especially the delight in eccentric characters and human oddities, the eye for the grotesque, and the gift for pin-pointing aspects of personality in peculiar habits and expressive turns of speech. Like other Victorian novelists, he measured himself against Scott, and, in so doing, tried to beat the master at his own game when he turned his hand to the historical novels *Barnaby Rudge* (1841) and *A Tale of Two Cities* (1859).

Dickens's own personal experience gave him a peculiar fittedness as a commentator upon his age. He was born in Portsea, Hampshire, the son of a clerk in the Navy Pay Office, but the family moved to London two years later, and then to Chatham, Kent, in 1816. By the time Dickens was nine they had gone back to London. His father was a feckless, impoverished fellow who probably provided the portrait for Mr Micawber in *David Copperfield*. In the Chatham days Dickens had some education and began to delight in the novels of Smollett, Fielding, Goldsmith (?1730–74) and Defoe (1660–1731), but when the family moved back to London in 1821 Charles was sent to work in a blacking factory, a squalid, rat-infested place that left an indelible mark on his imagination. Moreover, his father was imprisoned for debt in the Marshalsea and most of the family moved in to join him. The imprisonment in the Marshalsea lasted only a few months, but Dickens's imprisonment in the blacking factory continued until better times enabled the elder Dickens to send his son to Wellington House Academy in Hampstead in 1824. In 1827 the boy started work as a clerk for a firm of attorneys at Gray's Inn. He studied shorthand and eventually worked as a reporter, first dealing with law cases in the Consistory Court of Doctor's Commons, then with parliamentary debates. Such was Dickens's literary apprenticeship, but from the time of the publication of *The Pickwick Papers* (1837) he enjoyed increasing fame and affluence.

Dickens's personal life contained its disappointments and emotional tensions. After four years of wooing he was rejected by Maria Beadnell with whom he had fallen rapturously in love. He married Catherine Hogarth in 1836. Her sister Mary died in his arms. Her sister Georgina lived with the couple and Dickens was deeply attached to her. Catherine bore him ten children but the pair were separated in 1858. By that time Dickens had become acquainted with a young actress, Ellen Ternan, and she secretly became his kept mistress.

In Dickens we see a writer who by the age of twenty had experienced the rigours of dire poverty and of child labour under the most squalid and repressive conditions, who had roamed the London streets and seen Marshalsea life from the inside. He had also worked in a legal office and familiarised himself with the mysteries of litigation. Moreover, he had spent hours in the House of Commons as a reporter. When he reported debates on the Poor Law Bill he really knew something about those paupers for whom it catered. Hence his dislike of parliamentarians and hatred of the official institutions their legislation established. Dickens shot to fame and fortune when he was twenty-four years old. Thereafter he travelled, was lionised, and eventually took to giving public readings from his works in which so much nervous energy was expended that he died of exhaustion.

Dickens's own experience thus gave him an overview of English life at many social levels at a time when class distinctions were so sharp that real familiarity with life at more than one level was very difficult to attain. Indeed Dickens suffered his share of criticism for concerning himself with low life. 'I know that there are such unfortunate beings as pickpockets and street walkers,' said Lady Carlisle, 'but I own I do not much wish to hear what they say to one another.' Dickens brought to his survey of the world about him a keen sense of moral rectitude that made nonsense of preferences and evaluations based on social status and financial competence, a passionate demand for a social justice disentangled from class prejudice, and a fiercely defensive compassion for the victims of what he saw as institutionalised injustice. 'It's the system,' exclaims a victim of the protracted proceedings in the Court of Chancery which deprive him of his rightful inheritance in *Bleak House* (1853). 'Kill me sooner than take me there,' says the struggling, poverty-stricken Betty Higden of the official Poor-House in *Our Mutual Friend* (1865). 'Take this pretty child under cart-horses' feet and a loaded waggon, sooner than take him there!' She vows to die 'without that disgrace' of committal to the Poor Law's protective arms. 'Absolutely impossible, my Lords and Gentlemen and Honourable Boards, by any stretch of legislative wisdom to set these perverse people right in their logic?'

The fierce sarcasm is only one aspect of what is Dickens's most endearing gift, his sense of humour. It is exercised in appreciation of amiable and cheerful characters; it is exercised at the expense of pompous and dislikeable characters. It gives charm to his portraiture of odd, eccentric and grotesque characters, especially when he fixes them in the reader's mind by some obviously repetitive habit of speech, such as Uriah Heep's claim to be ''umble' in *David Copperfield* (1850). But it also assumes a more 'literary' or rhetorical guise when there is a carefully phrased riposte or rebuke in which wit gets the better of pretentiousness, meanness, or even of plain politeness and respectability. Thus, in *David Copperfield*, when Mr Micawber determines to put an end once for all to the tale of debt-ridden impecuniosity by emigrating with his family to Australia, his wife naturally enough seeks before parting from her homeland to bridge the gulf with her own family that her husband's behaviour long ago opened up. Mr Micawber, as usual, has the last word: 'All I would say is that I can go abroad without your family coming forward to favour me, – in short, with a parting shove of their cold shoulders.'

The comic element is strong in Dickens's first novel, *The Pickwick Papers*, which appeared in monthly sections between April 1836 and November 1837. It is a book that exudes zest and ebullience. It records the adventures of Mr Pickwick and his companions as they journey about the country. Pickwick is a benevolent if somewhat naïve gentleman with a tendency to get into scrapes. He stumbles inadvertently into the wrong bedroom one night and the eventual upshot is an appearance before a magistrate on a charge of intending to fight a duel; his landlady brings an action against him for breach of promise, and he is committed to the Fleet for refusing to pay damages. But Pickwick has a devoted servant, Sam Weller, a former boot black, resourceful in coming to his master's rescue, and ceaselessly entertaining in his colourful commentary upon life. (It is said that his appearance in Chapter X multiplied the sales a hundredfold to forty thousand a month.) The successive episodes scarcely constitute a 'novel', as generally understood, but the whole is rich in caricature and in farce.

The success of *The Pickwick Papers* led naturally to the composition of the more cohesive biographical novels, *Oliver Twist* (1838) and *Nicholas Nickleby* (1839). These are like the picaresque novels of Smollett, *Roderick Random* (1748) and *Peregrine Pickle* (1751), where the hero's adventures are recorded chronologically and the personal story provides the principle of continuity. Oliver Twist, a foundling, born and brought up in a workhouse, where he commits the outrageous impropriety of asking for a second helping of gruel, runs away from a miserable apprenticeship to London and falls into the company of a gang of thieves led by Fagin. He is forced to go with Bill Sikes on a burglary and is wounded as a result. In the end Oliver is adopted and educated; and he emerges as the victim of a wicked half-brother who tried to ruin him in order to keep his father's property to himself. In *Nicholas Nickleby*, the hero, his mother and his sister Kate are left penniless on the death of Nicholas's father. Nicholas tries to make a living as an usher and thereby comes to Dotheboys Hall, a school run by a brutal headmaster, Mr Wackford Squeers. Other experiences include a period in a theatrical company run by Vincent Crummles and a period as clerk in an office run by the benevolent brothers Cheeryble. Nicholas's grasping uncle, Ralph Nickleby, is the arch-villain of the tale, refusing to aid his nephew, conspiring to ruin his chances of marriage, and finally, when exposed, hanging himself. As in *Oliver Twist* a current of moral indignation against institutionalised inhumanity courses through the book. Cruelty to children in cheap private schools is recorded as it was to be later in *David Copperfield* (1850). The school at Bowes (the model for Dotheboys Hall) was only some forty miles away from Cowan Bridge where the young Brontë sisters went to the school which provided the model for Lowood in Charlotte Brontë's *Jane Eyre*.

In *The Old Curiosity Shop* (1841) the conflict between good and evil is expressed in situations and characters so intensely polarised that the book has always been the subject of critical controversy. Little Nell Trent is devoted to her grandfather who keeps the dismal curiosity shop. His resources have been squandered by his son-in-law and his grandson; he has borrowed heavily from Daniel Quilp, an evil and hideous dwarf, and has gambled everything away in the attempt to recover money for Little Nell's sake. Quilp dispossesses them of their home, and they roam the countryside, haunted remorselessly by their evil oppressor. When rescue at last arrives, Nell has already died. The inhuman figure of Quilp, a being cancerously infected by covetousness and lust, is so powerfully counterbalanced by the angelic goodness and virginal purity of Little Nell that Dickens's insistent rhetoric of emotion topples over into sentimentality, and his description of Nell's death has been regarded as an extreme example of melodramatic Victorian excess.

Dickens made his first attempt at a historical novel in *Barnaby Rudge* (1841), seemingly anxious to do for London what Scott had done for Edinburgh in *The Heart of Midlothian* (1818). In the previous century legislation removing restrictions on Roman Catholics provoked an anti-Catholic backlash and a demand for repeal of the legislation. Lord George Gordon led a movement under the slogan 'No Popery', and in 1780 protesters rioted in London, damaging property and burning Newgate prison. These 'Gordon riots' form the centre-piece of Dickens's novel. Barnaby Rudge is a half-wit who gets involved and is mistakenly condemned to death. The somewhat tangled plot has its awkward artifices. Some of Dickens's gravest faults – his over-strained plotting and the disproportionate enthusiasm with which he harries certain individual characters and their obsessions – are apparent here and they seem to arise from the very fertility and vitality of his creative gift which so abundantly overflowed the banks of discipline and order. Defects inevitably rose from his practice of publishing very long novels section by section in serialised form. In this respect it has been suggested (by John Lucas in *The Melancholy Man*, 1970) that the composition of *Martin Chuzzlewit* (1844) represents a crisis point in Dickens's development in that this work, richly studded as it is with vivid studies like that of the canting hypocrite Pecksniff and the disreputable nurse Sarah Gamp, is nevertheless so flawed by discrepancies and confusions that Dickens thereafter plotted his books in advance with far greater thoroughness. The relationship between character and plot must be firm and clear-cut if the characters are not to seem so tied to the plot or hampered by it that it begins to seem like an unnecessary burden for living human beings to endure. Neither Othello nor Iago could be said to have a life apart from the pattern of action – that is, the plot – in which Shakespeare involves them. We do not feel that Shakespeare invented Othello and Iago and then asked himself 'Now what kind of thing can I make them do?' Their personalities, their roles and their actions are one and indivisible. Yet, as G. K. Chesterton said of Dickens's characters in *Martin Chuzzlewit*, 'the best figures are at their best when they have least to do', and added, 'while Pecksniff is the best thing in the story, the story is the worst thing in Pecksniff'. Words like 'muddle' and 'mess' have been applied to *Martin Chuzzlewit*, implying that on the road of swift, unplanned composition Dickens drove himself into a cul-de-sac.

Dombey and Son (1848) was the first fruits of the more disciplined process of composition. Where *Martin Chuzzlewit* tells the story of a young man whose adventures and misfortunes in America eventually purge him of his selfishness, *Dombey and Son* is a story of the humbling of pride. Mr Dombey, a shipping magnate, focuses all his love and hope on his son Paul, whose mother died at his birth, and neglects his daughter Florence. The ambition to see his firm called 'Dombey and Son' is an obsession, and Paul, a sensitive boy, is quite unequal to the burden of affection and aspiration laid upon him. He dies, Mr Dombey remarries, but his second wife leaves him. The firm fails, and, bereft of all else, Mr Dombey is finally rescued by the daughter he alienated.

David Copperfield (1850) may be considered the first of the master-pieces of Dickens's full maturity which he published in the 1850s and 1860s. It was Dickens's own favourite novel, no doubt because of the substantial autobiographical element which gives vividness and intense emotional authenticity to many episodes and relationships. Dickens's own childhood was such that he was able to write a chilling exposé of the inhumane treatment to which children could be subjected in Victorian schools and factories. When David's affec-tionate but weakly impressionable mother marries again after the death of his father, she provides her son with a ruthless, overbearing step-father and step-aunt who drive her to an early grave and David to a school run by a tyrannical bully, then to a factory where he toils in squalor and misery. He rescues himself by running away to his aunt, Betsey Trotwood, who has him educated at a good school at Canterbury. David rises, like Dickens, through work at a firm of attorneys to parliamentary journalism and to authorship. His first marriage is to Dora Spenlow, a charming but childishly scatter-brained girl quite unfitted to run a home, and she dies after a miscarriage. Finally David recognises his true mate in Agnes Wickfield, the daughter of the lawyer who gave him lodgings in his Canterbury school days. It is Mr Wickfield's employee, the fawningly calculating Uriah Heep, who dishonestly entangles the lawyer in a net of business compromises so that he can virtually take over his firm as his official partner. Other characters include the irrepressibly impecunious Mr Micawber, the schoolboy idol Steerforth, the affec-tionate Traddles, the indomitably devoted Peggotty whose family is resident in a boat at Yarmouth, and the carter Barkis who conveys through David to Peggotty by way of marriage proposal the cryptic message that 'Barkis is willin''. This gallery of warmly conceived and often hilariously portrayed men and women is so rich in human reality that, had Dickens died after the composition of *David Copperfield*, his literary career would have been seen as a gradual ascent to the climactic production of one of the rarest masterpieces of literature. But *David Copperfield* proved to be only a beginning. What followed matched it repeatedly.

Bleak House (1853), for instance, is considered by some critics to be his finest work. In terms of social criticism its great theme is the ridiculous protraction of litigation in the Chancery Court. Dickens underlines the acute misery it can cause to expectant heirs and heiresses who may be kept as wards of court and deprived of access to funds while lawyers dispute points of detail at great profit to themselves. Lawyers' opportunities are especially lucrative when wealthy men have died intestate or when more than one will of a deceased testator is extant. Dickens treats the court to his most withering contempt:

> . . . to behold the Lord Chancellor, and the whole array of prac-titioners under him, looking at one another and at the spectators, as if nobody had ever heard that all over England the name in which they were assembled was a bitter jest; was held in universal horror, contempt, and indignation; was known for something so flagrant and bad, that little short of a miracle could bring any good out of it to anyone; this was so serious and self-contradictory . . . that I could not comprehend it.

The central interest focuses upon Esther Summerson, friend of two wards – cousins – who marry each other, and whose lives are ruined because the husband is lured into false prospects from the unending case of Jarndyce and Jarndyce. Another aspect of the plot is the network of intrigue which has been fabricated around the unhappy person of Lady Dedlock. The ingredients of mystery and the devices of suspense are cunningly employed here, and revelations are fed to the reader in judiciously measured stages.

What strikes the modern reader about both *David Copperfield* and *Bleak House*, and indeed about Dickens's later works in general, is that they are packed full of moral judgements: judgements by the author on his characters, judgements by the characters on each other, judgements by characters on themselves. True, a good deal of the first two categories of judgement are favourable. People are always being praised for virtue, benevolence, unselfishness, generosity and the like. But there is plenty of condemnation too, of meanness and hypocrisy, pretence and humbug, cruelty and rapacity. And self-judgement often involves agonised outpourings of remorse such as those to which the prostitute Martha gives way in *David Copperfield*, and acts of extravagant self-torture such as those Lady Dedlock undergoes in *Bleak House*. Dickens's world is a moral world, and, where sexual issues are concerned, a rigorously unbending one. Not that Dickens himself is hard on the fallen woman or the unfaithful wife, far from it; but he depicts a world where others are hard upon them and they are hard upon themselves.

In *Hard Times* (1854) Dickens turned to the contemporary industrial scene. Thomas Gradgrind of Coketown, a hard-headed utilitarian, nurtures his children on his own principles in defiance of imaginative or spiritual dimensions, and learns too late how he has blighted their lives. Ruskin (1819–1900) praised the book as Dickens's greatest for its social and political implications. There is harsh satire in Gradgrind's marriage of his daughter Louisa to the manufacturer Josiah Bounderby, a coarse and egotistical humbug, and in her shallow brother's attempt to frame an innocent mill-hand for a robbery he has himself committed. *Little Dorrit* (1857) has been called Dickens's darkest novel. William Dorrit, like Dickens's own father, is confined in the Marshalsea prison for debtors with his three children, Edward, Fanny and Amy (Little Dorrit) who is devoted to him. She alone of the family keeps her sweet and generous character when an unexpected inheritance makes the family affluent. The others become wilful and pretentious. The plot is one of immense complexity, but Little Dorrit's devotion to her father, then to Arthur Clennam who has returned to London after twenty years in the East, is a liberating and hopeful influence in a story in which imprisonment, external or internal, physical or spiritual, seems to corrode the fabric of human vitality. An air of oppressiveness and weariness hangs broodingly over the book.

After *Little Dorrit* Dickens turned for the second time to write a historical novel, *A Tale of Two Cities* (1859), but this novel does not, like *Barnaby Rudge*, bear the marks of a too conscious attempt to match Scott. The two cities of the title are London and Paris. The subject is the French Revolution, and the source was Carlyle's (1795–1881) *The French Revolution* (1837). Dickens uses all his rhetorical powers to picture both the miseries which a too powerful and insensitive aristocracy inflicted on the French people and the hideous revenge which was exacted. His heroine Lucie is daughter of a French doctor, Manette, who has been held in the Bastille for eighteen years simply because he came upon dangerous knowledge of an aristocrat's treatment of a peasant and his sister. Lucie herself marries a French aristocrat who is ultimately saved from execution only by the heroic self-sacrifice of his double, the wastrel English lawyer, Sydney Carton. The message which is pressed home by Dickens is that what has happened in France could happen here in

England if the lesson is not learned: 'Crush humanity out of shape once more, under similar hammers, and it will twist itself into the same tortured forms. Sow the same seed of rapacious licence and oppression over again, and it will surely yield the same fruit according to its kind.' The Victorian age may seem in hindsight a period of great assurance and self-confidence, but it is plain that people were not free of the fear of revolution. And indeed the whole tenor of Dickens's attacks on absurd or unjust institutions and the misery they inflict suggests awareness of how precarious civilisation may be.

Dickens's last two completed novels, *Great Expectations* (1861) and *Our Mutual Friend* (1865), are among his finest. Both are concerned with the effects on the human character of sudden access to wealth. Pip, the hero of *Great Expectations*, brought up by his overbearing sister and her warm-hearted husband Joe Gargery, the village blacksmith, comes to the home of the half-crazy Miss Havisham, who was abandoned on her wedding day and in revenge has brought up the girl Estella to attract, charm and torment men. Pip falls in love with her. Suddenly he is enriched by a mysterious inheritance. His head is turned. He goes to London and becomes ashamed of his lowly connections. There is a long purgation by renewed poverty and adversity before he learns his lesson and a happy ending is contrived. The moral subtlety of the book lies in the way Pip narrates his own story from the point of view of one who has learned his lesson. Thus he does not spare himself in recording the foolish or mean things he thought, said and did. Indeed the ruthless self-criticism, like the confessions of the converted sinner, tends to overstate the faults and follies of the past, leaving the reader to modify for himself the older Pip's judgements on the young Pip's dreams. For there are plenty of excuses to be found by reference to the extraordinary personalities that impinge on his life.

The damage done to human character and human relationships by a cash-oriented social order is even more comprehensively examined in *Our Mutual Friend* (1865). A fortune made, symbolically enough by a dealer in dust, is bequeathed to his son John Harmon on condition that he marries the girl Bella Wilfer. John Harmon returns from abroad determined to become acquainted with Bella without being known for what he is and what he brings. His adoption of disguise leads to the murder of a mate by mistake for himself. Since he is presumed drowned, the alternative clause of his father's will becomes operative and two delightfully genuine former servants of the dust-contractor, Mr and Mrs Boffin, succeed to the estate. Eventually the Boffins and John Harmon conspire in a complex plot to test Bella Wilfer – who has seemed flighty in some respects – by putting John Harmon in her way as a seemingly poor suitor. Ultimately the soundness of her heart is made clear. An account of one thread in a complex action can do little to suggest the panoramic richness of a book whose scenes and characters show Dickens's imagination at its most fertile. On the one hand we go out on the river Thames at night with a scavenger and corpse-robber about his grizzly task; on the other hand we attend dinner parties given by the vulgarly rich Veneerings, whose money-conditioned circle shows society rotten with shallowness and pretentiousness. There is an earnest but emotionally warped schoolmaster, Bradley Headstone, whose obsessive love for the poor waterside girl, Lizzie Hexam, conflicts with the fancies of a self-indulgent young lawyer, Eugene Wrayburn, to the point of attempted murder. We can read through a list of forty-two characters in *Our Mutual Friend* at the beginning of the volume in the Oxford Dickens, and there is scarcely a name that does not bring a sharply delineated personality leaping from the page. Only the very greatest authors are capable of such astonishing prodigality of invention and inspiration.

There has always been criticism of Dickens's sometimes over-strained plots and particularly of the artifices and improbabilities seemingly involved in strange bequests. At the end of *Our Mutual Friend*, on the strength of his experience in the legal world, Dickens assures his readers 'that there are hundreds of Will cases . . . far more remarkable than that fancied in this work; and that the stores of the Prerogative Office teem with instances of testators who have made, changed, hidden, forgotten, left cancelled, each many more wills than were ever made by the elder Mr Harmon. . .'

Benjamin Disraeli

It is not surprising that a writer with Dickens's experience of poverty should be able to represent the lives of the poor with sympathy and vividness, and to espouse their cause with passion; but the twentieth-century reader may well be surprised to discover the degree of sympathy and understanding with which Benjamin Disraeli (1804–81) espoused their cause. Disraeli, Prime Minister briefly in 1868 and then from 1874 to 1880, published several novels of which perhaps *Coningsby* (1844) and *Sybil* (1845) are the two most celebrated. They are political novels, the first tracing the youth and young manhood of Coningsby from boyhood at Eton to his embarkation on a parliamentary career. The period is the 1830s and the intrigue and infighting during and after the Reform Bill controversy is described in detail. Though some living figures are named (such as the Duke of Wellington, Earl Grey and Sir Robert Peel) a key is needed to identify the rest of the political cast. Disraeli was disgusted with the

Whig and Tory parties (forerunners of the Liberal and Conservative parties) alike. He is scathing in his denunciation of political jobbery and place-seeking. He denounces the aristocracy for their blindness to social change, their blinkered materialism and their shallow culture. In this respect, Disraeli's scenes of aristocratic society intriguing and back-biting, indulging their flippant witticisms and bitchy gossip, have an authentic ring which, say, Dickens's comparable portraiture lacks. This is not remarkable. At the same time, Disraeli's picture of the down-trodden workers, though it lacks the imaginative passion which Dickens's fervid rhetoric supplied, is astonishingly informative in a factual sense. We learn a lot from *Sybil*, for instance, about the way employers tricked their workers by paying in goods instead of in cash. We are taken through a ceremony of initiation into a Trade Union. We hear the Chartists planning their campaign. For *Sybil* covers the years leading up to and away from the Chartist disturbances of 1838–40. Like *Coningsby*, it traces the developing young manhood of an aristocratic hero, Charles Egremont. And like Coningsby, Egremont is utterly disillusioned with the decadence of the rich and the total lack of principle in the conduct of political parties. Both heroes are thinkers in a world of grabbers, idealists in a world of self-seekers. The subtitle of *Sybil* is *The Two Nations*: the nations are the rich and the poor, and the gap between the two is widening. Disraeli's view is distinguished by its human and moral aspects. He sympathised with the Chartists. He did not want to destroy aristocracy but to purge it. Indeed in his view a truly effective monarchy together with a truly inspired aristocracy, the natural leaders of society, ought to rescue the masses from the wicked manipulation of corrupt parliamentarians, greedy industrialists and hot-headed agitators. Such was the inspiration behind his 'Young England' group which was formed to rescue the Conservative party from the cynics and the pragmatists.

The emphasis in *Coningsby* is on the widening gap between the land-owning aristocracy and the new-rich industrialists. Young Coningsby defies family and protocol by marrying across the gap: his wife is Edith Millbank, daughter of a Lancashire mill-owner. The emphasis in *Sybil* is on the widening gap between rich and poor. Young Egremont falls in love across the gap but is saved from marrying across it by the fact that Sybil, daughter of an intelligent workman, turns out to be an heiress after all. For Disraeli's plots are highly artificial, employing the most melodramatic devices. In making his fictional surveys of public and political life he falls back on the device of the young hero who, by conscience and sympathy, is alienated from the party to which he naturally belongs, and finds virtue in the 'enemy' camp. This is the pattern which Scott adopted in *Waverley* and in many subsequent novels. It is a good recipe for presenting an honest, thoughtful hero who agonises over the condition of his world and wins the reader's sympathy for his magnanimity and humanity. Disraeli's heroes do so preeminently.

Writing at the end of *Sybil*, Disraeli said:

> A year ago, I presumed to offer the public some volumes that aimed to call attention to the state of our political parties; their origin, their history, their present position. In an age of political infidelity, of mean passions, and petty thoughts, I would have impressed upon the rising race not to despair, but to seek in a right understanding of the history of their country and in the energies of heroic youth – the elements of national welfare. The present work [*Sybil*] advances one step in the same emprise. From the state of the parties it would draw public thought to the state of the People whom those parties for two centuries have governed . . . In the selfish strife of factions, two great existences have been blotted out of the history of England – the Monarch and the Multitude; as the power of the Crown has diminished, the privileges of the people have disappeared; till at length the sceptre has become a pageant, and its subject has degenerated into a serf.

In his own day Disraeli achieved his most popular success as a novelist with *Lothair* (1870). One of Lothair's guardians, a Catholic convert, has become a cardinal, and, seeking his ideal, Lothair explores the Anglican, Roman Catholic and Jewish traditions, travelling to Italy and to the Holy Land. In Italy his status and wealth as an English aristocrat make him sought after by Garibaldi's patriots and by the Catholics. The novel as a whole displays a significant movement in Disraeli's fiction from concern (in the earlier novels) with young heroes who are seeking success and power, to concern, at a time when the author had established his own public position, with a hero whose patronage is being sought. Of the women who attract Lothair, Theodora is an Italian patriot and Lady Clare Arundel is a Roman Catholic, but ultimately Lothair rejects fanatical ideologies, marries Lady Corisande, and settles down on his estate at home.

Disraeli's last novel, *Endymion* (1880), takes us back to the English political scene in the days when Disraeli was a young politician, and the canvas is a wide one, taking in the social setting of high politics at one extreme and the Radicals' concern with the condition of the poor at the other.

George Eliot

The vast social overview of Victorian life to which Dickens, and to a lesser extent Disraeli, aspired in their novels did not permit of the thorough and intense exploration of individual experience within any sphere of it such as was achieved by George Eliot and Thomas Hardy. These two were country folk, born and bred, and they knew their respective segments of provincial rural society inside out. George Eliot (1819–80) was christened Mary Ann Evans but later telescoped 'Mary Ann' into 'Marian'. She was the daughter of a yeoman farmer knowledgeable enough in practical matters to have made good as estate agent to a Warwickshire landowner. As the youngest child of his second marriage, she seems to have craved for affection to a demanding degree and to have found the person fully able to return her whole-hearted love and trust only after years of passionate inner restlessness, and then, ironically enough, only in the person of an already married man, George Henry Lewes (1817–78). It was not that Marian was neglected by her parents. Indeed her father made a pet of his youngest child; but Marian worshipped her brother Isaac, three years her senior, and her devouring affection for him, together with her acute sensitivity to neglect or rebuff, produced inevitable frustration and suffering. What the imaginative, passionate and demanding young girl endured is made plain in the story of Maggie Tulliver in George Eliot's most autobiographical novel, *The Mill on the Floss* (1860).

Among other powerful influences that played on Marian's girlhood was that of her schoolmistress, Miss Lewis. Miss Lewis had thrown herself heart and soul into the movement of the Evangelical Revival which swept the Church of England, and Marian was soon infected with her teacher's enthusiasm. It gave direction and discipline to her naturally upright and earnest character. The death of her mother, when Marian was only fifteen, imposed on the now devout young lady the grave duty of running the family home for her father and her brother. It was some six years later, when Isaac had left home and father and daughter had moved to a smaller house in Coventry, that Marian made contact with people whose intellectual interests transformed her outlook. One of these was Charles Bray (1811–84) in whose company she met various social and philosophical thinkers. They, and the books she studied under their encouragement, under- mined her belief in Christianity as revealed truth. The development was to stimulate her to break out of the bonds of accepted Victorian religious practice and codes of conduct. It was in 1851, after her father's death, while she was still living in the home of the publisher and editor John Chapman (1821–94), that Marian was introduced to the philosophical writer George Henry Lewes, and the couple fell deeply in love. Marian had already entered the literary world. She had written reviews for Chapman's *Westminster Review* and had translated D. F. Strauss's (1808–74) *The Life of Jesus Critically Examined* (1846). She later translated L. von Feuerbach's (1804–72) *The Essence of Christianity* (1854), the only one of her works to appear under the name 'Marian Evans'.

Lewes and his wife Agnes already had records of infidelity, and Lewes was not the actual father of all his supposed sons. In 1854 Lewes and Marian went off to the continent together and their twenty-four-year long liaison began. Marian's emotional dependence on Lewes was total, but he was known for his sensuality and whether he continued faithful to her is open to doubt. Be that as it may, the ironies of George Eliot's career cut deeply. She was essentially a fervent moralist and a believer in marital fidelity, yet her behaviour scandalised her family, and, though it was eventually accepted and understood by those who valued her work, it cut her off permanently from playing the social role she was fitted to play. Gentlemen came to visit her salon, but would leave their wives at home. George Eliot's appearance was not attractive. Flattering observers compared her heavy, large-featured face to those of Savonarola and Dante. Less kind observers said she had the face of a cab-horse. 'Magnificently ugly – deliciously hideous,' said Henry James. And somehow, as a woman, Marian Evans does not excite among admirers of her work the personal regard which warms the hearts of Jane Austen's readers or Charlotte Brontë's. There is often a personal coolness in critical response to her. Describing the love between Marian and Lewes, Marghanita Laski writes, 'They had much in common, not only intellectual and artistic interests, but also a streak of moral coarseness, of emotional vulgarity, already apparent in George and increasingly so in Marian' (*George Eliot and Her World*, 1973). Yet the settled relationship answered Marian's emotional need so fully that her creative urge was released in the sequence of novels which, in spite of her ambiguous social standing, had made her by the 1870s and 1880s not only celebrated for her literary artistry but also, like Browning, acknowledged somewhat portentously as a sage moral and religious teacher.

It was soon after Lewes and Marian returned to England that she wrote a story, 'Amos Barton', that appeared in *Blackwood's Magazine* under the name George Eliot. Two other stories followed, and the three were published in book form as *Scenes of Clerical Life* (1858) – stories of town and village life in the Midlands. In the third story, 'Janet's Repentance', Janet is driven to drink by the brutality of her husband but is rescued from moral deterioration by an evan-

gelical clergyman, Mr Tryan. The frank realism here in George
Eliot's study of Victorian womanhood is notable. So, too, is the
powerful moral didacticism. Dickens immediately detected 'womanly
touches' which showed the writer to be an authoress.

The success of the stories led George Eliot to dig more deeply
into memories of provincial life in a full-length novel, *Adam Bede*
(1859). She had heard from an aunt the story of a girl condemned
to death for the murder of her child. The aunt, a Methodist, had
accompanied the girl to the scaffold on the day of execution. This
was the germ of George Eliot's tale of Hetty Sorrel, condemned for
the murder of her illegitimate child and comforted in prison by the
Methodist preacher Dinah Morris. The similarities between *Adam
Bede* and Scott's *The Heart of Midlothian* have often been pointed
out, and we know that Marian was in the habit of reading the
Waverley Novels aloud to her father in the evenings in his later
years. In both novels the central contrast is between a pretty, vain,
impulsive girl whose head is turned and who is seduced, and an
earnest, upright girl whose religious commitment and personal
charity pervade the book. In Scott the two are sisters, Effie and
Jeanie Deans. Although in Dinah George Eliot attempts an interesting representation of the effect of Methodism on English life,
her struggle to make Dinah's piety, directness and unselfishness
convincing and attractive is not wholly successful. Adam Bede
himself emerges as a warmly conceived workman on the pattern of
Marian's father, Robert Evans. He is a man of upright character and
sturdy self-respect. By contrast, Arthur Donnithorne, the young
squire who steals the affections of Adam's beloved Hetty, is an easy-
going fellow spoiled by too readily getting his own way in life.
Adam's brother Seth, gentle, pious and long-suffering in his hopeless
devotion to Dinah, is a study in virtuous self-abnegation, and it is
ultimately Adam who finds happiness with Dinah. Queen Victoria,
who confessed that she liked to fancy a likeness between George
Eliot's sturdier rural characters and her 'dear Highlanders', was so
impressed by *Adam Bede* that she commissioned the artist, E. H.
Corbould, to paint scenes from it. There is one of Dinah preaching
to the villagers and one of Hetty being visited by Arthur in Mrs
Poyser's dairy. Mrs Poyser, of course, is one of George Eliot's most
appealing creations, a shrewd, down-to-earth countrywoman whose
garrulity is rich in vivid shafts and homely phrases.

It is the sobriety and accuracy of George Eliot's portrayal of life
that distinguishes it from the heightened intonation and intensified
colouring of Dickens's fictional world. Critics have drawn comparisons between her studies of rural and small-town life and those found
in the poets Crabbe (1754–1832) and Wordsworth (1770–1850).

Indeed George Eliot laid great store by truthfulness of the kind which delighted her in Dutch paintings. 'I find a source of delicious sympathy in these faithful pictures of a monotonous homely existence which has been the lot of so many more among my fellow mortals than a life of pomp or of absolute indigence, of tragic suffering or of world-stirring action.' So she wrote in *The Mill on the Floss*. Her thoroughness in pursuit of such truthfulness inevitably means that her novels contain a good deal of the humdrum in event and dialogue. Over-laden with such freight, they move heavily forward with a sluggishness that is intensified by George Eliot's habit of intervening in the unfolding story to moralise or philosophise. It is this ever-intrusive and instructive authorial voice which for her own age established her as the venerated, high-minded sage. In reaction, in the earlier decades of our century she was often dismissed as oppressively didactic and governessy. But critical attitudes change and George Eliot's psychological realism is now recognised for its rare insight and authenticity.

The Mill on the Floss (1860) is a full-scale story of developing girlhood. Maggie Tulliver's adoration of her elder brother Tom proves to be a dominant influence, eventually inhibiting relationships with others. The subtlety lies in the contrast between the adored brother's stupidity and narrowness of outlook and the adoring sister's evident superiority in imagination, sympathy and understanding. This is what gives ironic force to Tom's continuing grip upon Maggie's loyalty and devotion. The family life of the Tullivers, much dominated as it is by the overbearing Dodsons – Mrs Tulliver's sisters and their husbands – is brilliantly portrayed. The Dodsons are petty-minded pillars of respectability over-ready to criticise deviations from family standards and practices which have been hallowed by time and by habit into unalterable laws of propriety. The portraiture gives George Eliot excellent opportunities for sly humour in tartly puncturing pretentious self-righteousness. The whole human back-ground to Maggie's growth and development is one of seemingly impregnable solidity in defence of a limited system of values which Maggie's deepest urges would reject. But then she is a remarkable child, and, though her father pets her fondly, there is no one of her calibre in mind and spirit. Her two abortive love-affairs, with the young artist Philip Wakem, son of a deadly family enemy, and with her cousin Lucy's suitor, Stephen Guest, scarcely offer the whole-hearted fulfilment which her emotionally starved nature craves; and it is no doubt artistically appropriate that brother and sister should ultimately be drowned in each other's arms.

Silas Marner (1861), George Eliot's shortest novel, is a kind of fable, for here the pressure of moral judgement, instead of being applied to a full-scale exploration of human experience, is gently channelled through the symbolism of a romantic fairy-tale. Silas Marner, a keen dissenter, has been ruined and disillusioned by a false accusation of theft. Moving to a new locality, he settles down to restore himself laboriously by toilsome solitary work as a weaver. He makes money and turns miser, treasuring his gold obsessively. Half blind, and subject to cataleptic fits, he one day finds that his hoarded gold has been stolen, and he is driven to despair; but sometime later he imagines that it has been restored to his cottage. In fact what he sees is the golden hair of a baby girl who has wandered in from beside her dead mother's body. Marner adopts her and his love for her redeems him.

It was no doubt the shadow of Scott that caused George Eliot, like Dickens, to attempt a full-scale historical novel, and she put an enormous amount of work into gathering material for *Romola* (1863) which is set in Florence in the time of Savonarola. The documentation is thorough, the historical background painstakingly researched, but, insulated from the provincial world George Eliot knew at first hand with its familiar and long-observed personalities, the novel fails to catch fire and remains only a lifeless monument.

Felix Holt (1866) has many defects which principally arise from its elaborately contrived plot about a country estate and an inheritance tangle of intolerable legal complexity. Moreover, there are various melodramatic mysteries over parentage locked up in the long-concealed secrecies of hidden indiscretions. Even so it is an immensely readable book with a substantial political interest relating to the period of the 1832 Reform Bill. The central human issue is the choice of husband which Esther Lyons ultimately has to make between the good-natured and comfortably-placed country gentleman, Harold Transome, and the idealistic, self-educated radical, Felix Holt, who identifies himself with the workers and opts to share their privations. Ultimately, Esther follows the dictates of her own heart which reverse the valuations of contemporary society so far as the relative standing of Harold and Felix is concerned. For she recognises that 'whatever Harold might think, there was a light in which he was vulgar compared with Felix'. She cannot feel inferior to Harold, but she feels an undoubted sense of dependence on Felix.

'The best part of a woman's love is worship' says George Eliot of Esther Lyons's devotion to Felix, and it is woman's need to give herself to some cause greater than herself that she explores in the study of Dorothea Brooke, heroine of her masterpiece, *Middlemarch*. It was published serially in 1871–2. Dorothea, a grown-up Maggie Tulliver, seeking an outlet for her intense and ardent yearnings and fulfilment for her powerful aspirations, marries an elderly scholar, Casaubon, in the belief that she can thereby achieve a life of fruitful service. In fact she finds herself tied to a dessicated, pedantic grubber among other people's ideas who escapes from reality into useless and uncompletable research. (Marian and George Lewes were hereafter to call each other Mr and Mrs Casaubon in fun.) In parallel, a lively-minded young doctor, Tertius Lydgate, comes to Middlemarch with high ideals and reforming zeal, and marries a thoughtless, selfish social-climber, Rosamond Vincy. Alongside these studies of thwarted aspiration, there are other powerful themes together constituting a searching survey of life in a Midland country town. Mr Bulstrode, a banker, conceals a fraudulent past behind the externals of a life of evangelical piety. The unmasking of Bulstrode is subtly tracked and its effect on his wife is registered with rare poignancy.

Daniel Deronda (1876), George Eliot's last novel, is more often praised than read. Though the heroine, Gwendolen Harleth, is another fine study of a spirited young woman who marries an arrogant egotist, her story is but clumsily related to the other central theme, Daniel Deronda's discovery of his Jewish parentage and his commitment to Zionism. Nevertheless George Eliot reveals again, and in very large measure here, that mastery of the subtler complexities of psychological analysis which points forward from the age of Dickens to the age of D. H. Lawrence (1885–1930).

Thomas Hardy

With Thomas Hardy (1840–1928) we reach another writer whose literary stature seems to have the immensity of Dickens's. Yet in literary character the two are not similar. Dickens's immensity is that of verbal wizardry and imaginative profusion that bewitch by their variety and prodigality. Hardy's immensity is that of emotional profundity and moral strenuousness that overawe by their grandeur and intensity. If Dickens seems to wave a magic wand to bring his fictional world to life with the histrionic ease of the conjurer, Hardy seems to construct his fictional edifice with the plodding thoroughness of the stone-mason, though he certainly did not lack skill or finesse in the management of words. Indeed it is an aspect of his immensity that he is the only front-rank English novelist to be also a front-rank poet. Moreover, his monumental grandeur as a literary figure is, like Wordsworth's, related also to his sheer longevity. Hardy was an investigator of human society who sought to explore the inner and outer experience of individuals in terms of their relationship to a historic process and in terms of the larger philosophical view of human destiny. For such a writer, such a thinker, a long span of years seems not just desirable but necessary. Norman Page (in *Thomas Hardy*, 1977) has pointed out that Queen Victoria had been on the throne only three years when Hardy was born, yet he lived to play host at his Dorset home to her great-grandson King Edward VIII when he was Prince of Wales. Moreover, though he was born before the railway came to his native Dorset, when he died in 1928 the news was telephoned to London and then broadcast by the BBC a few minutes later.

The village of Higher Bockhampton where Hardy was born lies a few miles east of Dorchester. His father was a builder, an employer of labour who, we are told, talked to his men in dialect and spoke standard English in the home. Hardy's mother had been a servant, and he was not proud of his humble origins. He was educated at the village school, then at school in Dorchester, and went to work at the age of sixteen for Hicks, a local firm of architects and church-restorers. Six years later he joined a firm of architects in London. Throughout this period he studied languages, literature, history, philosophy and art assiduously in his spare time. By 1867 he was back in Dorchester with Hicks and working on his first novel, *The Poor Man and the Lady, By the Poor Man*, which was never published. When George Meredith read the manuscript for Chapman and Hall, he interviewed Hardy and advised him to try again. It was in 1870 that the comparatively 'poor man' met and fell in love with his 'lady', Emma Lavinia Gifford, niece of an archdeacon. The couple were married in 1874. How happy the relationship was to begin with, how bitter it later became, and how tenderly and ruefully it was reconstituted after her death, was made evident with startling candour in some of Hardy's finest poems.

Hardy's first success as a novelist was with *Under the Greenwood Tree* (1872), and hereafter his novels were issued in serial form before being published as volumes. In Hardy's case the effect of this method of publication was marked. There were weighty objections by magazine editors and publishers to Hardy's directness and frankness in dealing with sexual relationships and with other aspects of the lives of the 'lower orders'. He therefore adopted the practice of thoroughly bowdlerising his own work for serial publication and then reconstituting it in the form he preferred for publication in book form.

There is a temptation to picture Hardy as a Wessex countryman immersed in observing rural and small-town life; but it was not until he was in his mid-forties that he designed and built his own very ugly house, Max Gate, just outside Dorchester and settled there. By then he was a literary celebrity, and, even after building Max Gate, he continued to visit London for long periods. He was lionised at society dinner parties and made the acquaintance of famous figures in the literary and artistic worlds, including Tennyson and Browning, Matthew Arnold and Henry James. Honorary degrees were showered upon him along with honorary fellowships at both Oxford and Cambridge, and ultimately he was given the Order of Merit.

The subtitle of *Under the Greenwood Tree, A Rural Painting of the Dutch School*, reminds one of George Eliot's professed attempt to capture the detailed realism of Dutch paintings in her novels. It suggests that Hardy was consciously seeking after the same effect. Indeed when the first instalment of *Far from the Madding Crowd* (1874) appeared at least one reviewer suggested that the anonymous author must be George Eliot. But the basis of much of George Eliot's realism lay in celebration of the humdrum and even the monotonous, and Hardy did not seek any such effect. The common interest in faithfully portraying rustic life does not itself bring George Eliot and Thomas Hardy close together as artists, any more than their common rejection of Christian revelation and common attachment to the Christian ethic brings them close together as thinkers. George Eliot stamps upon her fictional world the impress of an unfailingly alert moral intellectualism which impels the reader to harsh judgements on the petty-minded, the selfish and the mean, and to worried sympathy with frustrated idealists and saddened victims of others' misdeeds. Hardy involves his characters, selfish and unselfish alike, conscientious and thoughtless alike, in the long saga of injustice which is the age-old human lot. The crucial dilemma of a heroine in George Eliot is one from which she could escape to seeming joy or affluence if she could bring herself to snatch selfishly at what only moral rectitude urges her to deny herself. No such options are open to Hardy's afflicted heroes and heroines. No ticket to an escape route to immediate fulfilment at the cost of integrity is ever dangled temptingly before Michael Henchard, Tess or Jude.

Under the Greenwood Tree does not, however, bring contrasts of this kind to mind. The most unfailingly cheerful of Hardy's novels, it is a delightful pastoral idyll, a village love story of Dick Dewy, son of the local carrier, and Fancy Day, the schoolmistress. Dick is a frank, honest young man while Fancy has just sufficient innocent flightiness to give plausibility to a brief potential rivalry on the part of the Vicar himself. But what excited readers from the first was the portrayal of village characters and village life, and perhaps especially of the Mellstock church choir and the rebellious instrumentalists whose performances in the gallery are under threat from the newfangled harmonium.

The prevailing sunniness of *Under the Greenwood Tree* is darkened by more sombre and tragic themes in *Far from the Madding Crowd*.

Fancy Day has matured into Bathsheba Everdene, a rural heiress who owns a substantial farm and would like to prove herself in the masculine world. Three men fall passionately in love with her in their diverse ways. Gabriel Oak, ruined as an independent farmer and now Bathsheba's shepherd, is the steady, sober, loyal man of utterly unselfish integrity who would do anything for her except flatter her by hiding the truth from her when she acts foolishly. He serves and waits in silence until the happy ending gives him his reward. By contrast, Sergeant Troy is a flashy intruder on the rural scene who seduces Bathsheba's servant girl and then mesmerises her mistress into marriage. Meanwhile a third, tragic figure hovers in the wings: Farmer Boldwood, a bachelor in his forties, stirred from long years of repression to a frantically obsessive passion for Bathsheba. The irony is that the stirring up was initiated by an idle prank on Bathsheba's part in sending this most unlikely character a Valentine. In the upshot it is Boldwood, driven to madness by Bathsheba's marriage to Troy and Troy's ill-treatment of her, who murders the selfish husband and leaves the way clear for faithful Gabriel.

From the start reviewers of Hardy's novels tended to expend most of their admiration on the portrayal of rustic life which provided the background to the careers of his major characters. He was praised for conveying knowingly what happens at lambing time or harvest time and for bringing to life the gossip and banter of the ale-house and the farmyard. Yet early reviewers pointed, too, to the artificial element in the dialogue of farm-labourers – Hardy's way of giving them utterance above their capacity:

> The whole class of hoers, sowers, ploughmen, reapers, &c, are – if Mr Hardy's pictures may be trusted – the most incredibly amusing and humorous persons you ever came across, full of the quaintest irony and the most comical speculative intelligence . . . These poor men are quizzical critics, inaccurate divines, keen-eyed men of the world, who talk a semi-profane, semi-Biblical dialect full of veins of humour which have passed into it from a different sphere.

So wrote R. H. Hutton (1826–97) in a *Spectator* review of *Far from the Madding Crowd* in 1874. Hardy certainly intensified the drama of his central figures by supplying an imaginatively enriched commentary from the lips of his local peasantry. They perform some of the functions of the chorus in Greek drama, off-setting the grand passions and awesome agonies of the main participants by the voice of earthy, pedestrian humanity that has other things than grand passions to think about and has long ago reconciled itself to the contrariness of things and to the irony to be savoured in it.

In this respect Hardy brings to his novels the mind and artistry of the poet. It may be argued that what have been considered to be his main defects – his over-reliance upon coincidence in turning lives tragically awry, and his tendency to pictorialism that sometimes strains his diction with an awkward pretentiousness – are aspects of a dramatic and poetic vision that has to be imposed at any cost on the form of the Victorian novel, a form whose conventions of presentation were more fitted to the more prosaic representation-alism of a George Eliot or a Trollope. *The Return of the Native* (1878), for instance, stamps the impress of a fatalistic Greek tragedy on the love lives of Wessex country folk, and a good deal of the authenticity of the prevailing atmosphere of doom derives from Hardy's use in the background of Egdon Heath, a sombre, baleful presence casting a spell on its scattered inhabitants. The complaint was voiced by contemporary reviewers that Hardy was involved in absurdity in using as his dramatis personae people of such modest social standing as Clym Yeobright, whose blindness causes him to end up as a furze-cutter, and Damon Wildeve, the philandering publican with whom two contrasting women fall in love. They are the gentle, worthy Thomasin Yeobright and the selfish, ambitious Eustacia Vye.

The Trumpet Major (1880) is an altogether more cheerful story, a novel set in the period of the Napoleonic wars. Two contrasting brothers, John and Bob Loveday, are rivals for the love of Anne Garland. The trumpeter, John, is the unselfish, earnest fellow, while Bob the sailor is the breezy, light-hearted one. There is also a third contender for Anne's hand, a braggart too stupid to be taken seriously. Bob wins the prize; John goes off to blow his trumpet for the last time on 'one of the bloody battlefields of Spain'.

The Mayor of Casterbridge (1886), one of the century's finest novels, traces the rise and fall of Michael Henchard, a tough, egotis-tical fellow who, having committed the folly of drunkenly selling his wife and baby at a fair, turns teetotal and by sheer perseverence rises to wealth as a corn-factor and to respectability as Mayor of Casterbridge (Dorchester). After eight years his wife comes home believing herself a widow and bringing a daughter, Elizabeth Jane, whom Henchard assumes to be his own. Henchard's masterfulness and wrong-headedness drive his assistant, Farfrae, into competition in the corn business. Personal and business disasters crowd in upon Henchard to ruin him. On his wife's death he learns that Elizabeth Jane is not his daughter; worse still, her true father returns to claim her. A desolate, disgraced, impoverished figure, Henchard eventu-ally dies in a hut on Egdon Heath. It could be argued that *The Mayor of Casterbridge* is Hardy's least flawed achievement in fiction.

The emotional force sustained in tracing the development of Henchard's relationships, amicable and hostile alike, gives dramatic intensity to the work. Henchard, proud, obstinate, inflexible, bestrides the pages with the compulsive grandeur of Shakespeare's great tragic heroes. Through the chorus of rustic commentary from the lesser peasantry in the background runs a sombre and searching vein of ironic humour. And, as in *The Return of the Native*, Nature herself is sometimes less a background than a presence and participant, a living force intervening in human affairs in the form of rain and storm ruinous to harvest prospects. Hardy's survey of the human scene, unlike George Eliot's (except perhaps in *Silas Marner*), has the quality of a poetic vision. The same could of course be said of Dickens's; but whereas Dickens's poetic artistry creates multifarious idiosyncratic human beings against diverse social and natural backgrounds, Hardy's poetic artistry tracks the working out of destiny in the lives of a handful of men and women whose heroic stature arises simply from intensification of the ordinary and the everyday.

In *The Woodlanders* (1887) the faithful love of Giles Winterbourne for Grace Melbury is as frustrated as is the faithful love of Marty South for Giles Winterbourne. The obstacles to Giles's happiness are, firstly desire for social superiority which unites Grace to a philanderer, Fitzpiers, and then the restrictive Victorian *mores* which keep Giles and Grace apart when Fitzpiers deserts her for a time. Powerful as this novel is, it was eclipsed by *Tess of the D'Urbervilles* (1891), subtitled *A Pure Woman*, and focusing with intensity on a poor village girl, Tess, who is seduced by the well-to-do Alec D'Urberville, a thoroughgoing Victorian villain. Tess gives birth to a child, but it dies, and eventually, while working on a dairy farm, she falls in love with Angel Clare, son of a clergyman. Tess delays revealing her past to Angel until their wedding night, after he has made a comparable confession of his own and been forgiven. Angel, however, is pitiless and immediately deserts her. Alone and forsaken, she eventually succumbs to Alec's pressure upon her to accept his protection, and thus, when Angel returns repentant to reclaim her, her prospect of happiness has for the second time been ruined by the same man, Alec. Driven to madness, she murders him. The book ends with her execution. The pattern of action has again the remorseless fatalism of Greek tragedy and Hardy's last paragraph in the book underlines the point:

> 'Justice' was done, and the President of the Immortals (in Aeschylean phrase) had ended his sport with Tess.

The novel, of course, represents a powerful protest against the double standard of moral judgement in sexual matters which the

Victorians applied to men and to women. So the President of the Immortals is not the only source of injustice.

There were many who recognised the quality of Hardy's masterpiece from the start. Sir William Watson (1858–1935) reviewed the book favourably in *Academy*, noting especially the moral gravity of its subject:

> The great theme of the book is the incessant penalty paid by the innocent for the wicked, the unsuspicious for the crafty, the child for its father . . .

On the other hand, the over-riding pessimism and the sexual frankness of the novel inevitably provoked a critical backlash so sharp that Hardy noted in his diary: 'Well, if this sort of thing continues no more novel-writing for me. A man would be a fool to deliberately stand up to be shot at!'

In fact Hardy braved Victorian disapproval in fiction only once more and then with such provocative thoroughness that the hostile reception of *Jude the Obscure* (1895) put an end to his career as a novelist. Jude, an aspiring Wessex stone-mason, is frustrated in his intellectual ambitions and blighted in his sexual life. Trapped by sheer sensuality into an incompatible marriage to Arabella, and subsequently deserted, he falls in love with a lively-minded schoolmistress, Sue Bridehead. Jude has dreamed of a life in the priesthood, but when Sue leaves her husband and joins Jude, this possibility is removed. The low point of Hardyesque gloom is reached in the study of 'Little Father Time', Jude's son by Arabella, who is sensitively moved by the miseries of Jude and Sue. He contrives to help them by hanging himself, his step-brothers and step-sisters in a cupboard and leaving the cryptic explanation, 'Done because we are too menny'. In terms of effective propaganda it was perhaps a pity that the crucial protest against the unequal opportunities for educational development which is at the heart of Jude's dilemma should have been combined with a study of what Hardy himself called 'the deadly war . . . between flesh and spirit' waged on a battle-ground so overcast with contrived miseries. Yet little can have been lost by Hardy's forsaking of the novel at this point compared to what was gained by his turning to poetry.

The Brontë sisters

Like Hardy, the Brontë sisters are classed as 'regional' novelists. If the Dorchester of Hardy's childhood had a life far removed from the life of the metropolis, the moorland village of Haworth, Yorkshire, in which the Brontës were reared must have been even more remote to the London mind. The Reverend Patrick Brontë was an Irishman who had been educated at Cambridge. Bernard Shaw said, 'I am a typical Irishman: my family came from Yorkshire', and in fact Jonathan Swift could have said exactly the same. Charlotte Brontë would not have thought of saying, 'I am a typical Yorkshire woman: my father came from Ireland'. Nevertheless the cross-fertilisation between Ireland and Yorkshire has clearly proved fruitful in literature. Much has been made of the Celtic element in the Brontës' novels. It could be argued that the Yorkshire character, with its heavy irony, its dead-pan humour, its delight in deflation, its taste for self-parody, and its unfailing awareness of its own distinctiveness is in some ways more Irish than the Irish.

Patrick Brontë brought his Cornish wife and their first two daughters to a curacy at Thornton near Bradford in 1815. Maria Brontë (née Branwell) bore her husband six children, five girls and a boy, in seven years, and four of them were to survive to adulthood, Charlotte (1816–55), Branwell (1817–48), Emily (1818–48) and Anne (1820–49). Mr Brontë became incumbent of Haworth, a moorland village eight miles from Thornton, in 1820; his wife died early the following year, and the widower's attempts to remarry failed. His sister-in-law, Miss Branwell, took over the household, and it is not surprising that in 1824 Mr Brontë responded with eagerness to an advertisement which offered education peculiarly fitted to clergymen's daughters at a cost peculiarly fitted to clergymen's pockets at the Clergy Daughters' School at Cowan Bridge, some forty miles away in Westmorland. The Reverend Carus Wilson, the school's founder, presumably recognised the problem faced by widowed clergymen, but he seems to have tried to cater for it on a shoe-string at Cowan Bridge. Food was unhealthy, the water tainted, the building cold. Typhus and consumption took their toll of the children. Patrick Brontë sent his two eldest daughters, Maria and Elizabeth, there first. Charlotte and Emily followed in their turn shortly afterwards. When Maria and Elizabeth were sent home to die in 1825 their sisters were withdrawn.

The loss of their mother, then of their sisters, their committal to the care of Aunt Branwell, a rigorous-minded Methodist, and the absence in the locality of a congenial neighbouring circle of acquaintances, left their marks on the children. They constructed their own imaginative worlds and wrote their own chronicles. However, as they grew older, they did come to taste life outside Haworth. Charlotte was at a school at Roe Head near Dewsbury first as a pupil, then as a teacher. She and Anne both worked for a time as governesses. The sisters planned to open and run their own school, and in order to equip themselves with enough knowledge of French and German for this purpose, Charlotte and Emily went early in 1842 to a school in Brussels run by M. Héger. After coming home on their aunt's death in November 1842, Charlotte returned alone to Brussels for another year. She fell in love with M. Héger, so deeply indeed that she suffered long and miserably, and the experience, of course, left its mark on her work. While the sisters took refuge in writing, Branwell, at first a would-be artist, declined from one failure to another. He became addicted to alcohol and laudanum, and his death in 1848 at the age of thirty-one relieved the family of a depressingly intolerable burden. By this time Charlotte had published *Jane Eyre* (1847), Emily had published *Wuthering Heights* (1847), and Anne had published *Agnes Grey* (1847) and *The Tenant of Wildfell Hall* (1848), the three of them concealing their identities under the pseudonyms, Currer, Ellis and Acton Bell.

Successful authorship did not inaugurate a period of cheerfulness, for Emily died at home of consumption in December 1848 only three months after Branwell, and Anne died at Scarborough five months after that in May 1849. Charlotte became a celebrity; she visited London and made the acquaintance of Thackeray; but her last years were spent at Haworth where finally, in 1854, she married her father's curate, the Reverend Arthur Bell Nicholls, only to die after a brief period of great happiness nine months later. Her father outlived her for six years; her husband, who returned to his native Ireland and eventually remarried, outlived her by fifty years.

Charlotte was the dominant personality of the three sisters, though Emily's gifts were perhaps rarer and her achievement in *Wuthering Heights* more astonishing. In hindsight the immediate success of *Jane Eyre* looks predictable. There have been writers since who, before settling down to write a novel, have asked themselves, 'What ingredients will guarantee big sales?' and have contrived to manufacture those ingredients. *Jane Eyre* was not so written; if ever a novel was written from the heart, this was; but its ingredients are such that one hundred and forty years after its first appearance an advertisement for a paperback edition can proclaim it 'the finest of all romances'. Jane tells her own story. Orphaned, harshly brought up by her aunt, she is sent off to Lowood school where the privation, cruelty, and disease rampant at Cowan Bridge are endured by girls whose fortitude in suffering stirs the reader's fury at the meanness and hypocrisy of those responsible for it. In this respect Charlotte Brontë's assault on the injustices perpetrated by well-to-do adults and her compassionate portrayal of the agonies endured by their young victims more than match Dickens's, for, of course, little girls are even more vulnerable than little boys. Jane becomes a teacher at Lowood and then takes a post as governess to a little girl at Thornfield Hall. Charlotte Brontë had seen the life of the gentry from the point of view of the governess, and the status of the governess in Victorian society was an ambiguous one. In the role of governess, as in the role of curate, people of slender means could impinge on the lives of the well-to-do with such dignity as education could impart to sometimes otherwise socially unacceptable persons; for to such posts as those of governess or curate the young of the comparatively poor might aspire and the young of over-prolific middle-class families might be condemned. Thus, through the eyes of Jane Eyre, Charlotte Brontë has left some scathing portraiture of the society life of which the Victorian governess would be a witness rather than a participant.

The vitality of the Thornfield Hall section of the book relies chiefly, however, on the character of Jane's master, Edward Rochester, and on the way it impinges on her own. He is a proud, masterful, sardonic character, seemingly harsh and morose. Jane is plain and slight in build, but she has a wilfulness and spiritedness of her own and can give as good as she gets in a war of words, even with her domineering master. The two fall in love. But Rochester, at forty, has a mysterious life behind him, and strange events at Thornfield Hall cast an ominous light on developments. It is gradually revealed that there is a raving mad woman in the attic who has to be physically restrained from doing damage. Only on Jane's wedding day does the truth emerge: the marriage ceremony is interrupted by a stranger who declares Rochester married already. The lunatic is his wife. A tense personal struggle ensues for Jane. Rochester implores her not to forsake him, but moral rectitude triumphs and she flees the Hall. She is rescued in her distress by the Reverend St John Rivers and his sisters. Rivers, a man of great piety, is preparing to go to India as a missionary and he begs Jane to accompany him as his wife. Thus the struggle between duty and passion recurs in converse form, for though Jane admires Rivers and understands his need for companionship and support, she does not love him. At the second crisis of decision a telepathic message calls her back to Rochester. She discovers that Thornfield Hall has been destroyed by fire; Rochester has been blinded in vainly trying to save his wife from the flames, and Jane finds him desolate and hopeless. The last chapter of the novel begins, 'Reader, I married him.'

There is an intensity in Charlotte Brontë's novels very different from that of Hardy's. Hardy's is a sombre, brooding intensity; Charlotte Brontë's is a warm, glowing intensity. Waves of passion wash over the reader. A strange magnetism envelops the heroines as they move about the lofty rooms of Victorian vicarages and country houses. They live at a pitch of emotional sensitivity that sends a current of quivering fervour coursing through their otherwise humdrum lives. This is evident in *Shirley* (1849) in which Charlotte Brontë goes back to the days of the Luddite riots which took place some fourteen years before she was born. Progressive mill-owners were struggling to introduce new, labour-saving machinery into their factories at a time when the Napoleonic wars had cut the country off from its export markets and gravely damaged the textile industry. The activities of machine-breakers, who waylaid the loaded wagons on lonely moorland roads at night, provided exciting background material for fiction, and the obdurate persistence of far-sighted mill-owners in the face of organised local hostility naturally appealed to Charlotte Brontë's penchant for portraying wilfully masterful men of forbidding exterior, an interest dating back to her acquaintance with Paul Héger and no doubt influenced by the figure of the Byronic hero popular in her young days. Her hero, Robert Moore, significantly half-English, half-Belgian, is determined to make his Yorkshire mill up-to-date and prosperous in the teeth of violent opposition. He proposes marriage to a wealthy lady, Shirley Keeldar, to secure his financial position, although he is devotedly loved by Caroline Helstone, the rector's niece. Shirley, a high-spirited, independent woman, loftily rejects Robert Moore. Caroline, a sweet and gentle, patient and charming heroine, is her foil. In Shirley Charlotte Brontë strove to bring to life something of the firm, inspired, almost masculine temperament of Emily, for whom the family nickname was 'the Major'. In Caroline no doubt she presented a career of wish-fulfilment, for it is Caroline to whom Robert Moore turns finally for a wife, and by that time she has even rediscovered her long-lost mother. There is no doubt that Charlotte Brontë detaches herself from her own experience more fully in this novel than in the others, not only in the sense that Caroline and Shirley are conceived as objective portraits, but also in the sense that a larger and more varied cast of local characters is portrayed with some detail in the background. Nevertheless the dominant theme to come to life is that of the steady, devout Caroline Helstone undergoing the strains of deeply wounding emotional disturbance *en route* to happiness and fulfilment.

In *Villette* (1853) Charlotte Brontë re-works material from her earlier and then unpublished novel, *The Professor*, which was published posthumously in 1856. She returns, too, to the autobiographical method of presentation and to a more direct and impassioned use of her own experience. Her heroine, Lucy Snowe, is another plain, unattractive girl, poor and friendless, who takes a teaching post in a girls' school in Brussels. A less assertive and a lonelier figure than Jane Eyre, she suffers keenly to the point of a

nervous breakdown. A contrast is drawn between her deep seriousness and the shallowness of the flirtatious Ginevra Fanshawe. But
the dominant issue becomes the transformation of the seemingly
despotic and ill-tempered Paul Emmanuel into Lucy's benefactor
and lover. She who has known so little happiness is finally drenched
in the man's bounty and the reader is left to draw his own
conclusions. Paul Emmanuel, of course, is a portrait of M. Héger.
Mme Héger is represented in the headmistress, Mme Beck. Here as
elsewhere in Charlotte Brontë's novels it is the tingling responsive-
ness of the heroine's emotional antennae that evokes the reader's
sympathies. The sense of good and evil at war in the choices which
life presents is that of a deeply devout Christian for whom this
life may often be a vale of tears but for whom only obedience to
God can possibly bring peace. This is one aspect of Charlotte
Brontë's profundity. Another is the poetic sensibility which sees
the natural background in terms of the human drama enacted before
it. The use of symbolism is often searchingly apt, as when, on
the night after Rochester's proposal of marriage in *Jane Eyre*, the
horse-chestnut tree in the garden is struck by lightning and split in
half.

Emily Brontë was the most distinctively gifted of the three sisters.
She was neither a naturally sociable nor, seemingly, an actively
ambitious woman. She did not like being away from home. She
loved her native moorlands. She was something of a mystic and
wrote some fine poems. Her family clearly regarded her as the odd
one out, but admired her staunchness and inner resourcefulness. The
story of her novel, *Wuthering Heights* (1847), is complex in that it
follows family histories through three generations. Wuthering
Heights is a bleak farmhouse on the windswept Yorkshire moors.
Mr and Mrs Earnshaw bring up their two children, Hindley and
Catherine, there. One day Mr Earnshaw comes back from a business
trip to Liverpool with a poor waif he has rescued from the streets.
This is Heathcliff, who is brought up at the farm, becomes Mr
Earnshaw's favourite, is passionately befriended by Catherine, but
hated and bullied by Hindley. When Mr Earnshaw dies, Hindley,
who has been away to college, comes home with his young wife to
take over the farm and to reduce Heathcliff to the status of a menial.
When Edgar Linton of Thrushcross Grange proposes to Catherine,
she accepts him, recognising the degradation of Heathcliff. Yet the
passionate relationship which developed between Catherine and
Heathcliff as youngsters sends a powerful current coursing fatally
through the rest of the story. On the eve of her marriage to Edgar,
Catherine can say of Heathcliff:

'My great miseries in this world have been Heathcliff's miseries, and I watched and felt each from the beginning: my great thought in living is himself. If all else perished, and he remained, I should still continue to be: and if all else remained, and he were annihilated, the universe would turn to a mighty stranger.'

The intertwining of the Earnshaws and the Lintons provides the basis for Heathcliff's terrible revenge. Having disappeared on Catherine's marriage, he eventually returns to take calculated and systematic vengeance. He ruins Hindley with drinking and gambling, and inherits the farm on Hindley's death. He marries Edgar Linton's sister Isabella for her money and brings up Hindley's son Hareton as a brute. Catherine dies giving birth to a daughter and eventually Heathcliff forces a marriage between this daughter, also called Catherine, and his own ailing son, Linton, whose will brings Thrushcross Grange also into Heathcliff's hands on the son's expected early death.

As in Hardy Nature is a living force in *Wuthering Heights*, and there is an overshadowing fatalistic sense of human destiny worked out at a frightening cost. Yet fate does not work here, as in Hardy, by impersonal acts of God like thunderstorms that destroy crops or by accidentally undelivered letters whose contents could have saved lives. Disaster springs from human passion, the strangely irresistible mutual self-identification of Heathcliff and Catherine, Catherine's seemingly rational thwarting of it in conventional marriage, and Heathcliff's unflinching determination to exact vengeance that will match the enormity of this challenge to what is deepest in the lives of the two of them. Emily Brontë was no Hardyesque pessimist. At the end, when Heathcliff has done his worst, the demonic wilfulness is spent, and after his death Hareton Earnshaw and Catherine Linton marry happily. When the new tenant of Thrushcross Grange visits the graves of Catherine, Edgar and Heathcliff, it is to sense peace after the storm:

I lingered round them, under that benign sky, watched moths fluttering among the heath and harebells, listened to the soft wind breathing through the grass, and wondered how any one could ever imagine unquiet slumbers for the sleepers in that quiet earth.

Anne Brontë (1820–49), though no doubt the least gifted of the three sisters, wrote two novels which have a special fascination for readers interested in the Brontës themselves. *Agnes Grey* (1847), a short novel, was published alongside *Wuthering Heights* to make up the normal Victorian three-volume package. Anne herself frankly admitted its autobiographical character. The story is simply told in the first person. Agnes, daughter of a clergyman, goes to be a governess in order to help her family financially. She has two posts in succession, at Wellwood House and Horton Lodge. In each case she is badly treated by arrogant employers and has to handle disobedient, ill-brought-up children. While at Horton Lodge she falls in love with a curate, Mr Weston, and, after she has started a school of her own with her now widowed mother at a seaside resort, the curate turns up and marries her. There is unflagging force and directness in the story. No doubt George Moore exaggerated when he called it 'the most perfect prose narrative in English literature', but the heroine's sufferings, hopes and dreams are conveyed with such heartfelt conviction that any reader must find it a moving record, and doubly so in the knowledge of its autobiographical truth.

Wellwood House is in reality Blake Hall near Dewsbury where Anne Brontë took her first post with the Inghams ('Bloomfields' in the novel). The Bloomfield children are horrors, indeed monsters. They are selfish, undisciplined and cruel. They delight in tormenting their governess. They will spit in her handbag, they will throw it on the fire, and hurl her writing desk out of the window. Anne was indeed appalled at the behaviour of the Ingham children, at their ignorance, and at the way their mother indulged them. Horton Lodge, the place of Agnes's second appointment, was based on Thorp Green Hall, Little Ouseburn, twelve miles from York, and in an altogether mellower and less rugged countryside than that of Haworth or Dewsbury. In the novel Agnes's handling of the two elder girls, a flirt and a hoyden, makes entertaining reading and gives a clear satirical picture of country house life where the parents lack culture and the children are grossly spoilt. But most moving of all is the wish-fulfilment indulged in bringing the love-affair with the curate Mr Weston to a happy ending. For Mr Weston is undoubtedly a suitably modified portrait of Willy Weightman who was curate at Haworth from August 1839 to September 1842. He was a well-educated man with a good heart, a generous readiness to help others, and a charming presence, so charming that he gained a reputation for philandering, as Charlotte made plain. Though Anne became early attached to him, it seems that it was only late in his time at Haworth that the feeling was fully reciprocated. Anne's partiality seems to have been fuelled by Weightman's generous efforts to befriend and help Branwell after he had been dismissed in disgrace from a post with the railway at Luddenden Foot. Weightman, however, died from cholera while Anne was away at Thorp Green.

The genesis of Anne's second novel, *The Tenant of Wildfell Hall* (1848), lies deep in her first-hand experience of suffering. Anne came to Branwell's aid by recommending him as tutor to the Robinsons at Thorp Green Hall. An extraordinary series of events followed, not all of which are even now fully understood. It appears that Mrs Robinson flirted with Branwell and he fell in love with her. Mr Robinson became terminally ill and Branwell got the idea that Mrs Robinson would marry him on her husband's death, he would succeed to the estate, and all his worries would be over. Somehow Mr Robinson was made aware of the liaison and Branwell was ignominiously dismissed. Branwell continued to believe in Mrs Robinson, and indeed it seems that she may have sent him money from time to time; but on her husband's death a mysterious messenger rode to Haworth to announce that Mr Robinson's will forbade his widow to remarry and that Branwell must not appear again at Thorp Green. The information about the will was false, but the warning to Branwell to keep away was serious. Already dissipated in his habits, he drank and drugged himself to death.

Anne Brontë had been her aunt Branwell's favourite and had been imbued with an evangelical piety which she retained until her death. No doubt she felt a degree of responsibility for having introduced Branwell to Thorp Green. Certainly she devoted herself with resolute zeal to the earnest composition of a novel laden with moral instruction and pious exhortation. It traces the gradual descent to total degeneracy of a country gentleman, Huntingdon, whose faithful wife is alienated by his brutality and has to take refuge from him and from others who would take advantage of her unprotectedness by moving well away from him and living with her little boy under an assumed name in the Wildfell Hall of the title. The story opens as Mrs 'Helen Graham', alias Huntingdon, known as a widow, takes up the tenancy of the Hall. Her independence and spiritedness in thus defying Victorian convention is another aspect of a book which, for all its longueurs, has great authority. Its frank picture of a Victorian household where a shooting party might degenerate after a night's drinking into a vulgar brawl reminiscent of a low-class tavern is significant. The book sold well, partly because some reviewers condemned it for its coarseness and brutality in picturing scenes of debauchery, and so ensured that it enjoyed a measure of notoriety. To the modern reader it is restrained indeed in this respect, and even evasive when, for instance, Huntingdon makes his new governess his mistress. The reader has to infer this crucial development from the fact that Helen's maid has revealed something about the governess which justifies Helen's decision to depart from under the same roof and leave her husband forthwith.

Elizabeth Gaskell

After Anne's death Charlotte was left alone in the parsonage with her father, and a period of great nervous strain ensued. Nevertheless she was now known as the celebrated author of *Jane Eyre* and *Shirley*, and among those who sought her acquaintance were Sir James and Lady Kay Shuttleworth. Sir James was a Lancashire doctor whose experience of work among the industrial poor turned him into an advocate of large-scale improvement in public education, and he became Secretary to the Committee of the Privy Council on Education. The Kay Shuttleworths lived at Gawthorpe Hall near Burnley, and in 1850 Charlotte was invited to stay with them at Briery Close, a house they had taken overlooking Lake Windermere. On August 10th Charlotte wrote to her father from Briery Close that Mrs Gaskell (1810–65) was expected among the guests. Thus began a relationship matched in literary fruitfulness only by the relationship of Dr Johnson to Boswell and Scott to Lockhart. Both writers have told how they were respectively met at Windermere station by Sir Thomas's coachman and driven to the meeting which was so decisive in their lives. Mrs Gaskell noted Charlotte's plainness and slightness of build, her nervousness and her inner power, and was deeply impressed by the apparent cruelty and desolation of her experience. And indeed the contrast was sharp between Charlotte's current situation at Haworth and Mrs Gaskell's situation in Manchester where, married now for eighteen years to a Unitarian minister and the mother of six children of whom four girls survived, she was at the centre of a warm, lively, busy household with a devoted husband known for his good works. Moreover, she was as handsome, graceful and cheerful as Charlotte was plain, nervous and melancholy. The two women were drawn to each other, they visited each other's homes and spent long hours in conversation. It was natural that Charlotte's father should ask her to write an account of his daughter's life and work after her death.

The Life of Charlotte Brontë (1857) is Mrs Gaskell's most triumphant success. The technique of presentation is skilful. Preliminary sketches of the Yorkshire background and the Yorkshire character, of local traditions and local clergy, are done with the imaginative dexterity of the novelist. As the family history unfolds Mrs Gaskell's anecdotal tit-bits enliven a deep sensitivity to the natural environment, the home situation and the idiosyncrasies of the family and its hangers-on. Mrs Gaskell has sometimes been accused of excessive timidity in suppressing what might have struck her contemporaries as scandalous revelations. Certainly she did not open up the subject of Charlotte's relationship with M. Héger; but

surely it was too soon to do so within a few years of her death and
in the earliest years of Arthur Bell Nicholls's bereavement. What
strikes the modern reader is rather Mrs Gaskell's fearlessness in
telling the truth as she saw it. Indeed she landed herself in hot water
both for her frank revelations about the Reverend Carus Wilson and
his Clergy Daughters' School at Cowan Bridge, and for her account
of the behaviour of Mrs Robinson of Thorp Green, who was, of
course, still alive and who threatened action for libel. By the end of
the century standard critical opinion was that Mrs Gaskell had been
too impressed by Charlotte's own account of Branwell's last years
and his death. She had accepted uncritically, it was urged, the version
of a biased sister who had preferred to regard her brother as ruined
by a wicked woman rather than as simply the victim of his own
folly. Clement Shorter, in *Charlotte Brontë and Her Circle* (1896),
described the account of Mrs Robinson as 'one long tissue of lies
and hallucinations' on Branwell's part; and it became fashionable to
condemn Mrs Gaskell for her damaging credulity in relation to Mrs
Robinson and to praise her for so devotedly, tenderly and accurately
bringing her subject to life. And indeed Mrs Gaskell's effectiveness
in telling Charlotte's story from the inside by judicious use of letters
and by careful enquiries among those who knew her produced a
classic which in one respect perhaps surpasses what she achieved in
her novels, and that is in gripping and holding the reader's imagination from beginning to end.

When Mrs Gaskell greeted Charlotte Brontë for the first time, she
was known for her first novel, *Mary Barton, A Tale of Manchester
Life* (1848). It portrays Manchester life at the time of the Chartist
agitation of 1838–40 with which Disraeli was concerned in *Sybil*.
John Barton, an honest, intelligent, industrious cotton worker, is
distressed by the sufferings of the underpaid and the unemployed,
outraged by the contrast between their privations and the luxuries
of their employers' daily life which is dependent on the labour of
others, and totally baffled by the fact that these same employers are
supposed to be Christians. He joins a Trade Union and becomes
one of the men's leading representatives when a strike thrusts them
into bitter conflict with their bosses. Frustration and insult drive the
union members to plan an assassination. Barton draws the fatal lot
and kills Henry Carson, son of a tough mill-owner. Mary Barton,
his daughter, has been, first foolishly responsive to, then more wisely
resistant to young Carson's attempt to win her. Jem Wilson, whose
love she has foolishly rejected and who has on one occasion knocked
his rival Carson down in the street, is charged with his murder, for
it is Jem's gun that Barton borrowed for the crime. Stumbling on
the truth, Mary has to try to save Jem without implicating her father.

This part of the story is well-handled. Mary's heroic efforts, which involve tracking down a sailor, already aboard ship, who can guarantee Jem's alibi, match those of Jeanie Deans in Scott's *The Heart of Midlothian*, a novel whose influence Victorian novelists seemed incapable of resisting.

What gives conviction and authenticity to many episodes in the book is Mrs Gaskell's close knowledge of how workers live, the contents of their homes, the details of their daily struggle to make ends meet and to combat the weather, the diseases, and indeed the temptations to theft or to prostitution which could so readily destroy them. Mrs Gaskell strives hard to be fair in presenting the conflict between masters and men, and, indeed, manages to convey a sense of the essential sameness of human agony in bereavement whether felt by the boss or the penniless worker. In this respect she covers ground to be trodden again sixty years later by John Galsworthy (1867–1933) in his play *Strife* (1909). Nevertheless she was, not unnaturally, accused of bias against the employers, for it is the sufferings of the poor that tug most forcefully at the heart.

A defect of this and some other novels by Mrs Gaskell is the excessive sentimentality and the appetite for melodramatic plotting. Thus Mary's Aunt Esther, having once succumbed to seduction by one of higher social class, has been inevitably dragged down to prostitution. A gaudily decked, remorseful, whimpering street-walker, she flits in and out of the story, alternately moving the plot forward and shivering away from human touch in shame. Such heavily didactic studies fail in authenticity. And scenes at sick-beds or death-beds are delineated in over-heated rhetoric and are decorated with conventional pieties. Yet for all this, and rightly, Mrs Gaskell is celebrated for her sheer good-nature and her sheer common sense. George Moore labelled her 'the most commonplace of all English writers'.

She turned in *Ruth* (1853) to make a plea for sympathetic treatment of a seduced girl and her illegitimate child. Ruth is taken in by a Dissenting minister. Her long-drawn-out penance culminates in death, so that, at the time, her fate offended progressively-minded readers while moral reactionaries put the book on the fire. Modern readers will notice Mrs Gaskell's implicit protest against the Victorian double-standard of morality for men and for women. In *North and South* (1855) she returned to the theme of two nations, rich and poor, capital and labour, but her greatest achievement in fiction was to come in a very different form from that which allowed either for earnest economic argument or for high-flown melodrama. *Cranford* (1853) takes us to Knutsford in the Cheshire countryside in which Mrs Gaskell was brought up by her aunt (her mother having died soon after her birth). Her uncle, Dr Holland, used to take her with him on his country rounds. This was her home until she was sent to school at Stratford-upon-Avon at the age of fifteen. *Cranford* is not a plotted novel but rather a series of episodes in the lives of a group of Cranford's inhabitants. Mrs Gaskell employs a sly but compassionate irony in depicting the uneventful lives of genteel spinsters for whom palpitating sensations, such as the news of a forthcoming marriage or a visit to the aristocracy, give substance and excitement to their days. The delicacy with which Mrs Gaskell smiles at the devices by which poverty is concealed while all conspire in the deception is characteristic of a skill which makes comparison with Jane Austen appropriate:

> When Mrs Forrester, for instance, gave a party in her baby-house of a dwelling, and the little maiden disturbed the ladies on the sofa by a request that she might get the tea-tray out from underneath, everyone took this novel proceeding as the most natural thing in the world, and talked on about household forms and ceremonies as if we all believed that our hostess had a regular servants' hall, second table, with housekeeper and steward, instead of one little charity-school maiden, whose short ruddy arms could never have been strong enough to carry the tray upstairs, if she had not been assisted in private by her mistress, who now sat in state pretending not to know what cakes were sent up, though she knew, and we knew, and she knew that we knew, and we knew that she knew that we knew, she had been busy all the morning making tea-bread and sponge-cakes.

Cousin Phillis (1864) is a comparable *tour de force*. A short novel of less than one hundred pages, it has the qualities of a parable. The new railways are encroaching on the countryside, and into tranquil rural circles stride the bright young engineers of the new order with disturbing results. Phillis, daughter of an educated farmer who is also a Dissenting minister, has derived book-learning from him but otherwise at seventeen she is an unspoilt innocent, 'like a rose that had come to full bloom on the sunny side of a lonely house, sheltered from storms,' says her cousin Paul, who thinks she can be fitly compared with the Lucy of Wordsworth's love poems. Paul, brought to the area by his work on the railway, introduces into the minister's family group his brilliant young superior, Holdsworth. Holdsworth's knowledgeableness and sophistication charm more than they disturb the minister and touch Phillis's heart. She is so deeply and evidently distressed when Holdsworth is suddenly called away to work on the Canadian railway that Paul, out of sheer compassion, reveals how Holdsworth confided in him at parting his intention to return and marry her. Bloom and peace of mind are restored. When news comes that Holdsworth has married abroad Phillis is desolate and her health breaks down, but finally she recovers to announce her determination to put it all behind her. *Cousin Phillis, Cranford*, and the later novel, *Wives and Daughters* (1866), show Mrs Gaskell at her best. The knowledgeable concern she shares with the reader in her fictional studies of industrial conditions could not conceal the crudities of *Mary Barton* and *North and South*. She seems to have found her true vein in fastening on the foibles of Victorian country society with a blend of sympathy and satire that has polish and poise. She exudes warmth, moderation and goodwill, and her sensitivity is both subtle and perceptive over crucial – if limited – areas of human experience.

William Makepeace Thackeray

A name which keeps appearing in Mrs Gaskell's *Life of Charlotte Brontë* is that of William Makepeace Thackeray (1811–63). Charlotte admired him so much that she dedicated the second edition of *Jane Eyre* to him: 'I see in him an intellect profounder and more unique than his contemporaries have yet recognised.' He responded by sending her a copy of his *Vanity Fair*. The two met in London and he seems to have been the only celebrity who really overawed her. Yet when, after one of his public lectures, he introduced her to his mother as 'Jane Eyre', she laid into him next morning in her publisher's office with anger. 'They put the fear of God into each other', wrote Ann Monsarrat (in *The Uneasy Victorian, Thackeray the Man*, 1980).

In a memorable review in the *Quarterly Review*, headed '*Vanity Fair, Jane Eyre*, and Governesses', the two novels were classed together as having 'equal popularity'. Yet the two writers had little in common except, perhaps, in the way life had supplied them at first hand with the material for fiction. Indeed the story of Thackeray's own mother reads like the plot of a novel. Anne Becher was fifteen years old and in the care of her grandmother at Bath when a young army officer, Henry Carmichael-Smyth, fell in love with her. His prospects did not impress the grandmother, who put an end to their secret love affair by telling Anne that Henry had died of fever and had sent her a last message of love. Similarly Henry was told that Anne no longer cared for him and his letters to her were returned unopened. To give the heart-broken girl a chance to recover, her mother, home from Calcutta, took her back with her, and a year later, in 1810, she married Richmond Thackeray, the wealthy Secretary to the Calcutta Board of Revenue. One day in 1812, a year after the novelist's birth, Richmond Thackeray announced to his wife the arrival of a 'delightful and interesting' young man whom he had asked to dinner. The guest turned out to be Henry Carmichael-Smyth. After an agonising meal the stunned couple managed to share talk of how they had been duped, and when Richmond Thackeray died of fever in 1815 the couple were married. In 1817 when William was five years old he was sent back to England in the care of a servant, and preserved afterwards a notable memory of the journey. The boat called at St Helena and the servant pointed out to the boy a man walking in a garden: 'That is Bonaparte. He eats three sheep every day, and all the little children he can lay hands on.' In England Thackeray was sent to boarding schools and eventually to Charterhouse, where brutality was rampant. 'Torture in a public school is as much licensed as the knout [whip] in Russia,' he was to observe in *Vanity Fair*. At Cambridge, where he became acquainted with Edward Fitzgerald (1809–83) and with Tennyson, he wasted money in dissipation. He made a start on legal studies at the Middle Temple in 1831 and shared rooms with the future dramatist, Tom Taylor (1817–80), but the interest did not last long. He visited France and Germany. But his addiction to gambling eventually cost him a large part of his fortune and the rest of his father's wealth was lost through shaky investments by his stepfather. Thackeray married Isabella Shawe in Paris in 1836. She bore him three daughters of whom two survived; but after the birth of the third she suffered a mental breakdown which became permanent insanity. Thus the Thackeray who established himself as mentor of the 1840s had run through a fortune and been left with two daughters to bring up and a wife in a private mental home.

The need for money drove Thackeray into journalism and he moved by stages into the role of novelist. Early fiction included comic satiric magazine pieces such as the *Yellowplush Correspondence* in *Fraser's Magazine* which projects the life of society from the angle of the footman, and the exploits of *Major Gahagan* in the *New Monthly Magazine*. The comic periodical *Punch* was founded in 1841. Many writers were wary of it, but Thackeray contributed *The Snobs of England*, the pieces later collected as *The Book of Snobs* (1848), in 1846–7. They are hilarious sketches of society types. But it was the publication of *Vanity Fair* (1848) that gave Thackeray the status of a literary giant.

In this book all Thackeray's powers as a stylist and as an observer of the human scene suddenly came to fruition in a display of glowing creative energy. The basic pattern of the story relies on the well-worn contrast between the career of a flighty girl and that of an earnest one. But this time the flighty girl, Becky Sharp, meets with no retributive disaster of the kind that Scott's Effie Deans (*The Heart of Midlothian*) and George Eliot's Hetty Sorrel (*Adam Bede*) bring down upon themselves. For Becky Sharp is equal to the official world whose ethos she challenges. Daughter of a poor artist and an actress, she is bold, quick-witted and unscrupulous. A governess in the house of an aristocrat, she manages to marry his son and thereby lose him his inheritance. But as Mrs Rawdon Crawley she exploits a range of stratagems to establish herself in high society, where her amorous adventures eventually bring about a break with her husband and a loss of respectability. Her foil is Amelia Sedley, daughter of a wealthy London businessman, a gentle, attractive, affectionate, but not over-clever girl. She worships George Osborne, a young army officer who is scarcely worthy of her adoration and indeed has a liaison with Becky Sharp after his marriage to Amelia. He is killed at the Battle of Waterloo. Captain Dobbin, the worthy, unselfish fellow who has been Amelia's faithful advocate, benefactor and adorer, makes no headway with the grief-stricken widow until Becky disillusions her about Osborne's behaviour and his supposed fidelity. Then he is accepted.

The brilliance of the portraiture in this novel is indisputable, both in depth, in range and in variety. Undoubtedly the study of Becky Sharp, a vital, scheming, heartless temptress, is a *tour de force*. But the quality of the book lies also in the sheer immensity of coverage. From the households of London families Thackeray casts his eyes over the European scene at the time of the Battle of Waterloo, and the total effect is a vast panorama held under the gaze of omniscience. For though Thackeray works in the tradition of Fielding in standing back from his created world, the authorial angle is scarcely that of the amiable fellow-spectator at your elbow, but of the Olympian observer whose judgements reverberate with divine scorn. Charlotte Brontë called him 'an intellectual boa-constrictor', because 'he does not play with his prey, he coils round it and crushes it in his rings'. She sensed that he was terribly earnest in his war against the falsehood and follies of 'the world'. The barbed prose in which he flayed the mean and the arrogant bespeaks a lofty scorn, yet, in fact, Thackeray is neither a scoffer nor a sneerer. His chosen title from Bunyan's (1628–88) *The Pilgrim's Progress* (1684) and his subtitle, *A Novel without a Hero*, suggest the seriousness of his moral purpose. And indeed the authorial view achieves a philosophic dimension in the melancholy awareness of the mutability of those things on which men and women set their hearts.

It is not surprising that Thackeray failed to sustain in any of his later novels the emotional intensity and the inspirational sweep of *Vanity Fair*. The *History of Pendennis* (1848–50) has neither the tautness of concentration nor the unflagging narrative impetus of

Vanity Fair. It traces the growth of the writer, Arthur Pendennis, and is the nearest equivalent Thackeray left to Dickens's *David Copperfield*. Again there is a rich and varied gallery of characters and a full survey of upper-class London life. The novel is the first of what is called the 'Pendennis sequence', for Arthur Pendennis is the 'author' of two later novels, *The Newcomes* (1853–5) and *The Adventures of Philip* (1862). But more attention has been paid to Thackeray's success as a historical novelist in *The History of Henry Esmond* (1852), in which his minute knowledge of eighteenth-century history and his enthusiasm for eighteenth-century literature have full play. The hero serves in the campaigns of the Duke of Marlborough but also gets involved in the cause of the Stuart Pretender. Thackeray's style sustains the flavour of eighteenth-century prose and he actually had the first edition printed with the long eighteenth-century 's'. *The Virginians* (1857–9) is a sequel tracing the later history of the Esmond family. Henry Esmond's daughter Rachel having married an American, Thackeray transports us to America and does his best to win the sympathy of the American public when he comes to deal with the War of Independence. The tamer qualities of the books subsequent to *Vanity Fair* and perhaps especially the less critical outlook upon upper-class life, make it tempting to picture Thackeray as the man who, once his reputation was made and his financial and social position re-established, came to terms too readily with the moneyed world whose follies he had once mocked and scourged.

Edward Bulwer-Lytton

The lure of the historical novel and the challenge to vie with Scott led Thackeray, like Dickens and George Eliot, to produce works which were less than his best. It seems odd that it was a vastly inferior talent than theirs, that of Edward Bulwer-Lytton (1803–73), which in market terms most successfully assumed the mantle of Scott.

Bulwer-Lytton had published several novels by the time that Victoria came to the throne, first essaying the Byronic vein in *Falkland* (1827), and then focusing on the study of intelligent men who turn to crime in such novels as *Eugene Aram* (1832). Indeed, by the time the Victorian age proper began, Bulwer-Lytton had found his true forte as a historical novelist in *The Last Days of Pompeii* (1834), a love story reproducing the life in the doomed city immediately before its destruction by the eruption of Vesuvius in AD79. Moreover, the new reign was scarcely begun before Bulwer-Lytton had an immense success with an extravagantly romantic play, *The Lady of Lyons* (1838), which will concern us in the chapter on Victorian drama.

Bulwer-Lytton's later historical novels include *The Last of the Barons* (1843), about Warwick the Kingmaker, the power behind the Lancastrian king Henry VI who lost his throne to the Yorkist Edward IV in 1461. The novel deals with the period 1467–71. Warwick managed to restore Henry VI briefly in 1469, but was killed at the battle of Barnet in 1471, and Henry's cause was finally crushed at the battle of Tewkesbury in the same year. *Harold, the Last of the Saxon Kings* (1848) introduces us in the first chapter to Edward the Confessor playing host to William, Duke of Normandy in May 1052 on the old Kent Road outside London. The story of Harold's short reign is told to its end at the battle of Hastings, and Harold's love for Edith the Fair provides a romantic interest. The list of Principal Characters of the Story contains over eighty names and the list of Other Historical Persons mentioned in the text contains over fifty names. This gives some idea of the thoroughness of research and documentation behind the work. Yet, when all is said, the fatal addiction to a prose weighed down with false archaisms and laden with all manner of stylistic prolixities and affectations detracts from readability. A rhetoric which seems to have evoked reverence from the popular readership of the day now invites ridicule.

George Meredith

George Meredith (1828–1909), like Hardy, lived long enough to outlast the Victorian era, though his first novel, *The Ordeal of Richard Feverel* (1859), came out in the same year as George Eliot's *Adam Bede* and Dickens's *A Tale of Two Cities*. Meredith certainly bestrode two ages. His first wife was friendly with Mary Shelley (1797–1851), the poet's widow and author of *Frankenstein* (1818), and Thomas Jefferson Hogg (1792–1862), the poet's biographer, yet Meredith lived to be visited by Lloyd George (1863–1945) and to receive the Order of Merit from Edward VII. He was the grandson of a Portsmouth tailor, Melchisedek Meredith, who played the grandee, danced and drank and hunted and womanised, and was called 'Great Mel'. His mother died when he was five, and his father, also a tailor, took his young housekeeper as a mistress, later married her, went bankrupt, and emigrated to South Africa. Young George's education included a two-year spell at the Moravian School at Neuwied-sur-Rhine in Germany when he was fourteen to sixteen years of age. This was a significant period in his life. English society at the time was governed by men brought up in the public school and Oxbridge traditions, and influential writers such as Thackeray and Trollope shared this background. Meredith, by contrast, was nurtured at a crucial stage at a school with a clear philosophy that replaced the instructional principles, the crude discipline and the spartan ethic of English public schools with an emphasis on individual learning and unfettered informal development.

Meredith's personal story was for many years a sad one in that from the age of twenty he devoted himself to earning his living as a writer and had to endure some ten years of struggle and privation. Moreover, at the age of twenty-one, he married the daughter of the novelist Thomas Love Peacock (1785–1866), Mary Ellen Nicolls, a young widow whose first husband, a marine, had been drowned two months after their marriage, leaving her pregnant. She was twenty-five and Meredith eighteen when they met, which suggests that the initiative may have been on the widow's side. She was beautiful, witty and cultured. She had imbibed from her father libertarian notions of love and marriage. There was bound to be strain in a marriage where the husband deliberately gave himself heart and soul to writing which brought in so little, and in the long run it was Mary Ellen who proved unfaithful. Eight years after their marriage she broke the news to her husband that she was leaving him and that she was pregnant by the Pre-Raphaelite painter Henry Wallis (1830–1916) who had used Meredith for his model in his famous picture, 'The Death of Chatterton'. (It gives us an interesting view of what Meredith looked like with his beard shaved off.) Meredith's disastrous marriage sparked off the composition of his celebrated sonnet sequence, *Modern Love*, which is considered later in this volume. Mary Ellen lived only another four years, dying of kidney disease in 1861, and Meredith married his second wife, Marie Vulliamy, in 1864. He had a son, Arthur, by his first wife, and a son and a daughter, William and Marie, by his second.

Meredith lamented late in life that though he had achieved fame his books were little read. So it was, and so it has remained. The cause lies in Meredith's style. He believed that plain prose was appropriate for scientific or philosophical writing where stylistic novelty would be obtrusive, but that fiction does not require a 'perfectly smooth surface': it needs to draw on the poetic freedoms accepted in verse. (T. S. Eliot (1888–1965) once praised a novel for being 'so good a novel that only sensitivities trained on poetry can wholly appreciate it' (Introduction to Djuna Barnes's *Nightwood*, 1936).) Even so Meredith has been called 'a prose Browning'. Virginia Woolf (1882–1941), reading Meredith in 1937, found his prose 'so rich, so knotted, so alive and muscular after the pale little fiction I'm used to'. Certainly Meredith's style is never 'pale' and never plain. Oscar Wilde (1854–1900) acknowledged its influence and James Joyce (1882–1941) explored its innovations and admired the 'philosophical' substance of the novels. Meredith is a master of irony; he strives to load his books with wit and wisdom; many of his characters are people with ideas who are determined to voice them. If we compare his characters and their conversation with those of, say, Trollope, then, for all the charm and emotional solidity of Trollope's men and women, we have to confess that, compared with Meredith's, they have little of the life of the mind except when rationalising the struggle for wealth or place.

The Ordeal of Richard Feverel, subtitled *A History of Father and Son*, surveys the disastrous results of a father's determination to rear his son on an educational 'system' of his own. Sir Austin Feverel is a baronet whose wife has left him. Overbearingly confident of his own wisdom and of the corrupting effects of schools, he focuses on his son's upbringing a set of fixed notions of which real life makes nonsense. It is characteristic of Meredith's method that many quotations are given from Sir Austin's own book of aphorisms, 'The Pilgrim's Scrip'. Meredith's talent for witty epigram gets full play in such compilations. Richard's ingenuously idyllic love affair with Lucy Desborough is described in rapturous rhetoric; but she has not the birth required of Sir Austin for his son. The couple marry in secret, but then Sir Austin's moral blackmail separates the two. Richard is briefly seduced into infidelity, but after the agony of separation the way to reconciliation of father, son and daughter-in-law lies open. Richard, however, has an account to settle with a villain whose designs on Lucy lay behind his own involvement in infidelity. He is killed in a duel. Lucy goes mad and dies.

Evan Harrington (or *He Would Be a Gentleman*) (1861) is a more cheerful novel that takes Meredith's own grandfather and turns him into Melchizedek Harrington, 'the great Mel' whose distinguished comportment and social pretensions earn him the nickname 'the Marquis'. His daughters have married well, notably the 'Countess de Saldar'. Their anxiety to conceal their lowly origins, and, above all, their schemes to launch their brother Evan into society, conflict with Evan's native honesty and with his mother's determination that he should carry on the tailoring business. The autobiographical element in the book is evident, but it was in *The Adventures of Harry Richmond* (1871) that Meredith actually adopted the autobiographical pattern to tell in the first person the story of a boy who has to cope with an even more extraordinary and demanding father than either Richard Feverel or Evan Harrington has to deal with. For Roy Richmond, illegitimate offspring of royalty and an actress, is an overpoweringly flamboyant personality, compulsively fascinating, both resourceful and unscrupulous in forwarding outrageous schemes for establishing his son Harry in the exalted status he craves for him. But Harry's mother is the daughter of a down-to-earth English squire, whom Roy Richmond mesmerised, carried off, and drove to an early grave. So once more the struggle for the hero's soul is between the pretentious and the pedestrian. The fascination, then the burden, of having to deal with a devoted father determined to ennoble his son at any cost, is subtly registered. *Harry Richmond* is one of the most entertaining novels of the age, rich in characters and in moments of high comedy.

The Egoist (1879) is generally accounted Meredith's supreme masterpiece, and indeed in shapeliness of plot, in density of texture, in virtuosity of psychological analysis, and in the scintillation of the wit, the novel is an astonishing achievement. It traces the humbling of the arch-egotist, the insufferably conceited and vain gentleman, Sir Willoughby Patterne, whose search for the woman truly worthy to be his wife eventually lights upon Clara Middleton, the daughter of Dr Middleton, a character modelled on Meredith's father-in-law, Thomas Love Peacock. A notable study is that of the scholar Vernon Whitford, modelled on Leslie Stephen (1832–1904) in his younger days, which the reader will wish to compare with Mr Ramsay, modelled on the older Leslie Stephen by his daughter Virginia Woolf in *To the Lighthouse* (1927). The central theme, the dissection and unmasking of arrogance, involves a good deal of acerbity, but Clara Middleton is an attractive character who thinks for herself, is conscious of woman's rights, and fiercely resistant to acceptance of Victorian feminine submissiveness.

Meredith championed the cause of the modern woman again in *Diana of the Crossways* (1885). Diana, an exceptionally intelligent woman, is married to Mr Warwick, a man of limited understanding. A young politician, Percy Dacier, falls in love with her, but she leaks an important secret to the press which he has confided to her. A special interest attaches to this story which is based on what happened when the writer Caroline Norton (1808–77), Sheridan's granddaughter and mistress of Lord Melbourne (1779–1848), the Victorian Prime Minister, was reputed to have leaked to the *Times* Peel's (1788–1850) plan to repeal the Corn Laws. The reverberations of this scandal boosted the sales of the novel.

Anthony Trollope

In October 1857 Meredith reviewed Trollope's *Barchester Towers*, urging his readers to get hold of *The Warden* and *Barchester Towers* as soon as possible, and describing Trollope as a 'caustic and vigorous writer, who can draw men and women, and tell a story that men and women can read'. In common with Meredith, with Thackeray and with the Brontës, Anthony Trollope (1815–82) had in his parentage and upbringing the stuff of which fiction is made. His father, a learned barrister, seems to have been temperamentally incapable of making a success of life. It is now believed that excessive doses of calomel for the relief of asthma contributed to the conversion of a bad-tempered eccentric into a near-madman. At any rate he failed in his practice, then in farming. Hare-brained schemes to rescue his family included a plan to open a bazaar in Cincinnati. An exotic building was constructed but cash ran out before it could be stocked. It fell to Trollope's mother, Frances Trollope, to rescue the family from bankruptcy by her pen. Of her seven children only Tom (the eldest) and Anthony (the third) escaped the family scourge of consumption which killed off five of them in childhood or early adulthood. As the family died around her, Fanny Trollope wrote indefatigably and had published one hundred and fifteen volumes when she died in Florence in 1863 at the age of eighty-three. She was a woman of indomitable spirit and it is sad to read Robert Browning's letter to his wife discouraging her from meeting 'that vulgar pushing woman, who is not fit to speak to you'; but the warning opens our eyes again to the ingrained class-consciousness of Victorian England with which Trollope's own novels are so much concerned.

He suffered a great deal from it when young – sent to Harrow as a day-boy, then to Winchester, by parents who could neither afford to clothe him respectably nor to pay the school fees. The brutality of the Victorian public school is made evident in Trollope's account of the scorn with which he was treated, not to mention the 'care' with which his elder brother Tom, five years his senior, looked after him at Winchester. 'As part of his daily exercise, he thrashed me with a big stick,' Trollope laments in his *Autobiography* (1883), where he also confesses that he was awkward, ugly and dirty. Desperately friendless and lonely, he early began to live mentally with imaginary characters. His mother got him a job with the Post Office. At first an unsatisfactory, slovenly clerk in the General Post Office, he escaped to a post in Ireland in the town of Banagher, King's County (Offaly), where, incidentally, Charlotte Brontë's husband took her on their honeymoon and where he settled after her death. There Trollope worked hard, gained promotion, and was eventually given responsible administrative tasks in Ireland and in England. He married in 1844 and had two sons. Trollope was fifty-two before he left the Post Office. Like his mother, he rose early in the mornings to do a daily stint, aiming at three hours work and three thousand words before breakfast. His Post Office work involved a good deal of travelling and he wrote *en route* in railway carriages. His fiction output alone runs to fifty-seven titles.

'His great, his inestimable merit was his complete appreciation of the usual.' That was Henry James's comment on Trollope in *Partial Portraits* (1888). Trollope himself told how, when he was inventing his imaginary worlds, 'for weeks, for months, if I remember rightly, from year to year, I would carry on the same tale, binding myself down to certain laws, to certain proportions. Nothing impossible was ever introduced, – nor anything which, from outward circumstances, would seem to be violently improbable.' Thus his two great sequences of novels, the 'Barsetshire' novels and the 'Palliser' novels are rooted in the commonplace life of Victorian England. Nevertheless Trollope made some false starts before he found his true *métier* in *The Warden* (1855), the first of the Barsetshire cycle. The genesis of this novel lay in the correspondence columns of the *Times* – letters about the medieval almshouses of St Cross, Winchester. The charitable trust set up long ago to serve the needs of a number of aged men had been invested so successfully over the centuries that by this time a warden, inhabiting a spacious and beautiful house, was drawing a large income for nominal duties, utterly disproportionate to the modest provisions made for the inmates. Would not the original benefactor's intentions have been better served if the provisions made for the inmates had been augmented instead of enriching a sinecure for a clergyman? Trollope accepted that there was need for reform but resented the blame that accrued to the hapless warden, whose lucrative office had been handed to him by a long-standing tradition. Thus he invented the Reverend Septimus Harding, Warden of Hiram's Hospital, a mild, sensitive, unworldly widower devoted to his home and to his bedesmen (the residents of the almshouse), driven by the press campaign and the threat of legislation to resign his position and opt for comparative poverty. Of Harding's two daughters, the elder, Susan, is the wife of Archdeacon Grantly, the Bishop's son, and the younger, Eleanor, marries the young doctor, John Bold, who initiated the campaign out of his reforming zeal and sense of justice.

The Warden is a short novel but the acorn it planted grew quickly into an oak tree in *Barchester Towers* (1857). The gentle Mr Harding's foil is his son-in-law, Archdeacon Grantly, a wealthy, ambitious and pushy fellow, indeed a commanding, loud-voiced, quick-tempered and self-important dignitary who has ruled the Cathedral Close during the last years of the revered Bishop, his father. On the old Bishop's death, he would like to succeed him but, alas, a change of ministry brings a change in episcopal churchmanship, and the successor chosen, Dr Proudie, is a weak, comfort-loving fellow hen-pecked by a domineering termagant of a wife. Mrs Proudie's bullying presence at clerical discussions with the Bishop raises hackles and sets teeth on edge in all the parsonages not inhabited by place-seeking toadies. The struggle between Mrs Proudie and Archdeacon Grantly continues through other volumes of the cycle. Of the three main issues in *Barchester Towers* one concerns rivalry for the now vacant wardenship of Hiram's Hospital, another traces the gradual unmasking of Mrs Proudie's ally, the Bishop's chaplain, Obadiah Slope, as greasy a hypocrite and as cunning a schemer as fiction contains, and the third traces the trials of Mr Harding's younger daughter Eleanor Bold, now widowed but financially well-off and highly attractive to gold-digging bachelors. After rejecting such unworthy candidates as Mr Slope himself, Eleanor is finally married to a scholarly clergyman, Mr Arabin; and Mr Harding, offered the Deanery in compensation for his self-sacrifice in *The Warden*, nobly and selflessly manages to have the offer transferred to his new son-in-law. In later Barsetshire novels the psychological analysis plumbs deeper levels of motivation, but *Barchester Towers* is especially rich in sparkling humour – not just in witty irony but also in sheer slapstick, much of it connected with the daughter of Canon Stanhope, long resident in Italy, married but separated, and calling herself Signora Madeline Vesey-Neroni. She is carried from sofa to sofa by virtue of a damaged limb, and queens it over every eligible male with a hilariously outrageous apparatus of seduction.

In *Doctor Thorne* (1858) we move to the village of Greshambury for a finely organised story of a penniless illegitimate girl, Mary Thorne, brought up by her uncle, the Doctor. Mary has intelligence and generosity of spirit and attracts the love of Frank Gresham, heir to an estate so much impoverished by his father that it is deemed essential for him to marry for money. Here Trollope keeps the reader consistently aware, as no other novelist does, of the pressures of financial need and the way the Victorian obsession with inherited property could collide with the demands of the heart. Again, in *Framley Parsonage* (1861) a young gentleman, Lord Lufton, finds his wish to marry a fortune-less girl fiercely resented by his family. And again the young lady, Lucy Robarts, is a finely presented study in genuineness and subtle forcefulness. She is ready totally to efface herself for the well-being of the man she loves and of his own loved ones. But she has wit, resilience and a devastatingly shrewd way of mocking herself. Trollope's young heroines are vividly drawn. 'Trollope settled down steadily to the English girl,' said Henry James; 'he took possession of her, and turned her inside out. He never made her the subject of heartless satire.'

The Last Chronicle of Barset (1867), the longest of the cycle, contains a moving study of a poor, scholarly, pious but sometimes absent-minded clergyman, Josiah Crawley, against whom a false charge of stealing a cheque is brought. Obdurate and inflexible, he makes things worse for himself by the arrogance with which he projects his humiliation and self-judgement. Critics have seen in this portrait of one who seems half-mad even to his wife recollections of Trollope's own father. The study has a tragic grandeur, though a happy ending is contrived. The reality and solidity of the Barsetshire novels is as authentic as the daylight. Trollope's moral soundness gives profundity and wholesomeness to his satire. He can trace with great subtlety and precision the way in which an honest, open-hearted, likeable young man, such as Mark Robarts in *Framley Parsonage*, can gradually be all but ruined by cunning manipulation of his good nature and his wish to be thought not ungenerous. The very spaciousness of Trollope's coverage of thought-processes and conversations enables him to pin-point the way a good intention is perverted and overlaid by ulterior motive, leading to momentary acquiescence in what is unworthy. As author he will intervene to address the reader over the characters' heads or even, *sotto voce*, to remonstrate with one of his own characters at a moment when they are not being strictly honest with themselves.

Above all, the greatness of Trollope is proven in the way, with the massive achievement of the Barsetshire novels behind him and a massive public fascinated by his characters and their doings, he drew the series to a close and embarked upon another sequence, the 'Palliser' novels, this time centred primarily in London and focusing on the political world, but following its gentry and others to their country homes in due season. The novels are *Can You Forgive Her?* (1864), *Phineas Finn* (1869), *The Eustace Diamonds* (1873), *Phineas Redux* (1874), *The Prime Minister* (1876) and *The Duke's Children* (1880). It must be remembered that after leaving the Civil Service Trollope stood unsuccessfully as parliamentary candidate for Beverley. The life he could not enjoy in practice he chose to live on paper. Thus another concourse of characters was created with whom Trollope lived mentally as he had lived with his Barsetshire folk. A dominating figure is that of Plantagenet Palliser, nephew and heir of the Duke of Omnium, a conscientious, hard-working Whig statesman who becomes Prime Minister and succeeds to his uncle's title in *The Prime Minister*. It must be emphasised that just as the Barsetshire novels pay little attention to the real religious life and interests of the clergy, so the Palliser novels are not political novels as are, say, Disraeli's. The ecclesiastical set-up provided a backdrop for exploring the social life of the provinces, and the parliamentary set-up provided a backdrop for exploring the social life of the metropolis and of the great country houses. In each case the concern with money and property, place and power, love and marriage is constant. But from the first, in *Can You Forgive Her?*, there is a commanding mastery in analysing and recording the inner workings of the mind and heart, more especially in the female characters. This more than compensates for the loss of the more scintillating humour of *Barchester Towers*. Palliser's young wife, Lady Glencora, is one of the most fascinating figures in Victorian fiction, a woman bursting with half-repressed emotional vitality. Social pressures have torn her from the love of a dashing but worthless charmer and installed her as the wife of a soberly undemonstrative aristocratic politician. Irrepressibly talkative, provocative and defensive, she vents any soreness or frustration in unstoppable ridicule and banter. Yet she is honest and candid, and learns to appreciate her husband's qualities. With great ingenuity Trollope gives her as confidante a young woman even more wilful and rebellious but far more conscientious, whose heart oscillates between an earnest and wealthy but too 'perfect' gentleman and a scheming rogue. She is Alice Vavasor, member of a family with a home near Penrith (where Frances Trollope had a house for some years). As ever in these Palliser books, Trollope shows remarkable skill in tracing those subtle transitions by which the attitudes and pressures of others deflect a man or a woman from their thought-out purpose to its very opposite or at any rate to something widely divergent from their most earnest intentions. No novelist can more forcibly register how men can destroy themselves and how women can let their best purposes be undermined.

In *Phineas Finn* Phineas, the son of an Irish doctor, begins to make his way as a Member of Parliament on the English scene, much aided by Lady Laura Standish with whom he falls in love. Out of sheer prudence, however, Lady Laura marries instead an MP of great wealth and seeming benevolence to become Lady Laura Kennedy. The slow awakening to the folly of a choice which destroys her happiness and eventually turns sour even Phineas's continuing disinterested concern for her, is traced through this novel and through *Phineas Redux*, and gives a tragic dimension to Phineas's career. His Irish charm and inner resilience are tested to the utmost in the later novel where he is falsely accused of murder, but he finds happiness in marriage at the end and attains political re-instatement.

Perhaps the most intensely engaging themes in these novels are the stories of the women. At one extreme Lady Eustace of *The Eustace Diamonds* is a teasingly engaging but conscienceless intriguer and social climber. At the other extreme Lucy Morris of the same book is a devoted, self-sacrificing young woman sorely tested by her loved cousin's irresponsibility. Trollope is also brilliant at tracing gradual deterioration of character in the case of Ferdinand Lopez in

The Prime Minister and the gradual awakening to this deterioration in the one who loves and marries him, Emily Wharton. The expansiveness of the canvas allows Trollope to trace the changing and indeed fluctuating moods and insights which determine happiness or misery in personal relationships with an acumen and a sureness of touch that perhaps no other English novelist can match. A moving philosophical commentary upon the human situation emerges in the last of the Palliser novels, *The Duke's Children*, in which Lady Glencora dies and Palliser, now Duke of Omnium, faces alone seemingly rebellious marital choices by his children which re-awaken the tensions and worries of his own early days with the loved wife he has lost.

Charles Kingsley, Lewis Carroll

Trollope's critique of society is that of the detached moralist: he does not exude the fervour of the prophet inspired with the urge for social reform. Charles Kingsley (1819–75), on the other hand, was imbued with the zeal of the reformer. An Anglican clergyman who held the living of Eversley, Hampshire, for many years, he became Professor of modern history at Cambridge in the 1860s. He came under the influence of another Anglican clergyman, F. D. Maurice (1805–72), who was determined to bring orthodox theological presuppositions to bear on the field of social action. In this connection Maurice and Kingsley were involved in the movement which came to be called 'Christian Socialism'. Their efforts eventually resulted in the foundation of the first Working Men's College in London in 1854. Tracts on Christian Socialism were published by the movement, which was basically an attempt to come to the aid of the English working class after the failure of the Chartist movement in 1848. Its aim was not so much to institute a radical restructuring of society as to move individuals to bring Christian principles to bear on all social relationships and activities. An emphasis on the need for educational reform and improvement in public amenities such as hygiene and sanitation is evident in Kingsley's propaganda pamphlets, for he recognised that the Church of England had failed to tackle the human and social problems created by the vast spread of industrialisation. His novel, *Yeast, A Problem* (1848), focuses on the lot of the rural labourer, while *Alton Locke, Tailor and Poet* (1850) tells the story of a sensitive working-class boy in London apprenticed in a tailoring sweatshop, whose sense of injustice leads him to participate in a Chartist riot. The conditions of deprivation and hardship are forcefully pressed home.

Kingsley's reputation has not benefited from some of the controversies into which his espousal of so-called 'muscular Christianity', a brand of aggressive patriotic Protestantism, led him. In particular he was bitterly hostile to the Tractarian movement within the Church of England, which sought to re-emphasise the continuing Catholic inheritance of the Established Church. His venom against John Henry Newman after his conversion to Rome expressed itself in a jibe against him which had momentous consequences in Newman's composition of his *Apologia pro Vita Sua* (1864), a matter which will be dealt with in a later chapter.

Kingsley turned historical novelist in *Hypatia* (1853). The scene is set in Alexandria in the fifth century as the Roman Empire declines. The barbaric invading Goths are at the gates. The Prefect Orestes tries to keep the city in control with his legionaries. The patriarch Cyril governs an aggressive Christian church. A young Christian monk Philammon comes from the desert to be fascinated and converted by the beautiful Hypatia who expounds the Neoplatonic philosophy of moderation and who is killed by a fanatical mob of Christians. *Westward Ho!* (1855) tells the story of Amyas Leigh, a Devonshire boy who goes to sea in the reign of Queen Elizabeth I and is involved in the colonial struggle with Spain. This colourful, patriotic tale became very popular, though Kingsley's emphasis on Jesuit intrigue and on the cruelties of the Inquisition is not without its anti-Catholic propaganda message for his own day. *Hereward the Wake* (1866), Kingsley's last historical novel, deals with the eleventh-century outlaw who led a rising against William the Conqueror in 1070. But the most enduring of Kingsley's fiction turned out to be two works both of very different genres. The one, *The Heroes* (1855), tells the classical legends of Greek heroes for children. The other, *The Water-Babies* (1863), is an exercise in fantasy highly attractive to children but carrying also a graver message for the adult reader. It tells the story of Tom, a boy chimney-sweep who runs away from his bullying master, Mr Grimes, falls into a river, and is transformed into a water-baby to become acquainted with a submarine society whose doings are not all innocent. Kingsley was genuinely horrified by the use of little boys as sweeps. The practice flourished because boys were more popular than machines with the householders; for they made less dirt and cleaned the chimneys more thoroughly. A child could be considered old enough not to collapse fatally under the strain at the age of six, and there was no lack of unwanted boys, often orphans, to supply the market.

It was not long after the publication of *The Water-Babies* that an even more remarkable exercise in fantasy appeared, *Alice's Adventures in Wonderland* (1865), which was to be followed by *Through the Looking-Glass* (1871). Lewis Carroll (pseudonym of Charles

Lutwidge Dodgson) (1832–98) was a mathematics don at Oxford with an innocent affection for young girls. In *Alice's Adventures in Wonderland* Alice meets a white rabbit equipped with a watch one day and follows it down its hole into a land of wonders where there are magic potions to drink which will make you smaller or taller, and such creatures as a Cheshire Cat which vanishes, leaving its grin behind to fade tardily after it. Alice plays croquet with the King and Queen of Hearts, using flamingoes for mallets and hedgehogs for balls. Throughout, Carroll takes the familiar paraphernalia of a child's home life and liberates it from the cramping straitjacket of reality. Similarly the devices of logical deduction and dialectic are set free from enslavement to rationality. Thus the innocent imaginativeness of the child mind is allowed to run riot in a dream world whose freedoms make adult attachment to the humdrum mechanics of the possible seem drab and petty indeed.

George Gissing

Kingsley, like Mrs Gaskell, had become zealous for social reform through sympathising with the sufferings of the poor as one who enjoyed the comforts of middle-class life. A very different standpoint inspired the novels of George Gissing (1857–1903). His father had a chemist's shop in Wakefield, Yorkshire. He had moved there from East Anglia and to that extent was a 'foreigner' in the locals' eyes. His three sons and two daughters formed a harmonious family grouping which insulated George from contact with other shop-keepers' children. 'We hung between two grades of society – as I have done ever since in practical life,' Gissing later observed. The father died when George, the eldest child, was thirteen. Gissing was a bright boy and eventually won a scholarship to Owens College, Manchester. There he distinguished himself further and would no doubt have gone on to London University, but in 1876 he fell into a trap devised to identify the thief who had been stealing from the cloakroom. He was divested of his awards and sentenced to a month's hard labour in gaol. His excuse was that he wanted money to buy a sewing-machine for a girl called Nell Harrison in order to save her from resorting to the streets to keep herself alive. Certainly he fell in love with Nell; but she was no saint and in 1876 a college friend who had shared her favours was writing to Gissing to compare notes about signs of venereal disease. Nevertheless, though Gissing went off to America for a time after serving his sentence, he rejoined Nell on his return and married her in 1879. The act had something of the character of a decisive plunge into the lower class whose contact his own family had always shrunk from. But the couple were soon separated; she became an alcoholic, turned prostitute, and died in 1888. Gissing paid visits to France, Italy and Greece, then in 1891 made a second disastrous marriage to a girl he picked up in Oxford Street, Edith Underwood, an unbalanced, neurotic, unstable girl who was eventually to be confined in an asylum and to die of brain disease. It was not long before Gissing left her and formed the only seemingly happy such relationship of his life with Gabrielle Fleury, a Frenchwoman.

It is evident that the events of Gissing's life, superficially considered, had their share of melodrama. It might not be easy to exaggerate the psychological damage done by the lapse into thieving and the subsequent sentence on a young man brought up to a consciousness of superiority to the lower orders of society and endowed with all the intellectual gifts necessary to climb the social ladder. Gissing seems to have made a mess of his life in a uniquely wilful way. Picking up two wives from the streets and then having to watch them disintegrate as personalities, he appears to have been either hag-ridden by destiny or culpably foolish. It is not surprising that fiction produced by such experience sometimes conveys the envy and unease of the disappointed man, but he managed to publish thirty works of fiction and eventually succeeded in earning a satisfactory income with his pen.

In his first novel, *Workers in the Dawn* (1880), which he regarded as a vehicle of reformist radicalism and which sold only twenty-nine copies, he emerged as a realistic novelist of working-class life. 'In that book,' he said, 'I have, so to speak, *written off* a whole period of my existence'. *The Unclassed* (1884) was read for the publisher by George Meredith, who praised it enthusiastically and invited the author to meet him. It takes up a theme close to Gissing's heart, that of rescuing a fallen woman, and its heroine, the prostitute Ida Starr, is presented with great sympathy. Gissing's most celebrated novel, *New Grub Street* (1891), satirises the contemporary literary world, and in particular draws a stark contrast between the career of an unprincipled, self-seeking reviewer who makes a good thing out of his fluency and his ready adaptability, and the lives of writers with genuine artistic or scholarly ideals which are blighted by struggle and privation.

Gissing lacked the flair which turns talent into creative genius. He was painstaking in his realistic registration of the lives of the poor, but he was also, no doubt as a result of his own history, obsessed with a dread of the coarseness and brutality to which poverty could drag one down, and the struggle of those who aspire to escape to the refinements of middle-class life is a constant theme. What distinguishes him above all is his ability to bring home the overwhelming significance of class and to pin-point the differences by which class-distinctions are manifested.

Wilkie Collins, Charles Reade, Richard Blackmore, Sir Arthur Conan Doyle

Wilkie Collins (1824–89), a close friend of Dickens, enriched a field of fiction into which social problems never obtruded – except in the familiar form of the class-barrier which a drawing-master might face in falling in love with a country gentleman's daughter. Such is the initial situation of the hero in *The Woman in White* (1860), a novel of mystery, crime and detection, skilfully presented through the separate narratives of several participants, each of whom has a partial view of events and personalities. Collins's mastery of ominous atmosphere and suspense guaranteed popularity for this specimen of the new 'novels of sensation', a genre which includes the melodramatic stories of Mrs Henry Wood (1814–87), notorious for the tear-jerking extravagances of *East Lynne* (1861). There were dramatised versions of this novel to which we shall return in considering Victorian drama. The intricacy of the plotting in *The Woman in White*, which involves a villain's forgeries and his forcible confinement in an asylum of a woman who knows the truth is supported by one or two engaging character studies, but there is no great psychological subtlety either here or in the equally celebrated novel, *The Moonstone* (1868), a story revolving around the theft of a vast diamond from an Indian idol's forehead and its bequeathal to a young woman. In these novels Collins can be credited with having launched on its course the mystery novel of crime and detection which was to become so popular in the next century. Collins never married but had two mistresses and three illegitimate children. Dealing with the pains of gout turned him into a regular consumer of laudanum. His fictional world was no doubt an 'escapist' one.

Another highly popular novel published a year after *The Woman in White* and in the same year as *East Lynne* was *The Cloister and the Hearth* (1861) by Charles Reade (1814–84), the one novel to survive from a busy thirty-year-long output of novels and plays. Reade held a fellowship at Magdalen College, Oxford, for nearly twenty years; and he had an actress as mistress for twenty-five years. He cultivated a painstaking realism that was shot through with a vein of the romantic. *The Cloister and the Hearth* is a novel of picaresque spaciousness set in the fifteenth century, and it tells the story of the parents of the Dutch humanist philosopher Erasmus (*c.*1466–1536), a story remarkable enough as Erasmus himself told it. For, acutely sensitive to his illegitimacy (he was the product of an irregular alliance between a girl and a priest), Erasmus somewhat modified a story which anyway was based on childhood memories, his mother and his father having died when he was in his teens. In Reade's novel Erasmus's father, Gerard, is prevented from marrying Margaret, the girl he loves, is persecuted, leaves Holland, and eventually in Italy is falsely informed that she has died. In fact she has borne him a son and longs for him. After a period of dissipation he becomes a monk, returns to Holland, and then discovers the truth. No doubt the tense moral conflict involved by the collision between Gerard's love for Margaret and his religious vows took some force from Reade's experience as an officially celibate don with a mistress.

Another novelist remembered now for one book alone is Richard Doddridge Blackmore (1825–1900). *Lorna Doone* (1869) has survived – a tale of adventure and romance. Set at the time of the Monmouth Rebellion and its aftermath, it tells how a bold young yeoman deals heroically with a band of villainous robbers on Exmoor. As a historical novel, Reade's book was, of course, an altogether more substantial and researched work than Blackmore's. Indeed there was one distinguished contemporary who thought *The Cloister and the Hearth* the greatest novel in the English language because of its realism in recreating the period – 'not a conventional study-built Middle Age, but a period quivering with life, full of folk who are as human and real as a bus-load in Oxford Street'. So wrote Arthur Conan Doyle (1859–1930), the Edinburgh-born doctor. His medical training and interest in diagnosis led to the creation of Sherlock Holmes, the archetypal private, amateur detective, whose deductive skill and whose capacity to plumb a bewildering concatenation of events to its depths entranced readers of the *Strand Magazine* in the late 1880s and the 1890s. Doyle's enthusiasm for Reade was that of an ambitious historical novelist, but it was the detective stories that fascinated and still fascinate a vast reading public. Few fictional figures are better known or more thoroughly discussed than Sherlock Holmes, a man of quiet, penetrating reflectiveness, whose brilliance of insight is balanced by the stolid, humdrum companion and foil, Dr Watson. Watson can always share the reader's dazzlement at the great man's unerring ability to expose the fallacies in the seemingly commonsensical first reactions to the evidence of crime.

Robert Louis Stevenson

Conan Doyle's fellow-Scotsman, Robert Louis Stevenson (1850–94), also created some of the best-known characters in English fiction in *Treasure Island* (1883). Jim Hawkins, the narrator, a West Country boy, manages to get hold of a map jealously sought by a bunch of seafaring rogues. Squire Trelawney and Dr Livesey take Jim with them on a voyage in the *Hispaniola* in search of the hidden treasure whose site is located on the map. A knowing, one-legged sailor, Long John Silver, has managed to pack the crew with a view to seizing the ship mutinously and gaining the treasure. The thrilling adventures are recounted with a vividness and economy that grip young readers still. Stevenson was here working in the tradition of a fellow Scot, R. M. Ballantyne (1825–94), whose vast output of adventure stories for boys included *The Coral Island* (1857). This was the book which was to inspire William Golding (1911–) a century later to turn the tale of marooned boys' heroism upside down in *Lord of the Flies* (1954).

Within three years of the publication of *Treasure Island*, Stevenson had produced another novel destined for equally extensive fame, *The Strange Case of Dr Jekyll and Mr Hyde* (1886). Dr Jekyll manages to devise a drug that will separate in a distinct personality all the evil impulses of his nature. The repulsive personality into which he is transformed by taking the drug commits a hideous murder. Eventually the efficacy of the antidote taken for re-assuming his original personality fails, and, as his crimes catch up with him, he commits suicide.

Stevenson's father and grandfather were both distinguished lighthouse engineers, and the father, a strong-willed man, wanted Robert Louis to follow the family trade. Robert Louis's interests lay elsewhere however, and there was considerable tension between father and son over Robert Louis's beliefs and way of living from his student days onwards. He was, in any case, physically unfitted for the family business and he did not improve matters by falling in love with a married American, Fanny Osbourne, in France. After her divorce he eventually sought her out in the United States and married her. Reconciliation with his family came, but Stevenson's developing consumption compelled him to seek a mellower climate than Scotland's, and he eventually settled in Samoa in the South Seas at Vailima. There he was acclaimed as 'Tusitala', the 'Story-teller'.

The title was apt, but Stevenson's yarns, whether spun in America or in the South Seas, tended to focus on the Scottish scene. *Kidnapped* (1886) and its sequel *Catriona* (1893) are exciting adventure stories set against the background of the conflicting loyalties of Jacobite and Hanoverian in the aftermath of the 1745 rebellion. But Stevenson's swift narrative thrust does not allow any subtle exploration of motive and ideology such as Scott made in *Waverley*, his novel of the '45, and other novels. G. K. Chesterton (1874–1936) hit the nail on the head when he observed that Stevenson 'simplified so much that he lost some of the complexity of real life'. This does not mean that his fiction was always limpid or lacking in dimension, for in *The Master of Ballantrae* (1889), one of his deeper studies, the dualism so forcefully represented in *Dr Jekyll and Mr Hyde* is explored with foreboding and suspense on a naturalistic level in the story of the rivalry of two brothers, the violent, wicked James, the elder, who fails to return from the battlefield of Culloden and is assumed dead, and the gentle, generous younger brother Henry, who has taken his estate and married his intended bride by the time James puts in an appearance to embark on vengeance which destroys them both.

Henry James

'Never let a long sentence get out of hand' was Stevenson's character-istic advice to a girl pupil. Yet Stevenson maintained a warm friend-ship for a fellow-stylist of totally opposite bent to his own in this respect. Henry James (1843–1916) was born in New York. His father was determined that his sons should not be moulded into stereotypes by accepted American educational institutions. Henry and his elder brother, William, the philosopher, consequently had the benefit of a variety of schools and tutors and were early taken to Europe to savour the culture of the Old World. Henry had had experience of living in Switzerland, France, Italy and Germany by the time he finally settled in England in 1876, making his home first in London, then in Rye, Sussex. When the First World War began James became increasingly desirous of being no longer officially an 'alien' and increasingly committed patriotically to the British cause. Thus he became a naturalised British subject in 1915. A year later he died, but not before George V had awarded him the Order of Merit. The story is that James was lying in bed when the news of the award was brought to him, and, when the messenger departed, he opened his eyes and said, 'Nurse, turn off the light and spare my blushes.'

James's output of fiction is generally categorised as the product of three successive phases, and it is an old joke to distinguish them as the ages of James I, James II, and the Old Pretender. It is the final period that produced James's greatest masterpieces, *The Wings of a Dove* (1902), *The Ambassadors* (1903) and *The Golden Bowl* (1904), but since these works belong to the twentieth century not only in chronology but also in literary technique, they cannot properly concern us here. There is a strong connection, however, between the novels of the first period and those of the last period, in that James is deeply concerned with the collision between the American and the European mentalities. James's acute sensitivity to the diversity of psychological and emotional motivation and to the effect of varied social nuances in confusing the flow of communication by word, by gesture, by tone and by behaviour made this a fruitful theme for fictional exploration. Moreover he had a bubbling sense of humour which enabled him to register the subtler collisions of ethos with ethos, temperament with temperament, and culture with culture, in dialogue and commentary that are underscored with wry irony. To pin-point slight subtleties of understanding or mood that complicate human relationships and to underscore them with the oblique resonances of authorial humour or irony, James perfected a verbal notation which, at its best, illuminates and entertains by the precision of its insights. But James's pursuit of exactitude in trying to define the evanescent kaleidoscope of the minute-by-minute mental life often put a strain on syntax which militates heavily against readability. He will sometimes cross the syntactical borderline and tax the reader too exactingly:

> It made me blush, the next minute, to see in my friend's face how much more unreservedly she had forgiven him than her anecdote struck me as presenting to my own tenderness an occasion for doing.
>
> (*The Turn of the Screw*)

A second reading of such a sentence gradually unravels it, but James was capable at times of pushing syntactical entanglements of this kind beyond the bounds of ready comprehensibility.

Roderick Hudson (1875) tells the story of a young would-be sculptor frustrated by having to make his living in a Massachusetts law office. Subsidised by a wealthy friend, he goes to study in Rome. There he is corrupted by the easy-going Italians, work gives place to dissipation, and he dies tragically. The somewhat simplistic distinction here between American innocence and European decadence was to be elaborated later; for the basic contrast between American innocence and European corruption eventually complements the equally impressive contrasts between American rawness and European culture, American enthusiasm and European world-weariness. In the shorter novel *Daisy Miller* (1879) James made his first sketch of the 'American girl' who was to exercise such a fascination upon him. Daisy comes to Rome to be destroyed. A flighty, exuberant girl, she has an honest openness in bringing her own values into play in stuffy alien societies. She and her young brother Randolph are taken about Europe by a mother who exercises discipline over neither of them. Randolph, who stuffs himself with sweets and charges about hotels, is a little horror, plainly the product of what James saw as a developing American permissiveness in bringing up the young. And Daisy, too, has no time for European conventions that limit contact between the sexes. She shocks the Italians and settled American expatriates alike.

It is in *The Portrait of a Lady* (1881) that James's study of young American womanhood produced a full-length masterpiece. Isabel Archer comes from her home in Albany to her wealthy expatriate uncle's English country house. 'Like the mass of American girls Isabel had been encouraged to express herself; her remarks had been attended to; she had been expected to have emotions and opinions,' James tells us. She has 'inflated ideals', is confident, 'innocent and dogmatic', vivacious, anxious to impress, exacting and above all determined 'to see, to try, to know' and not to lose her independence. She inherits her uncle's fortune, and, having rejected honest and sincere offers of marriage alike from a doggedly devoted if unromantic young American businessman who pursues her across the Atlantic and from an English aristocrat of impeccable character, charm, taste and means, she succumbs to an unscrupulous expatriate American dilettante in Italy, who marries her purely for her money. Finally resisting the temptation to leave him, she resigns herself to a life of fidelity devoid of happiness. Nowhere is James's skill shown more entertainingly than in the conversations which occur between Isabel, the American charmer, and her friend, Henrietta Stackpole, a blunderingly aggressive journalist, who is in search of copy on the one hand and of the English or Anglicised gentry on the other hand.

In his second period James is more concerned with specifically English subjects. In particular the contrast between innocence and sophistication assumes a more deeply moral aspect. The issues implicit in *Daisy Miller* about the education of the young are tackled head on. In this respect *What Maisie Knew* (1897) is a remarkably penetrating study of a young girl's awakening. Maisie is the daughter of parents who divorce and remarry; the settlement apportions Maisie's time between the two new households. James had heard of a case where a girl so placed was at first passionately wanted by each parent out of vindictiveness to the other, and later as passionately unwanted, finding herself 'practically disowned, rebounding from racquet to racquet like a tennis ball or a shuttlecock' (Preface).

In Maisie's case the father takes her governess as mistress, later marries her, then abandons her for a series of disreputable liaisons. Meanwhile her mother marries the charming but weak Sir Claude, but likewise deviates into other liaisons. By bringing her stepfather and stepmother together and taking childish delight in their immediate mutual liking for each other, Maisie innocently furthers another illicit relationship. The effectiveness of the study lies in James's touching capacity to tread the tightrope between over-grave emphasis on the damage done to the child by adult selfishness and insensitivity, and comic exploitation of the way Maisie in thought and talk misunderstands, then learns to half-understand, what is afoot in the adult world. Again the dialogue across the generation gap is beautifully resonant with wryly entertaining overtones.

In different vein James returned to portray adult corruption of children in the celebrated ghost story, *The Turn of the Screw* (1898). In this perhaps over-estimated tale a governess takes over the care of an orphaned boy and his sister in a country house only to discover gradually that a former valet and previous governess, now deceased, have evilly taken possession of them from the dead, having first corrupted them when they were alive. James's failure to evoke a real sense of corruption could be explained away only if it were assumed that the poor governess's experiences are subjective and hallucinatory. James seems to have allowed for this possible reading in calling his story 'a trap for the unwary'. But one does not need to be unwary to be uncomfortable with the ambiguities. More authentic is the sense of corruption evoked in James's picture of Mrs Brockenham and her circle in *The Awkward Age* (1899). She is at the centre of a decadent, amoral, worldly London clique given over to witty, malicious gossip. James presses the parallel between her daughter Nanda's lot in being given premature freedom at 'the awkward age' and that of her cousin Aggie who is kept out of such corrupting circles until she marries. 'To create a particular little rounded and tinted innocence had been aimed at' in Aggie's case. She had been 'deliberately prepared for consumption', whereas in Nanda's case 'the elements of that young lady's nature were already, were publicly, were almost indecorously, active'.

George Moore, Rider Haggard, Rudyard Kipling

In the final decades of Victoria's reign there were, of course, writers at work whose literary careers extended well into the twentieth century and whose maturer novels fall outside the scope of this survey. If one could not do full justice to Henry James while ignoring his post-Victorian output, still less could one deal fairly on that principle with younger writers such as George Moore (1852–1933). Indeed Moore is a very special case, for he changed and developed with the passing decades both as novelist and as imaginative commentator on himself and on his times. Nevertheless his Victorian output is distinctive. Son of a landowner in County Mayo, Moore went over to Paris to study painting, but then came to England to write, and in particular to apply the realism of Zola (1840–1902) and Flaubert (1821–80) to the Victorian novel. *A Mummer's Wife* (1885), a novel set in the Potteries, in which a provincial housewife is drawn into the corrupting life of the theatre, was followed by *A Drama in Muslin* (1886), in which Moore turned to his native Ireland to point the contrast between the wealth and comfort of the Anglo-Irish ascendancy and the miseries of the peasantry at a time when the country is ravaged by evictions and assassinations. The drama is in 'muslin' because the emphasis is on the role of women whose destiny is to find a husband in one of the drawing-rooms or ball-rooms of the well-to-do, and the heroine learns to see through the superficialities of the social set-up.

The most remarkable novel of Moore's early phase, however, is *Esther Waters* (1894). This novel is the anti-romantic reply to the standard fictional treatment of the seduced working-class girl by Victorian novelists. The erring girl was exalted into a tragic heroine in Hardy's *Tess of the D'Urbervilles*, hounded into criminality in George Eliot's *Adam Bede*, and reduced to squalor and prostitution in the novels of Dickens and Mrs Gaskell. Neither the poetic glorification of her destiny nor the intensification of its agony and sordidness will do for Moore the realist. Esther, his heroine, escapes from a squalid home into domestic service at Woodview, a house where everyone is obsessed with the racing stables and with gambling. Esther is a religious girl, a Plymouth Sister, but she is seduced by one of the staff and deserted. Pregnant, she is compelled to leave Woodview, and she endures great hardships and privations in her indomitable determination to look after her child. Relief comes when the child's father turns up again, marries her and proves a good husband. When he dies, she goes back into service at Woodview. Esther's sufferings are real enough, and so is her taste of comparative happiness, but both are tempered in their impact by her moral sturdiness and her religious faith. The undemonstrative, even drab record of her experience is a movingly authentic corrective to the extravagances of much Victorian fiction.

But as the age drew to a close, voices very different from Moore's were about the ears of the wider reading public. Rider Haggard (1856–1925) entranced a vast audience with spell-binding tales of stirring adventure, ingenious in their use of mystery. His experience of Africa supplied him with the backgrounds of *King Solomon's Mines* (1885) and *She* (1887), ennabling him to exploit the compelling fascination of its landscape and its tribal life, and to explore those weird, preternatural aspects most likely to appeal to readers seeking escape from their familiar world.

Rudyard Kipling (1865–1936) is another whose maturer fiction belongs to the post-Victorian era. In any case it is only as a short-story writer and not as a novelist that he excels. In the earlier volumes of short stories, *Plain Tales from the Hills* (1888), *Wee Willie Winkie* (1888) and *Life's Handicaps* (1891) India was for Kipling what Africa was for Rider Haggard. In Lahore he met the three soldiers immortalised in *Soldiers Three* (1888) – 'A Collection of Stories setting forth Certain Passages in the Lives and Adventures of Privates Terence Mulvaney, Stanley Ortheris, and John Learoyd'. They are soldiers who have been through the mill and known what it is to stand on your own feet in crisis and peril, and indeed the celebration of such endurance was to provide a dominant theme in Kipling's fiction. Here the stories are recounted with a cool realism, reflecting what Bonamy Dobrée has called Kipling's 'insatiable curiosity about ordinary men and common things'. The tales at this stage do not employ the more sophisticated techniques of presentation or the deeper analyses of states of mind that mark Kipling's twentieth-century story-telling. But it was to the last decade of the century that his *The Jungle Book* (1894) and *The Second Jungle Book* (1895) belong. These charming stories for children centre on Mowgli, a child nurtured by wolves and instructed by a bear and a panther in the ways of the jungle. On the other hand Kipling's school experience in England in his early teens provided the inspiration for his schoolboy stories, *Stalky & Co.* (1899).

Kipling's one really successful novel, *Kim* (1901), gives a packed picture of Indian life, its variegated culture and landscape. Kim is an orphaned Irish boy whose childhood on the streets of Lahore initiates him into the ways of its diverse inhabitants. He attaches himself to a travelling Tibetan lama but, in their wanderings, he falls into the hands of his father's old regiment and is sent to school. It is recognised that Kim's precocious experience of life, his adaptability in disguise and his quick-wittedness fit him for secret-service work, and his adventures eventually take him up into the Himalayas to grapple with Russian spies. The 'Great Game' played by British and native agents is a far cry from the 'Great Search' for spiritual release which the lama pursues, yet the two are oddly conjoined in Kim's zestful and testing pilgrimage.

Part 3

Victorian poetry

Lord Tennyson

Alfred, Lord Tennyson (1809–92) is generally regarded as not only the most distinguished but also the most characteristic Victorian poet. There is irony in the widespread assumption that Tennyson, who succeeded Wordsworth as Poet Laureate in 1850, is preeminently a literary symbol of Victorianism in all its splendour, its stability, its respectability and its confidence. For the man himself, at least until his late marriage, was notorious for wearing dirty shirts, was capable of flinging himself in an ungainly manner about the drawing-room, and, at the end of dinner with men friends, putting his feet on the table. So much for the finer points of Victorian respectability. Nor could Tennyson be regarded in any sense as a representative of Victorian stability. His family background was a hot-bed of instability. Tennyson's father, George Tennyson, though older than his brother Charles, had been passed over in favour of Charles by the wealthy grandfather. George Tennyson's subsequent career did much to justify his displacement. Pushed into holy orders and a country rectory at Somersby in Lincolnshire, an embittered, slack, though intellectually able man, he suffered from epileptic fits and mental aberrations, became addicted to alcohol and to laudanum, and occasionally threatened violence; it was a relief to his family when he died. Two of the poet's brothers went insane, one became an alcoholic, another an opium-addict, and the rest of the family of ten had their share of mental breakdowns. There was nothing calm or stable about life at the Somersby rectory when the rector was at home, and even the servants grew rebellious. One cook was burnt to death, though the rector injured himself in trying to save her. Nevertheless his reputation was such that local rumour had it that he ordered a water-butt to be kept thereafter in the kitchen 'so that any cook who caught fire could jump into it and extinguish herself without troubling her master'. This we have from the poet's grandson. Meanwhile Tennyson's favoured uncle was installed in the family home, eventually transformed it into a baronial castle, aspired to nobility, and heartily despised the Somersby Tennysons as utterly disreputable.

It was a remarkable career that transformed Alfred from the worried product of this ménage to the gentleman resident at Farringford in the Isle of Wight on whose door Prince Albert knocked informally one morning to announce that he would like to bring the Queen round to call. Tennyson was at Trinity College, Cambridge from 1828 to 1831. There he got to know William Brookfield, the future parson whose wife Jane was to win Thackeray's devotion; and indeed Thackeray himself overlapped with Tennyson at Trinity, as did Edward Fitzgerald who became a great friend. Tennyson attracted enough attention to be elected a member of a group of twelve young men called the 'Apostles', an exclusive society who met to discuss philosophical, political and aesthetic topics. One fellow Apostle who won Tennyson's friendship was Arthur Hallam (1811–33), generally accounted a brilliant young man of rare promise and accomplishment. Hallam eventually became engaged to Tennyson's sister Emily, and his early death from haemorrhage in Vienna in 1833 devastated brother and sister alike. Shaken by the loss, Tennyson wrote some verses which proved to be the first fragment of the long elegiac poem, *In Memoriam*, and the work was to occupy him intermittently until its publication in 1850. The modern reader might be tempted to be sceptical about the vaunted goodness and brilliance of Arthur Hallam, were it not that he won from the future Prime Minister, W. E. Gladstone, the same affection and the same praise that he evoked from Tennyson.

Nothing shows more clearly the nervous instability in Tennyson's make-up than the story of his approach to a marriage which, when it came, gave him a degree of happiness and poise that he had never had before. Yet it was a painfully protracted courtship, beginning in 1826 and becoming an official engagement in 1827, only to be broken – or at least to fade out by reason of Tennyson's tentativeness and unreadiness in 1840, and then to be renewed only after nearly ten years. This time friends and family were accomplices in making sure that Tennyson did not get cold feet again. His brother Charles was frank about it. 'After what happened last time, we kept a strict eye upon him, in case he should take it into his head to bolt!!!' The bridegroom was now forty-one and the bride thirty-seven.

One might reasonably consider 1850, the year of Tennyson's marriage, of *In Memoriam*, and of the Laureateship, as a dividing line in Tennyson's career. The output up to this point, in *Poems, Chiefly Lyrical* (1830), *Poems* (1832), *Poems* (1842) and *The Princess, A Medley* (1847), has astonishing technical variety. Tennyson seems to have at his fingertips the lush sensuous imagery of Keats (1795–1821) and the incantatory music of Coleridge (1772–1834). It is the latter which enables him to conjure up in 'Mariana' the vision of the weary, forsaken, forlorn young woman, heartsick with waiting in the moated grange where the 'clinking latch' is ever unlifted:

> She only said, 'My life is dreary,
>   He cometh not,' she said;
> She said, 'I am aweary, aweary,
>   I would that I were dead.'

The hopeless cry of the abandoned woman taps a neurotic vein that is to be frequently exploited in Tennyson's verse. A more culpable mood of utter self-abandonment is explored in 'The Lotos-Eaters', which follows Odysseus's mariners, on their way home from the Siege of Troy, to the land where they feed on the stupefying drug. It dissolves into somnolent inertia any desire for return home, still less for the strenuous struggle with the sea which would face them first. The mellifluous lines, weary with languorous imagery, opiate-laden in rhythm and rhetoric, create an atmosphere of uncanny narcosis. This atmosphere of trancelike enchantment is juxtaposed against the life of action again in 'The Lady of Shalott'. The Lady defies the spell laid upon her to view the world only through a mirror when she turns round to the window to see Sir Lancelot riding by, and pays the penalty of the curse by her death. In this case the dichotomy between the lady's allotted task to weave what she sees through her mirror into a magic tapestry and her urge to look upon the real world face to face has implications for the role of the artist. The poet may choose to immerse himself in the reflected pageantries of the imaged world or may turn aside to reality itself. The same issue is tackled at length in the more philosophical poem, 'The Palace of Art':

> I built my soul a lordly pleasure-house,
>   Wherein at ease for aye to dwell.
> I said, 'O Soul, make merry and carouse,
>   Dear soul, for all is well.'

The architecture and adornments of the palace are described in detail, but the soul cannot take pleasure in her isolation, for the 'riddle of the painful earth' flashes upon her till despair overtakes her, a sense of 'slothful shame' and exile from God, and she leaves the palace:

> 'Make me a cottage in the vale,' she said
>   'Where I may mourn and pray.'

Yet such poems as these give but a faint sense of the poet's own acquaintance with inner conflict compared to the remarkable poem, 'The Two Voices', which states its subject starkly in the first stanza:

A still small voice spake unto me,
'Thou art so full of misery,
Were it not better not to be?'

There could be no surer corrective to the false notion of Tennyson as a symbol of supposed Victorian complacency than to point to this long dialogue of some one hundred and fifty stanzas between the inner voice that counsels suicide and the responding voice which casts around on this side and on that for evidence and cause to sustain a case for going on with life. And it is a tribute to the poet's honesty and integrity that he concedes that the negative voice makes a powerful case indeed; the positive voice has to rescue itself from its dilemma by turning from hard logic to the spectacle of life lived in love by a simple church-going family, and by sensing the 'pulse of hope' in the living motion of the natural world:

The woods were fill'd so full with song,
There seem'd no room for sense of wrong.

The Princess set the pattern for Tennyson's longer works. He called it a 'Medley', and it was, like *In Memoriam, Maud* (1855) and *The Idylls of the King* (1859), not so much an organically constructed unity like Milton's (1608–74) *Paradise Lost* (1667) or even Wordsworth's *The Prelude* (1850), but rather a work put together from separately conceived pieces eventually assembled into a whole. One result of this method is that in both *The Princess* and *Maud* there are incidental lyrics, not all utterly essential to the narrative, which can stand alone as some of the best poems Tennyson wrote. Indeed Tennyson enriched *The Princess* with additional lyrics in the edition of 1850. It would be difficult to exaggerate the quality of the best of these lyrics which include 'Sweet and Low', 'The splendour falls', 'Tears, idle tears' and 'Now sleeps the crimson petal'. The subtle orchestral effects in 'The splendour falls', which Tennyson wrote after hearing a lone bugler playing by a ruined castle near the lake of Killarney in Ireland, are as moving as the uncanny garnering of sensuous imagery in 'Now sleeps the crimson petal', images so powerfully suggestive that sensitivities all but wilt in receiving them. Yet the story of *The Princess* has little staying-power. It concerns a princess, betrothed in childhood to a prince, who embraces the cause of women's rights, rejects marriage, and founds a feminine university. The prince and his companions gain admittance in female disguise. When a masculine army arrives the three intruders are wounded in defending the ladies, the ladies assume the feminine role of nurses, and the princess succumbs to love. Neither in substance nor in tone is the work a serious commentary on the rising issue of women's educational demands and other rights, but it is a high-spirited work, versatile in its craftmanship, and it proved fruitful in inspiring W. S. Gilbert (1836–1911) to transform it into a libretto for one of the Savoy operas written in collaboration with Sir Arthur Sullivan (1842–1900). Sullivan's unflagging inspiration turned *Princess Ida* (1884) into one of the pair's most accomplished productions.

It was to be *In Memoriam*, however, which set the seal on Tennyson's greatness. It is without doubt the greatest poem of the age. It contains over seven hundred quatrains disposed in one hundred and thirty-one sections, together with a prologue and an epilogue. Taking as its starting-point the need to come to terms with grief and find meaning and consolation, the poem tussles with the problems which are every man's, facing the challenge to faith which blind nature and human tragedy represent, but never, or rarely, losing itself in abstraction. For actual memories of the past are evoked, the present scene is described, and philosophical speculation is concretely embodied in wondering, for instance, about the personal experience of Lazarus, who was raised from the dead by Christ, and of Martha and Mary of Bethany, his sisters. The passages of grief have a profound simplicity and clarity that is as authentic as the daylight:

> Be near me when my light is low,
> When the blood creeps, and the nerves prick
> And tingle; and the heart is sick,
> And all the wheels of Being slow.

It is typical of the work that this lament leads quickly to the taxing question: Do we really want our dead to see us clearly as we are, with all our hidden shames? and thereafter to the argument that it would be wrong to attribute deficient faith or understanding to the dead in making allowances for us. In such sequences of thought the poet reasons, never reaching the abstruse to which the common reader cannot follow him, but vividly conveying the sheer tension of the self-questioning which pondered bereavement sets in train. At the same time, the passing of the seasons and the years is registered with that fine selectivity of observation which Tennyson was master of:

> Now fades the last long streak of snow,
> Now burgeons every maze of quick
> About the flowering squares, and thick
> By ashen roots the violets blow.

The simple metre and the stanza form – the quatrain with its lines folded in upon themselves by substituting the rhyme scheme *abba* for the more familiar *abab*, prove ideal for the brand of fitfully recaptured reflection and self-exploration which is the poem's characteristic. 'I did not write them with any view of weaving them into a whole, or for publication, until I had found that I had written so many,' Tennyson explained, and he added the warning that ' "I" is not always the author speaking of himself, but the voice of the human race speaking through him.'

Although *In Memoriam* probably represents the high peak of Tennyson's achievement, there were some justly celebrated poems to follow, notably *Maud*. This 'monodrama' is a collection of lyrics, multifarious in form, but all conveying the thoughts and feelings of the anonymous central character. He is a highly-strung, neurotic young man. His father failed in business and was driven to suicide, and he has fallen in love with Maud, the daughter of the lord of the hall who was chief agent of his father's ruin. Maud's family are determined that she shall marry a rich young lord. Her brother discovers Maud and the narrator in the garden at night, and the narrator kills the brother in a duel. Maud dies; the hero loses his reason and is restored only to go off and fight in the Crimean War – which to him seems to be but an extension of the personal struggle in which he has been immersed. The poem contains some of Tennyson's most celebrated lyrics, such as 'Come into the garden, Maud'. There are violent shifts of mood and tone between lyric and lyric from the extreme calm, say, of 'Go not, happy day' or 'Birds in the high hall garden' to the angry outburst of:

> This lump of earth has left his estate
> The lighter by the loss of his weight.

Rapture and hysteria are registered with a force which brings the reader into uncomfortable intimacy with a disturbed, self-absorbed personality. One is bound to recall what there was in Tennyson's own family's experience of persecution by the grandfather and his chosen heir to vivify the strange fiction.

In 'Locksley Hall' (probably written in 1837–8) Tennyson had already spoken through the mouth of an unstable character. The narrator's cousin, Amy, his childhood beloved, has proved faithless, bowing to the threats of a tyrannical father and being 'mated to a clown'. The sturdy rhythm of the monologue expresses the impassioned disgust of an outraged man, deeply conscious of his own superiority. Through him Tennyson projects a prophetic vision of the world as it will be, foreseeing the heavens filled with commercial aircraft, and then of war in the air, 'a ghastly dew/From the nations' airy navies grappling in the central blue'. It is in this vigorous poem that Tennyson made his oft-quoted proclamation:

Not in vain the distance beacons. Forward, forward let us range,
Let the great world spin for ever down the ringing grooves of
change.

It is said that the celebrated image can be traced to Tennyson's
journey on the first railway train from Liverpool to Manchester
when, owing to his short-sightedness, he failed to notice that the
wheels ran on rails and not in grooves. This poem and its sequel,
'Locksley Hall: Sixty Years After' (1886), together have a virile
thrust that is gripping and compulsive, though the harsh condem-
nations in the sequel voice the outrage of a staunch conservative at
movements in contemporary society:

Bring the old dark ages back without the faith, without the hope,
Break the State, the Church, the Throne, and roll their ruins down
the slope.

Tennyson's most ambitious work was the *Idylls of the King* which
began to be issued in 1859 and which were fully issued in a completed
version thirty years later. The plan to fashion a great work of epic
proportions on the Arthurian legends was a long-pondered one.
The seriousness of the poetic effort involved has something of high
vocation. It is tempting to mock a Laureate's master-work which
begins with a memorial tribute to the Prince Consort and ends with
a dedication to the Queen. It is tempting, too, to speak wryly of the
Victorianisation of values which seems to be involved in Tennyson's
study of Arthur and of the faithlessness of Guinevere. And certainly
if one thing above all is lacking in the vast work it is the imaginative
energy which gives life to *Maud* and to *Locksley Hall*. Nevertheless
the work as a whole is readable, readable almost to a fault through
the sheer smoothness of the blank verse. Sandwiched between 'The
Coming of Arthur' and 'The Passing of Arthur' are ten stories such
as 'Gareth and Lynette', 'Lancelot and Elaine' and 'Guinevere'. The
theme of Guinevere's unfaithful love for Lancelot casts its shadow
over other enterprises and finally marks the beginning of the disinte-
gration of the Round Table. Guinevere flees to a convent at Almes-
bury and Arthur follows her there:

She made her face a darkness from the King:
And in the darkness heard his armed feet
Pause by her; then came silence, then a voice,
Monotonous and hollow like a Ghost's
Denouncing judgment, but tho' changed, the King's.

Then Arthur turns preacher, sadly recounting the tale of high chiv-
alry corrupted by Guinevere's shameful sin with Lancelot and its

influence. The moral strain is lofty. Arthur has no choice but to root out the evil from his household for the infectious effects it might otherwise have:

'Better the King's waste hearth and aching heart
Than thou reseated in thy place of light,
The mockery of my people, and their bane.'

We are told that when Tennyson read this book aloud his voice would break with emotion and his listeners would wipe away the tears. It is not easy for us to enter sympathetically into a work in which the moral tone is so aggressively unyielding. It ill fits the archaic artificialities of the language. The blank verse too often lapses from a winning smoothness into a limp flaccidity. The narrative unfolds in a sequence of static pictures rather than in dramatic movement.

It is not possible to dismiss lightly works which bear the stamp of Tennyson's laureateship, for indeed occasional verses such as the 'Ode on the Death of the Duke of Wellington' and even 'The Charge of the Light Brigade' have both nobility and vigour, and the former has rhythmic subtlety too. Perhaps no one more aptly summed up Tennyson's greatness than the critic Edmund Gosse (1849–1928), speaking on the occasion of the poet's eightieth birthday:

He is wise and full of intelligence; but in mere intellectual capacity or attainment it is probable that there are many who excel him. This, then, is not the direction in which his greatness asserts itself. He has not headed a single moral reform nor inaugurated a single revolution of opinion; he has never pointed the way to undiscovered regions of thought; he has never stood on tiptoe to describe new worlds that his fellows were not tall enough to discover ahead. In all these directions he has been prompt to follow, quick to apprehend, but never himself a pioneer. Where then has his greatness lain? It has lain in the various perfections of his writing. He has written, on the whole, with more constant, unwearied, and unwearying excellence than any of his contemporaries.

Tennyson's great friend Edward Fitzgerald never hesitated to criticise the work of his contemporaries, often sharply. He watched Tennyson's career with some dismay for he felt that Tennyson's marriage and growing celebrity had diluted his inspiration. He thought it a waste of his talents that he should have devoted them to turning Arthur into Prince Albert and he thought *In Memoriam* self-indulgently ruminative over grief. 'It is full of finest things, but it is monotonous, and has that air of being evolved by a Poetical Machine of the highest order.' Yet Fitzgerald's essential respect for Tennyson never faltered. 'Tennyson,' he said, 'has stocked the English language with lines which once knowing one can't forgo.'

Robert Browning

If one were to seek in Victorian poetry for specimens to illustrate the extremes of limpid clarity and tangled obscurity one might well cite Tennyson's *Idylls of the King* on the one hand and Browning's *Sordello* (1840) on the other hand. Yet if the complexities of Browning's poetry contrast with the simplicity of Tennyson's, and indeed the intellectual content of much of Browning's work with the home-spun reflections embodied in Tennyson's, in terms of character and emotional life Browning is the straightforward one, Tennyson the man of complexity and inner conflict. In view of the two men's respective home backgrounds and early family life this is perhaps not surprising. Robert Browning's (1812–89) father was a cultivated, sympathetic, retiring man who, having had differences with his own father about the family plantations in the Indies, was determined to do well by his own son, gave him the run of his library, and encouraged him when he chose the poetic vocation. Browning had no need to work for his living. The generosity of relatives allowed him trips to Russia and Italy. His first poem *Pauline* (1833) was published at his aunt's expense. It gained reviews but no copies were sold. The subsequent pamphlets of poems and plays, *Bells and Pomegranates*, issued in the 1840s, were published at his father's expense. (The Old Testament High Priest has the hem of his robe bordered with bells and pomegranates. For Browning these symbolised poetry and thought, the blending of which was his aim.)

The climactic personal experience of Browning's life, his marriage after a far from easy courtship, was itself a triumph of sheer zest and will-power. Elizabeth Barrett (1806–61), herself already an established poet, had paid a compliment to Browning's work in 'Lady Geraldine's Courtship', mentioning it in the same breath as Wordsworth's and Tennyson's:

> Or from Browning some pomegranate which if cut deep down the middle,
> Shows a heart within blood-tinctured of a veined humanity.

Browning returned praise for praise, arranged to call on her, and almost immediately proposed marriage. But she was not well, and her tyrannical father, who was anyway utterly hostile to the idea of her marriage, encouraged an invalidism which Browning refused to accept as incapacitating. 'I had done with living, I thought, when you came and sought me out,' she confessed later; but Browning whisked her from her invalid couch and her immurement in the family to a secret marriage in London in 1846 and they subsequently fled to Italy where Mrs Browning enjoyed a remarkable revival in health. After her death in 1861 Browning returned to live in London. His later years, like Tennyson's, were those of an accepted genius, indeed a venerated prophet. The adulation of enthusiastic members of the Browning Society was amusingly depicted in a cartoon by Max Beerbohm (1872–1956).

In *Pauline* the narrator pays tribute to the great inspiration of his life, who is clearly Shelley: 'Sun-treader – life and light be thine for ever!' and the Shelleyan influence is certainly evident in this long monologue by a hero, passionate and self-absorbed, who has recovered faith only through the love and beauty of Pauline. *Paracelsus* (1835), a dramatic poem, tells the story of the sixteenth-century alchemist and astrologer who was eventually declared a quack. In so far as this work began to establish a reputation for Browning, the effect was totally undone by the publication of the massive poem *Sordello* which became at once a by-word for incomprehensibility. Tennyson quoted the first and last lines:

Who will, may hear Sordello's story told . . .
Who would has heard Sordello's story told.

They were the only two lines in the poem he could understand, he said, and they were both lies. The story of the 'development of a soul' is set in thirteenth-century Italy at the time of strife between Guelphs and Ghibellines. It is not only tangled in historical context but intolerably tortuous in argument and style. Browning's best work is scattered throughout *Dramatic Lyrics* (1842), *Dramatic Romances and Lyrics* (1845), *Men and Women* (1855), *Dramatis Personae* (1864) and the long poem, *The Ring and the Book* (1868–9).

The most felicitous thing to happen to Browning as a craftsman was the discovery of the dramatic monologue and the dramatic lyric. It enabled him to concentrate on portraying the individual in his exploration of himself and his world. He brought the individual to life by setting him at a particular point of interest or crisis in his own experience. The method gave him the chance for exploiting his unique gift for assuming a persona and living that persona's thoughts and feelings. To find previous dramatic monologues with anything like the vitality and immediacy of Browning's we have to turn back to the poems of John Donne (1572–1631). It is interesting, therefore, that Browning should remind us of Donne too in his capacity for translating passionate feeling into strenous reasoning without forfeiting urgency or vividness. Browning's wide sympathies enabled him to enter the minds of human oddities and eccentrics and probe the inner thoughts of imposters, hypocrites and criminals without necessarily alienating the reader from his subject. G. K. Chesterton noted what he called Browning's 'fierce charity' in this respect. 'He was a kind of cosmic detective who walked into the foulest of thieves' kitchens and accused men publicly of virtue.'

Thus in 'Porphyria's Lover' the narrator sits on a stormy night in his cheerless cottage with breaking heart until his beloved Porphyria glides in. She has so far failed to tear herself from her proud, wealthy family and give herself where her love truly is, but tonight she has come pityingly to take his head on her shoulder. What shall he do to make the most of this new-found joy and pride in possessing her?

> I found
> A thing to do, and all her hair
> In one long yellow string I wound
> Three times her little throat around,
> And strangled her.

So he sits, supporting her corpse, contemplating how she could scarcely have guessed in what way her love for him would be fulfilled. But if the psychopath is to be pitied, the arrogant, cruel, self-centred Duke of 'My Last Duchess' repels all sympathy. Again the revelation of the man's character is delayed. For the Duke is displaying his picture gallery, which includes a striking portrait of his 'last Duchess', to a visitor who, it emerges, has come to arrange the terms for the Duke's next marriage. It is only in somewhat defensively replying to questions about the portrait that, bit by bit, the Duke's domineering possessiveness emerges, and from his own lips we gather that he so bullied and persecuted a good-hearted wife that she fell into a decline and died. Ironically enough, it is out of his own mouth and with the open intention of making clear his deceased wife's demerits and his own concern for their dignity, that the Duke condemns himself. There is sharp symbolic, indeed ironic, relevance, in his proud final reference to one of the gallery's sculpted treasures: 'Notice Neptune though,/Taming a sea-horse, thought a rarity . . .'

Many of Browning's lyrics, though dramatic in setting, do not have much narrative content compressed into them; but in variety of tone and situation, mood and style, they are impressive. 'A Woman's Last Word' is a wife's conciliatory yielding after a dispute with her husband:

> Let's contend no more, Love,
>   Strive nor weep;
> All be as before, Love,
>   – Only sleep.

Its simple structure carries a flavour of wearied innocence and dutifulness, while the urgent rolling rhythms of 'How they brought the Good News from Ghent to Aix' ('I sprang to the stirrup, and Joris, and he') are alive with a desperate excitement, and the sturdy dactyls of 'The Lost Leader' ('Just for a handful of silver he left us') are charged with dignity and disgust. Techniques to match infinite modulations of mood seem to be at Browning's command. The percussive outbursts of the malicious monk in 'The Soliloquy in a Spanish Cloister' snarl with envious ill-will.

Browning achieved some of his greatest successes in dramatic monologues in the volume *Men and Women*, which includes the two contrasting studies of Florentine painters, 'Fra Lippo Lippi' and 'Andrea del Sarto'. Filippo Lippi (*c*.1406–69) was in early life a monk. He abducted a nun and was father of Filippino Lippi. Filippo Lippi's work has a detailed naturalism, and it was logical that Browning should turn him into a vital personality, abounding in energy, full of delight in life, alert at all times to the pictorial possibilities of what he sees around him. In Browning's poem Lippo is defending himself after having been caught by the watch sneaking back to Cosimo Medici's home in the early hours after a night's escapade. The story he tells of his upbringing, and, in particular, how poverty and hunger trapped him in the cloister, is a bubbling, bouncing record of exuberance and independence by one who can brook no constraints on his zest for life and art. By contrast Andrea del Sarto (1488–1530) earned the label 'Andrea senza errore' (Andrea the faultless) for the sheer perfection of his drawing. He went to the French court of Francis I in 1518 and returned a year later in disgrace, having appropriated money dishonestly. Browning made the contrast between the wayward vitality of Lippi and the inert perfectionism of Andrea the key to his poems. Andrea has the techniques that any master might envy, but he lacks the fire of inspiration. While Lippi talks excitedly with his captors as the dawn breaks, Sarto indulges defeatist reflections on what he might have been and is not, as dusk falls and his wife understandably prepares to go out for the evening with a less depressed and lifeless partner. Andrea recognises that in his art he has achieved a placid perfection, and that his technical accomplishment leaves no room for aspiration:

> Ah, but a man's reach should exceed his grasp,
> Or what's a Heaven for?

This theme became a dominant one in Browning's thinking: the need for earthly striving which is its own justification irrespective of attainment, and indeed acceptance of the finite sphere as one in which effort and aspiration can never meet with more than partial success, for the very good reason that fulfilment and realisation are only to be attained in the hereafter. It has been suggested that Browning too readily philosophises, indeed baptises, Victorian optimism. But in fact Browning's optimism is wholly unworldly. It is not based on the prospect of progress here below. On the contrary it glorifies failure when failure is the result of effort. There can be no grave failure except as the product of high purpose and endeavour; such failure is testimony to the significance of the realisations unachieved. In 'A Grammarian's Funeral' a sixteenth-century German scholar is celebrated as mourners carry his corpse to the height for burial and proclaim his greatness, the greatness of a man so devoted to learning that he never had time to get down to living. In so doing he was virtually staking his life on there being some use for his perfected intellect hereafter. The assumption is that it is better to aim high and fail than to aim at what can easily be achieved.

Browning develops this reasoning through the mind of a lover in 'The Last Ride Together'. The lover has failed to win his beloved and has accepted rejection on the condition that she will take one last ride with him. Her acceptance brings momentary rapture as he helps her to mount. In riding, he begins to measure his achievement mentally and sees all men labouring and failing, in public life, in poetry, in art, in music. He reflects that at least he has the joy of this present ride and even argues that, had he won his beloved, he would have had nothing to look forward to in the life hereafter. Perhaps indeed, he muses, heaven can be no more than an immortalisation, a permanent extension of such bliss as he now enjoys. The same thinking that is here applied to the experience of love is applied in 'Abt Vogler' to the experience of music. Music, like love, offers an opening to the transcendent. Vogler, a German organist, in extemporising at the keyboard, builds up a musical fabric of such mounting splendour that at the moment of climax earth touches heaven, indeed heaven transfigures earth, and Vogler recognises that he is tasting a transcendence which brings him into the spiritual company of beings from past and future alike. Time is swallowed up in eternity, and Vogler turns to praise God whose power can satisfy all the aspiration of the hearts he has made:

> There shall never be one lost good! What was, shall live as before;
>   The evil is null, is nought, is silence implying sound;
> What was good, shall be good, with, for evil, so much good more;
>   On the earth the broken arcs; in the heaven, a perfect round.

This kind of thinking being congenial to Browning, it is not surprising that Christian incarnational doctrine embeds itself in some of his work. In the poem 'Saul' it becomes explicit. One of the unique poems of the age, 'Saul' makes a lasting impact on the reader because Browning manages to thread through the dramatic presentation of the healing influence of David's songs upon Saul a sequence of logical reasoning that is inseparable from it. David tells how he was called upon to go into Saul's tent where for three days Saul has been in a trancelike black depression, speechless and motionless. David finds him in his agony erect against the tent-prop, his arms spread wide on the cross-supports. The symbolism of crucifixion is evident. David's task is to stir him to life by making him aware that life is worth living. To this end he sings in turn in praise of everything that is good – the country, marriage, battle and temple-worship – but he has to sing more urgently of life's delights and Saul's especial glory before he can produce a glimmer of response. Desperate to find something more stirring still, he sings the praise of immortal fame. Then, exhausting his resources, David yearns in agony to be able to comfort Saul by some more magnificent blessing still. Then suddenly the truth dawns upon him. In all respects God transcends man; but if God does not care for Saul as David now does, and would not give Saul the new life that David would gladly bestow on him even at the cost of his own life, then the Creator's love is less than the creature's, and that is nonsense. The logical necessity for divine love to take human form is established:

> O Saul, it shall be
> A Face like my face that received thee; a Man like to me,
> Thou shalt love and be loved by, for ever! a Hand like this hand
> Shall throw open the gates of new life to thee! See the Christ
> stand!

Browning's *The Ring and the Book* is one of those immense masterpieces that are more praised than read. It is not tempting to settle down to well over twenty thousand lines of Browningesque blank verse far from always easy on the ear or the eye, but the poem nevertheless has a surprisingly consistent vitality. One day Browning picked up a book in Florence recording a criminal case against a nobleman who was executed in Rome in 1698. The book's title page also announced, 'Roman Murder-Case. In which it is disputed whether and when a Husband may kill his Adulterous wife without incurring the ordinary penalty.' The case fascinated Browning, as well it might. It concerned Pompilia, the supposed daughter of Pietro and Violante Comparini, who had an inherited income. Count Guido Franceschini married Pompilia to win control over the inheritance. He then made her life a misery, so she fled and was able to find help in a handsome young priest Caponsacchi. Guido pursued Pompilia and Caponsacchi in the hope of finding evidence for a divorce.

He tracked them to an inn, and, though there was no evidence of impropriety, they were brought to court and found guilty of too close an intimacy. Pompilia was despatched to a convent, but eventually returned to her parents with her baby son. Hearing that he now had an heir, Guido took four companions and stabbed Pompilia and her parents to death.

Browning's story is that of the trial, and he uses his device of the dramatic monologue to new and startling effect. Thus in book II, 'Half-Rome', the speaker is a married Roman citizen who sympathises with Guido as the cuckolded husband up against a clever priest. In book III, 'The Other Half-Rome', the speaker is an unmarried citizen who sympathises with the pathetic victim, Pompilia. In book IV, 'Tertium Quid', an impartial speaker, an aristocratic Roman, tries to see right and wrong on both sides. In book V, 'Count Guido Franceschini', Guido pleads his innocence. In book VI, 'Giuseppe Caponsacchi', the young priest indignantly defends his innocence and Pompilia's. In book VII, 'Pompilia', there is a deposition from Pompilia whose stab wounds did not prove immediately fatal, but who survived briefly to make her case. In book VIII, 'Dominus Hyacinthus de Archangelis', the defence lawyer prepares his brief. In book IX, 'Doctor Johannes-Baptista Bottinius', the prosecution counsel reads proudly over his prepared speech, relishing its rhetoric. In book X the Pope weighs the evidence, because Guido has appealed to him on the grounds that he took minor orders, and passes judgement. In book XI, 'Guido', the Count, now deprived of his title, reveals his real nature in addressing friends who visit him in the death-cell.

In spite of the adulation of the Browning Society not everyone succumbed to admiration of Browning the Sage. Edward Fitzgerald mocked his philosophical vein as 'Cockney Sublime' and labelled him 'the great Prophet of the Gargoyle School', while Carlyle's (1795–1881) judgement on *The Ring and the Book* was almost as dismissive: 'It is full of talent, energy, and effort; but actually without *Backbone* or basis of Common-sense. I think it among the absurdest books ever written by a gifted man.' Browning's spirit, however, seems not to have faltered. In the Epilogue to *Asolando* (1889), which was published on the day of his death, he asks one who loves him not to pity him after death but to remember what he always was:

One who never turned his back but marched breast forward,
   Never doubted clouds would break,
Never dreamed, though right were worsted, wrong would triumph,
Held we fall to rise, are baffled to fight better,
   Sleep to wake.

Elizabeth Barrett Browning

It startles us today to learn that when Wordsworth died the suggestion was made that Elizabeth Barrett Browning (1806–61) should succeed him as Poet Laureate, no doubt the notion being abroad that a female sovereign might appropriately appoint a female laureate. Women poets had been too rare a phenomenon in the mid-nineteenth century for it to be possible for the popular mind to think of Elizabeth Barrett Browning as just another poet, as Mrs Gaskell was just another novelist. The Victorian prejudice was so strong that on Mrs Browning's death we find Edward Fitzgerald writing in a letter:

> Mrs Browning's death is rather a relief to me, I must say: no more Aurora Leighs [a reference to her most considerable work], thank God! A woman of real Genius, I know: but what is the upshot of it all? She and her Sex had better mind the Kitchen and their Children; and perhaps the Poor: except in such things as little Novels, they only devote themselves to what Men do much better, leaving that which Men do worse or not at all.

It is ironic that Fitzgerald's admission, 'A woman of real Genius' (which seems to make nonsense of the accompanying denigration), is in fact something which modern criticism, by and large, would dispute. Commendation for Mrs Browning, if any, is generally grudging, and wrapped about with qualifications. And it is easy to see why, for her unrestrained emotionalism and her verbosity are offensive to modern taste. When she gets into anthologies it is usually by way of her *Sonnets from the Portuguese* which first appeared in a collected edition of her works in 1859. These love poems, celebrating her love for and marriage to Robert Browning, were presented as translations because of their intensely personal character. Browning had playfully called her 'the Portuguese' because of his admiration for her poem, 'Catarina to Camoens', in which Catarina, 'dying in his absence abroad, refers to a poem in which he recorded the sweetness of her eyes':

> O my poet, O my prophet,
>   When you praised their sweetness so,
> Did you think, in singing of it,
>   That it might be near to go?
>   Had you fancies,
>   From their glances,
> That the grave would quickly screen
> 'Sweetest eyes, were ever seen?'

The sonnets are very uneven. Outbursts of imprecise rhetoric occur in sometimes tangled sentences which defy the sonnet form to bring them to heel. Yet in the best of them, such as the celebrated:

> If thou must love me, let it be for nought
> Except for love's sake only,

the intensity of feeling is blended with fineness of psychological discernment, giving the lines a moving authenticity.

Elizabeth Barrett Browning's great work, however, is *Aurora Leigh* (1857) which can only be called a novel in verse, and it is not a very good novel, though the blank verse is surprisingly readable and a good deal more energetic than the verse of Tennyson's *Idylls*. It proves a flexible instrument. The poem's eleven thousand odd lines are, of course, too many, but to pick the work up, once one knows the story, is generally to be interested. Aurora Leigh is herself a poet with a sense of vocation to her art, while her cousin Romney Leigh is a practically-minded social reformer who wants her to marry him. The trouble is that he does not take her poethood seriously, but wants her help in his own great work. The female sex is 'weak for art', he tells her, but 'strong/For life and duty'. This leads her to reject him indignantly:

> 'You misconceive the question like a man,
> Who sees a woman as the complement
> Of his sex merely. You forget too much
> That every creature, female as the male,
> Stands single in responsible act and thought,
> As also in birth and death.'

The plot thereafter is a complex one. Romney puts egalitarian ideas into practice, all but marries a tramp's daughter, and imports the riff-raff of the London streets to his hall in the country much to the resentment of the locals. The social experiment collapses, the hall is wrecked and burned, and Romney loses his eyesight. Ultimately Aurora brings him the devotion that Jane Eyre brought to Rochester. Both are chastened, he of his dogmatic arrogance, she of her pride. 'Art is much, but Love is more,' Aurora learns, and Romney exclaims, 'Thank God who made me blind, to make me see!'

Edward Fitzgerald

When the poet Edward Fitzgerald (1809–83) denigrated Elizabeth Barrett Browning, and for that matter when he denigrated her husband, he was expressing the view of one who was above all a literary craftsman of exquisite fastidiousness. His one remembered work, *Rubáiyát of Omar Khayyám* (1859), a loosely translated version of quatrains by an eleventh-century Persian poet, establishes that beyond doubt. Indeed his previously quoted comment on Tennyson, that he 'stocked the English language with lines which once knowing one can't forgo' has a special significance in that the *Rubáiyát of Omar Khayyám* is one of the most quoted poems in the English language and the *Oxford Dictionary of Quotations* gives it almost as much space as it does to Tennyson's *In Memoriam*.

Fitzgerald's character was a strange mixture of the generous and the querulous, the affectionate and the quirky. His father's family name was originally Purcell, but his mother was a Fitzgerald, indeed sole heiress to the enormous wealth of a distinguished and ancient Irish family, who set up home apart from her husband and who kept Edward at her beck and call when social engagements required it. Fitzgerald was fond of observing that all his family were mad but that at least he had the advantage of knowing he was insane. He was not the eldest son, but of course he was not required to work for his living and he was frequently self-critical of his own indolence. He was a staunch if sometimes difficult friend. Tennyson was only one among several whom he helped financially. He had many eccentricities. He was carelessly informal in his dress and so odd in his habits that locals near his Suffolk home at Woodbridge nicknamed him 'Dotty'.

The great blunder of Fitzgerald's life was his marriage in 1857 to Lucy Barton, the daughter of a Quaker poet whom he befriended and whose work he helped to edit after his death. Fitzgerald's passionate attachments were to men, though it is clear that such attachments in Victorian society (like Tennyson's attachment to Hallam) did not generally imply homosexual partnerships. Some kind of tacitly accepted obligation to marry Lucy Barton made him feel unable to escape when his mother's death gave him the required independence. He was then forty-seven and she a little younger. The two were totally incompatible and soon separated. The discovery of Omar's poem and his early work on it coincided with his marriage failure. 'Omar breathes a sort of Consolation to me,' he confessed at the time, and ten years afterwards was to say, 'Poor Omar is one I have great fellow feeling with.'

The consolation he found in Omar was at once personal and philosophical. Fitzgerald, like Tennyson, had been afflicted by the religious doubts of the age and had come down firmly on the side of unbelief. He went so far in the *Rubáiyát* as to throw the Old Testament God's handiwork in his face with a Hardyesque acerbity:

Oh, Thou, who Man of baser Earth didst make,
And who with Eden didst devise the Snake;
　　For all the Sin wherewith the Face of Man
Is blacken'd, Man's Forgiveness give – and take!

Such stanzas indicate, of course, how freely Fitzgerald adapted his original. 'Translation' is the wrong word for stanzas often composed mentally on country walks when the original texts were back home in the study. But the qualities of the work which, after many years of near total neglect, eventually turned it into a best-seller, were those of Fitzgerald's unerring craftsmanship in suggesting an oriental atmosphere and soaking the lines in sensuous evocation by image and cadence of rare felicity:

Think, in this batter'd Caravanserai
Whose Portals are alternate Night and Day,
　　How Sultan after Sultan with his Pomp
Abode his destined Hour, and went his way.

The brevity of life, the vanity of worldly hopes, the irrelevance of study, the fruitlessness of philosophical enquiry, to creatures whose universal end is the grave – these are the themes, along with the advice to make the most of life before it fleets away:

Here with a Loaf of Bread beneath the Bough,
A Flask of Wine, a Book of Verse – and Thou
　　Beside me singing in the Wilderness –
And Wilderness is Paradise enow.

The glorification of wine, women and song as life's great consolations was not calculated to chime in with the mood of Victorian England, but Fitzgerald's poem has never lost its appeal since. T. S. Eliot observed how, on his first reading of the poem, the 'world appeared anew, painted with bright, delicious, and painful colours'. It is only fair to add that some scholars have challenged Fitzgerald's basic reading of Omar. There is a theory that Omar was in fact a saintly Sufi ascetic whose imagery of wine represented the spiritual refreshment earned by the devout contemplative.

Matthew Arnold

In denigrating Tennyson's *Idylls of the King*, Fitzgerald observed that they might almost have been written by Matthew Arnold (1822–88). It is an apt observation in that Arnold's poetic vein was the reverse of the energetic; and the smooth verses of the *Idylls* often have a dispirited tone. Arnold, as a poet, is the arch-exponent of dispiritedness, though as a young man he could be lively and sociable enough. Indeed he had a reputation for adopting the grand manner and for display of conceit. When Harriet Martineau took Charlotte Brontë to visit his mother, Mrs Thomas Arnold, at her home near Ambleside in 1850, Charlotte found Arnold's 'foppery' displeasing, though she testified that he improved on acquaintance.

In his response to current scepticism which found the supernatural claims of Christian revelation untenable, Arnold more closely resembled Fitzgerald than Tennyson. The general decline of faith in the course of the era left him bewildered and melancholy. His reaction is neatly summed up in 'Dover Beach', where the poet stands watching a calm sea and a full tide, and hearing 'the eternal note of sadness' in the ebb and flow of the incoming waves:

> The Sea of Faith
> Was once, too, at the full, and round earth's shore
> Lay like the folds of a bright girdle furl'd.
> But now I only hear
> Its melancholy, long, withdrawing roar,
> Retreating . . .

For a man of Arnold's ethical earnestness there was no question of following Fitzgerald and celebrating the consolations of wine, women and song in a Persian garden. The prevalent mood of much of his work is that of despondency and discontent.

In this respect Matthew Arnold stands in strong contrast to his father, Thomas Arnold (1795–1842), in his own way one of the most influential of Victorian innovators. For when he was made Headmaster of Rugby School in 1827 he determined to change the face of education throughout the public school system, and indeed he achieved his aim. Much of what came to be recognised as the public school ethos derived from Thomas Arnold, a man of immense vigour and determination. He was profoundly convinced that intellectual and moral development must be bound together, that the educational process was insuperably bound up with the inculcation of Christian belief and practice. Arnold raised the status of teaching staff, brought breadth and imaginative appeal to the classical curriculum, and preached sermons in the school chapel to corroborate the ethical approach to academic and personal training. He also gave dignity and responsibility to his senior boys, laying on them obligations of moral and disciplinary leadership. The robust Christian zeal which Thomas Arnold exuded makes his son's worried lack of conviction seem like a gift for the psychologist's case-book. Certainly Matthew Arnold himself was aware of the contrast. In the poem 'Rugby Chapel' he mourns his lost father, emphasising his sturdiness and cheerfulness of disposition, while 'we' who are left struggle through life with compressed lips and furrowed brows.

The mood of Arnold's dramatic poem, *Empedocles on Etna* (1852), is suicidal. Based on the story of an ancient Sicilian philosopher, it tells how the formerly powerful Empedocles, 'half-mad/With exile, and with brooding on his wrongs', comes to Mount Etna and climbs to the summit, determined to die. He broods on human misery, on man's foolishness in imagining that the world exists for his welfare, and above all on the absurdity of postulating the existence of divinities and of happiness hereafter. He gives the lie direct to the Browningesque optimism which extrapolates success from failure, good from evil:

> Fools! That so often here
> Happiness mock'd our prayer,
> I think, might make us fear
> A like event elsewhere;
> Make us, not fly to dreams, but moderate desire.

Empedocles then plunges to his death in the volcano.

In unpeopling the universe of gods and preaching a discipline of moderated desire, Arnold was accepting the necessity of scepticism, and this left him with the question he tackled in prose works to be considered later in this book: how morality and culture could be preserved in the absence of the religion which had authenticated them.

Arnold's most celebrated poem is 'The Scholar-Gipsy', in which he takes up a legend recorded by a seventeenth-century writer, Joseph Glanville, in his book, *The Vanity of Dogmatizing* (1661). It tells of a poor Oxford scholar whose frustration drove him to join the gypsies to learn their lore. Arnold pictures the Oxford countryside still haunted by the scholar-gypsy, and there is a Keatsian luxuriance in this evocation of the landscape. He makes the scholar-gypsy a symbol of decisive faith, a man with '*one* aim, *one* business, *one* desire'. By contrast he laments the halting, faltering lives of his contemporaries, 'vague, half-believers of our casual creeds', obsessed with dwelling on their miseries. He bids the scholar-gypsy flee the 'infection of our mental strife' and the 'strange disease of modern life'.

Arnold was nothing if not lachrymose, and the modern reader is likely to find the pervasive mournfulness more palatable when tears are shed over a tale of tragedy than when they are shed over the griefs of a Victorian gentleman bereft of conviction and faith. Thus the fine epic fragment, 'Sohrab and Rustum', tells a tragic story of a great Persian hero, Rustum, whose son Sohrab joins the Tartar forces, and, many years later, when they attack the Persians, challenges their bravest warrior to meet him in single combat. In this way it comes about that, as Arnold reveals, all unknowingly the old warrior Rustum fights with his own son and kills him. Although the tragic catastrophe is a result of pure coincidence and there is therefore no question of analysing human motive or involving the reader in tense awareness of choice and conflict between good and evil, nevertheless Arnold manages to endow the tale with a stately if gloomy ominousness. The blank verse recreates the grand orchestration of classical epic, though with that tired, muted intonation which Arnold so rarely escaped:

> So, on the bloody sand, Sohrab lay dead;
> And the great Rustum drew his horseman's cloak
> Down o'er his face, and sate by his dead son.
> As those black granite pillars, once high-rear'd
> By Jemshid in Persepolis, to bear
> His house, now, 'mid their broken flights of steps,
> Lie prone, enormous, down the mountain side –
> So in the sand lay Rustum by his son.

The sombre note predominates again in 'Balder Dead', a tale from Norse legend. Balder, a son of Odin, was killed by Loki, the evil son of Hela, goddess of the dead who dwelt below the roots of the sacred Yggdrasil. Arnold's poem tells of the grief of the gods at Balder's death and of Hermod's journey to beg Hela to deliver him up. Hela's condition is that all things on earth must first weep for him, and Loki, disguised as an old hag, refuses to do so. The versification of 'Balder Dead' shows academic proficiency rather than either vigour or inspiration.

After 'The Scholar-Gipsy' perhaps Arnold's most quoted poem is 'Thyrsis', the elegy he wrote on the death of his friend, the poet Arthur Hugh Clough (1819–61). The elegy excels chiefly in the sensuous lushness with which the Oxford countryside is recreated and from which one can view 'that sweet city with her dreaming spires'. The line has become familiar through its use in travel brochures, while the later line, 'Lovely all times she lies, lovely tonight', has been heard on the lips of many an after-dinner speaker paying tribute to his alma mater. The poem is written in the classical convention which converts Arnold, Clough and their contemporaries into swains and shepherds. However, the poet's own mood of nostalgic melancholy is not encouraged by Thyrsis, whose voice is made to whisper:

> Why faintest thou? I wander'd till I died.
> Roam on! the light we sought is shining still.

Arthur Hugh Clough

Clough, in contrast to Arnold, rejected defeatism in his poetry. His most famous poem is a sinewy call to optimism in crisis, 'Say not the struggle nought availeth', and Winston Churchill quoted its final stanza in a war-time broadcast:

And not by eastern windows only,
  When daylight comes, comes in the light,
In front the sun climbs slow, how slowly,
  But westward, look, the land is bright.

Clough, however, had his share of troubles. He was one of Thomas Arnold's prize pupils at Rugby, and it is tempting to attribute some of his disabilities in maturity to his sensitive response to the burden of moral earnestness laid upon him in boyhood. 'I verily believe my whole being is regularly soaked through with the wishing and hoping and striving to do the school good,' he wrote at the age of seventeen, and it has been ironically observed of Arnold's hot-house moralism at Rugby that it ignored God Almighty's apparent intention 'that there should exist between childhood and manhood the natural production known as a boy'.

Certainly Clough's difficulties were those of a man brought up to an intense moral scrupulousness, who found himself having to discard intellectual conventions that had seemed unquestionable until he was infected by doubts about traditional religious beliefs. He was given to unceasing re-analysis of his own position in the light of current developments in the intellectual world. Though he obtained a fellowship at Oriel College, Oxford in 1842, he resigned it voluntarily in 1848 because he felt that he could no longer subscribe conscientiously to the Thirty-nine Articles of doctrine laid down in the Church of England Book of Common Prayer to which Oxford fellows were required to give formal assent. There were some years of unsettlement, including a brief attempt to settle in America, before he finally got a modest post in the Education Office in 1853, and he married Blanche Smith in 1854. She was a cousin of Florence Nightingale (1820–1910), the hospital reformer.

Not only was Clough's sturdy temperament out of tune with Arnold's brooding dejection, his attitude to poetry was also markedly different from his friend's. Whereas the cultivated artifices of Arnold's pastoral odes and the stately epic contrivances of 'Sohrab and Rustum' distanced poetry from contemporary life, Clough sought to bring it closer to everyday life in substance and style. Clough's *The Bothie of Tober-na-Vuolich* (1848), 'A Long Vacation Pastoral' written in hexameters, has something of a mock-heroic tone in telling how an Oxford tutor takes a student reading party on a vacation trip to Scotland. The hero, Philip, has radical egalitarian views which lead him to idealise working-class women. A thoughtful but rashly impulsive young man with a ready tendency to flirt, he falls seriously in love with a Highland lassie, Elspeth Mackaye, whose father owns the 'bothie'. His emotional development has a healthily stabilising effect on his political thinking. The poem is a spirited work of great freshness and naturalness:

> Philip returned to his books, but returned to his Highlands after;
> Got a first, 'tis said; a winsome bride, 'tis certain.
> There while courtship was ending, nor yet the wedding appointed,
> Under her father he studied the handling of hoe and of hatchet.

The couple fail to find a place in English society and go off to New Zealand.

Amours de Voyage (1858) is another exercise in hexameters. Its hero, Claude, is visiting Rome and meets a middle-class family of English tourists with a daughter, Mary. In contrast to Philip of *The Bothie of Tober-na-Vuolich*, Claude is so excessively scrupulous in introspection that he is incapable of commitment. Unable to make up his mind, he loses the opportunity to follow his inclination to court Mary, who loves him. Thus both poems explore the situation of the young intellectual who falls in love. Both are alive with mental reflection and rumination worked through in the concrete circumstances of real life in clearly defined environments. It was Clough's aim to dramatise personal feelings and dilemmas in this way, and they express the inner dialogue of mind and heart in an entertainingly objective form. Whereas *The Bothie of Tober-na-Vuolich* has a buoyant, often boisterous, exuberance, the *Amours de Voyage* by virtue of the preoccupation with a damagingly over-fastidious mentality, is sharper in its satire. Critics have seen in Claude's ineffective posturings, his evasion of commitment, and his self-irony, and especially in the sharply realised contemporary environment, an anticipation of the deflationary self-analysis found in twentieth-century poetry:

> Look you, we travel along in the railway-carriage, or steamer,
> And, *pour passer le temps*, till the tedious journey be ended,
> Lay aside paper or book, to talk with the girl that is next one;
> And, *pour passer le temps*, with the terminus all but in
>   prospect,
> Talk of eternal ties and marriages made in heaven.
>   Ah, did we really accept with a perfect heart the illusion!

Clough's irony in 'Dipsychus' often has a twentieth-century ring.

His concern with the intellectual hero whose values contradict those of contemporary philistine society is manifested again in Dipsychus, whose moral scruples alienate him from the materialistic society around him. (Dipsychus means 'Double-minded'.) He soliloquises and carries on a dialogue with a 'Spirit' who represents current trends. His despair is thus countered by the Spirit's accommodating cynicism, and the note of emotional crisis is balanced by the note of callous acceptance. Clough plainly had a capacity to handle conversational idioms and to give rhythmic force to the low-key by-products of casual musing which foreshadows devices of poetic understatement to be cultivated by such twentieth-century poets as W. H. Auden (1907–73). He had wit and a mastery of epigram too, as is shown in the celebrated poem 'The Latest Decalogue':

No graven images may be
Worshipped, except the currency . . .
Thou shalt not kill; but needs't not strive
Officiously to keep alive:

These are not poetic veins to be found in Arnold. Indeed Arnold believed that the concern of poetry was with 'great actions, calculated powerfully and delightfully to affect what is permanent in the human soul'. This might well seem a more appropriate formula for describing the tragic and heroic contest between Sohrab and Rustum than for describing the antics of contemporary undergraduates let loose in Scotland in the summer vacation. But then Clough believed that poetry should concern itself much more than it usually did in his day 'with general wants and ordinary feelings'. And Arnold himself conceded that *The Bothie of Tober-na-Vuolich* conveys to the reader the sense 'of having, within short limits of time, a large portion of human life presented to him, instead of a small portion.'

Algernon Charles Swinburne

Matthew Arnold, who spent most of his working years as an Inspector of Schools, also became Professor of Poetry at the University of Oxford in 1857 and in this capacity he once boldly prophesied that by the end of the century people would generally recognise that its two greatest poets had been Wordsworth and Byron (1789–1824). The pronouncement provoked a passionate response from the poet Algernon Charles Swinburne (1837– 1909), who denigrated Byron and declared that the century's two greatest poets were Coleridge and Shelley (1792–1822). While Browning, too, had a special devotion to Shelley, it must be observed that if Shelley had a poetic successor then Swinburne was the man. Yet, as H. J. C. Grierson has written, there is 'an essential difference between the poetry of Shelley and that of Swinburne. Shelley has something to say . . . He was a prophet as well as a poet.' Perhaps no poet's quality is easier to sum up than Swinburne's. His sheer technical accomplishment can be described only in superlatives. Yet the technique operated throughout his life at the service of what were at best second-hand radical postures and naïve outbursts against respectability.

It is significant that little needs to be said of Swinburne's life, of what he actually did. The son of an Admiral with aristocratic connections, he was born in Northumberland, spent much of his childhood on the Isle of Wight, and was educated at Eton and at Balliol College, Oxford. At Oxford he came into contact with Dante Gabriel Rossetti and the Pre-Raphaelite circle. He attracted favourable attention from the *cognoscenti* with *Atalanta in Calydon* (1865), a poetic drama in the classical style. Tennyson hailed it enthusiastically ('It is a long day since I have read anything so fine'), and Ruskin called it 'the grandest thing ever yet done by a youth – though he is a Demoniac youth.' A year later he burst rudely on the English public with the first series of *Poems and Ballads* (1866), the precursor of a second and third series in 1878 and 1889. The volume at once set outrageous phrases in swinging rhythms rocking in the heads of undergraduates, phrases designed to shock by their blasphemies and their sexual improprieties. Mid-century religious doubt had driven Browning into defiant celebration of faith, Tennyson into tortured brooding on the human lot, Arnold into dejected agnosticism, and Fitzgerald into the glorification of epicurean indulgence, but it drove Swinburne into a strident snarling denunciation of God and the Christian religion.

The role of the reckless shocker did not last him his lifetime, however – at least so far as his personal conduct was concerned. For when he was all but killing himself with alcohol and dissipation, his friend Theodore Watts-Dunton rescued him, settled down with him in 1879 at his home in Putney, and imposed a strict regimen that tamed and domesticated him. Whether it benefited his poetic output is another matter.

There is a party trick in which a person is asked to describe a spiral without using his hands. Perhaps only a fool, or a very clever person, would make the attempt. It might make an appropriate test of a similar useless ingenuity to ask a literary student to describe Swinburne's poetry without quoting it. A peculiarity of his verse is that it clamours to be spoken out loud, to have its vowels and consonants, its rhymes and its rhythms, its alliterations and repetitions sent rolling through the air from the lips and the tongue to the listening ear. For Swinburne's music mesmerises, drugs the mind. The mental and moral perverseness which sometimes accompanies it adds spice to a heady recipe. In 'Dolores' he parodies a litany to the Virgin Mary in hymning the sexual charms of a shameless seductress and *femme fatale*:

> Hast thou told all thy secrets the last time,
>   And bared all thy beauties to one?
> Ah, where shall we go then for pastime,
>   If the worst that can be has been done?
> But sweet as the rind was the core is;
>   We are fain of thee still, we are fain,
> O sanguine and subtle Dolores,
>   Our Lady of Pain.

In Swinburne's erotic outburst the 'Lilies and languors of virtue' are scorned in favour of the 'raptures and roses of vice'; kisses are bloody, they sting till one shudders and smarts; passion smites and slays; lips foam and the flesh is bruised. There is a sinister call to indulgence in unnameable vices, and talk of pain and chains conjures up imagery of sadism and flagellation. Having thus adopted the public role of a pagan celebrating sexual abandon, Swinburne could scarcely have been surprised to find himself labelled by a reviewer as a 'libidinous laureate' with 'a mind all aflame with . . . feverish carnality'. The carnality and the feverishness are evident enough. So too is the surge of sound that sets the reader's heart pulsing in sympathy. But in sympathy with what? It is doubtful whether reading 'Dolores' would send anyone in search of erotic satisfaction. Rather listening to Swinburne's music is like listening to any music. It stirs delight in itself and wonder at the virtuosity of its creator.

The rejection of Christianity is eloquently voiced in the 'Hymn to Proserpine', which purports to be composed on the official proclamation of the Christian Faith in Rome, and laments the dethronement of the old gods by the victory of Christ:

> Thou hast conquered, O pale Galilean; the world has grown grey
>   from thy breath;
> We have drunken of things Lethean, and fed on the fullness of
>   death.

The price paid for Christianity is the loss of what is vital and passionate, sensuous and joyful, and its replacement by a religion which exalts the pale maidenhood of a virgin over the flushed and fruitful goddesses of old. It is a question of life or death: 'O ghastly glories of saints, dead limbs of a gibbetted Gods!'

The critical estimate of Swinburne's work has never been steady.

In 1953 H. J. C. Grierson was saying, '*Poems and Ballads* are little read today' and claiming precedence for *Songs Before Sunrise* (1871), a collection of poems inspired by Mazzini's (1805–72) struggle for Italian independence, and bringing political assaults on the world's powers-that-be into concert with withering scorn of God and Christ. Yet Curtis Dahl in *Great Writers of the English Language: Poets* (1979) tells us that the political poems have 'faded with the liberal causes', and the *Oxford Companion to English Literature* (1985) remarks that the first volume of *Poems and Ballads* contains 'many of his best as well as his most notorious poems'. With this judgement the reader will probably concur. It is from his unreflecting paeans of acclamation for the sensuous appeal of the natural world and the human body that Swinburne's most memorable lines derive:

> I will go back to the great sweet mother,
>   Mother and lover of men, the sea.
> I will go down to her, I and none other,
>   Close with her, kiss her and mix her with me;
> Cling to her, strive with her, hold her fast;
> O fair white mother, in days long past
> Born without sister, born without brother,
>   Set free my soul as thy soul is free.

The intimate connection between response to the natural world and to the human body emerges in the stanza which follows the one above in 'The Triumph of Time':

> O fair green-girdled mother of mine,
>   Sea, that art clothed with the sun and the rain,
> Thy sweet hard kisses are strong like wine,
>   Thy large embraces are keen like pain.

Dolores and the sea, it seems, have much in common.

Yet who would not envy the power of such utterance as this? It scarcely seems to matter what is being said. Indeed when Swinburne turns in *Songs Before Sunrise* to write a philosophical poem, 'Hertha', in the form of a proclamation by the goddess of the earth, it is again the technical tricks of incantatory echo and repetition, rather than the cogency or penetration of the thinking, that appeal:

> Beside or above me
>   Nought is there to go;
> Love or unlove me,
>   Unknow me or know,
> I am that which unloves me and loves: I am the stricken, and I
>   am the blow.

Swinburne is a poet whose impact is greatest on first reading. After that there is nothing new to be gleaned, no depths to be sounded. The throbbing rhythms pulse in the reader's veins, the rhapsodical rhetoric intoxicates his brain, and that is the end of it.

Dante Gabriel Rossetti

One of the poems in Swinburne's first *Poems and Ballads* tells the story of Tannhäuser, who journeys vainly to Rome in search of absolution from the Pope for his sinful life with Venus under the Venusberg, the mountain supposed to have been her refuge after Christianity ousted the pagan divinities. Wagner's (1813–83) opera *Tannhäuser* (1845) tells the same story. Swinburne's poem on the subject, 'Laus Veneris', is his attempt to imitate the stanza of Fitzgerald's *Omar Khayyám*, a poem which became known only on its discovery by Dante Gabriel Rossetti (1828–82). Swinburne had first come across Rossetti and William Morris at Oxford in 1857, when the two artists, along with Edward Burne-Jones (1833–98), were painting murals on Arthurian subjects in the Union Debating Hall. This was one of the manifestations of what was called the 'Pre-Raphaelite' movement. The original Pre-Raphaelite Brotherhood had been formed by a group of artists, including Dante Gabriel Rossetti, J. E. Millais (1829–96) and W. Holman Hunt (1827–1910), who agreed in their disapproval of the current values of the artistic establishment. Like many such movements, the Brotherhood called for a return to nature. It considered that the immensely influential Italian Renaissance artist Raphael (1483–1520) had been over-rated, and that his idealisation of human beauty and human character falsified life. Its members criticised the romantic portraiture of his English disciple, Sir Joshua Reynolds (1723–92), and the academic tradition he founded. They advocated instead a return to the simplicity, the detail and the fidelity to nature found in medieval frescoes. The banding together in a 'Brotherhood', the Pre-Raphaelite Brotherhood, was at first something of a lark, but the element of secrecy and the air of revolutionary menace it suggested made the Pre-Raphaelites suspect so far as the world at large was concerned.

Ruskin, however, sprang to their defence in a letter to the *Times* in May 1850, and argued:

> They intend to return to early days in this one particular only – that, as far as in them lies, they will draw either what they see or what they suppose might have been the actual facts of the scene they desire to represent, irrespective of any conventional rules of

picture-making; and they have chosen their unfortunate, though not inaccurate name, because all artists did this before Raphael's time, and after Raphael's time *did* not this, but sought to paint fair pictures rather than represent stern facts; of which the consequence has been that from Raphael's time to this day historical art has been in acknowledged decadence.

The movement quickly spread from the artistic to the literary sphere. Both Rossetti and Coventry Patmore (1823–96) contributed poems to *The Germ*, a short-lived periodical founded in 1850 to advance the Pre-Raphaelite cause. But too many diverse personalities became involved with the movement for it to remain homogeneous. Some Pre-Raphaelites sought especially to cultivate moral seriousness and earnestness of message, whether religious, personal or social; in consequence the movement came to involve a curious blend of enthusiasm for medievalism and of concern for contemporary culture and even for social justice. Indeed the 'Pre-Raphaelite' label was eventually to cover a whole range of developments in the artistic and literary worlds. Ford Madox Brown (1821–93) painted a famous picture, 'The Last of England', in which a middle-class couple are seen sailing in a boat from shore to ship in the 1850s, sadness, bitterness and defeat in their expressions. It summed up the frustration of many at this time driven to emigrate in order to make good. Brown's later picture, 'Work', celebrates the dignity of honest manual toil. In both these pictures the narratives carry a social message. In William Holman Hunt's pictures, 'The Hireling Shepherd' and 'The Light of the World', by contrast, the narratives carry moral and religious messages respectively. Generally speaking, Pre-Raphaelite painting sets out to ensnare the spectator's attention by a frank use of bold colours, and then to shock, or at least surprise, the spectator by presenting an unexpected vision of how the world of the past or the present might look to a perceptive artist. Thus Millais's famous painting, 'Christ in the House of His Parents', roused bitter controversy because the faces of St Joseph, the Virgin Mary and the boy Christ are unmistakably those of everyday nineteenth-century life unglamorised.

Dante Gabriel Rossetti, like William Blake (1757–1827), became distinguished both as an artist and a poet. His father Gabriele was a political refugee from Italy who had married Frances, the daughter of another expatriate. Three of their children left names behind them: Dante Gabriel and his sister Christina as poets, and William Michael (1829–1919) as an art critic, editor and man of letters. Gabriele was a nominal Roman Catholic but really an agnostic. Frances was a devout Anglo-Catholic and brought up her children accordingly. There is a painting, 'The Girlhood of Mary Virgin', in which Dante Gabriel represents his sister Christina as the Virgin Mary, sitting with an embroidery frame in her hands, and his mother Frances as St Anne.

Dante Gabriel Rossetti's best remembered poem, 'The Blessed Damozel', was published in *The Germ* in 1850. It shows the influence of Dante in its portrayal of the transfigured ideal beloved leaning out from the rampart of Heaven:

> The blessed damozel leaned out
> From the gold bar of Heaven;
> Her eyes were deeper than the depth
> Of waters stilled at even;
> She had three lilies in her hand,
> And the stars in her hair were seven.

The simplicity of the form and the syntax, the stylised archaism in symbol and image, and the occasional hint of more realistic sensuousness – as when, in her stooping, 'her bosom must have made/The bar she leaned on warm' – these are characteristic of Rossetti's literary ventures into medievalism. The damozel is longing to be joined in Heaven by her lover. And indeed bracketed stanzas indicate that the lover is the narrator himself, for whom she has been dead ten years, and who is not at all sure that God will bring to her side one whose only claim to Heaven is his love for her.

This poem predates the love which casts its shadow over some of Rossetti's most moving poetry. In 1850 he fell in love with Elizabeth Siddall, a golden-haired milliner's apprentice. He was then in no position to support a wife, and it was to be ten years before they were married. The depth of Rossetti's early devotion to her is not in doubt, but the long years of waiting imposed a great strain on her. Certainly Rossetti postponed the wedding unnecessarily; for Lizzie began to be helped financially by John Ruskin with a view to facilitating it. Certainly, too, there were two other women to complicate life for him as the years passed and Lizzie's health and beauty and patience waned. One was a model, Fanny Cornforth, who later became his housekeeper after Lizzie's death. The other was Jane Burden, the wife-to-be of William Morris, whom he met in Oxford in 1857 and who was later to appear frequently in his portraiture. Finally, however, Dante Gabriel and Elizabeth were married in May 1860.

Though Christina Rossetti was not ultimately happy with the relationship, there is a sonnet of hers, written in December 1856, 'In an Artist's Studio', which gives a touching picture of her brother's beloved Lizzie:

One face looks out from all his canvases,
    One selfsame figure sits or walks or leans . . .
He feeds upon her face by day and night,
    And she with true kind eyes looks back on him.

The sonnet goes on to say that the glance she throws back on him
in the portraits is a 'joyful' one, 'not wan with waiting, not with
sorrow dim':

Not as she is, but was when hope shone bright;
    Not as she is, but as she fills his dream.

The poem seems to sum up the frustration and sadness of Lizzie's
protracted engagement. The couple had been married less than two
years when in February 1862 Lizzie died of an overdose of laudanum.
Though the verdict was 'Accidental Death', Dante Gabriel could not
escape the suspicion that it was suicide, and he was devastated by
remorse. He thrust a collection of manuscript poems he had intended
to publish into her coffin to be buried with her. It was many years
later before he allowed them to be retrieved for publication.

Christina's phrase, 'Not as she is, but as she fills his dream',
perhaps sums up one aspect of Dante Gabriel's character as man
and poet, the element of idealism which produced poems such as
'The Blessed Damozel'. There was another side to him, however,
and this produced the poem 'Jenny', the study of a prostitute. The
narrator has gone home with Jenny after an evening of wild dancing.
She seems too tired to go to bed, and, after a drink together, she
falls asleep resting against his knee. He broods through the rest of
the night on her lot, and slips away next morning, substituting
cushions for his knee to prop up her sleeping head. Rossetti's octosyllabics give a jaunty flavour to the poet's musings. The picture of the
prostitute may be sentimental, but the poem's conversational idiom
stands in strong contrast to the tapestried fineries of 'The Blessed
Damozel', the charmingly archaic rhetoric of the ballads 'Sister
Helen' and 'Eden Bower', and the Swinburnian exaltation of the
'Song of the Bower', which was apparently written for Fanny
Cornforth:

Say, is it day, is it dusk in thy bower,
    Thou whom I long for, who longest for me?
Oh! be it light, be it night, 'tis Love's hour,
    Love's that is fettered as Love's that is free.
Free Love has leaped to that innermost chamber,
    Oh! the last time, and the hundred before:
Fettered Love, motionless, can but remember,
    Yet something that sighs for him passes the door.

After Lizzie's death Rossetti renewed contact with William Morris and his wife Jane. He was in love with Jane, and Morris connived at the relationship. It seems clear that many of the poems in the sonnet sequence, 'The House of Life', recount his love for Jane, but there are also others which refer to his wife Lizzie and lament her death. The sequence contains one hundred and two sonnets; they appeared in two parts in *Poems* (1870) and *Ballads and Sonnets* (1881). It is said that some more intimate ones were lost because Jane Morris would not allow them to be published. At his best in these poems Rossetti can evoke a situation with simple directness, and the voice of passion rings through it with an almost mystical rapture, as in the first and last lines of 'Silent Noon':

> Your hands lie open in the long fresh grass –
> The finger-points look through like rosy blooms;
> Your eyes smile peace . . .
> Oh! clasp we to our hearts, for deathless dower,
> This close-companioned inarticulate hour
> When twofold silence was the song of love.

Rossetti, as poet and artist, seems to belong among the gifted but hag-ridden Romantics. His melancholy, his complex emotional make-up, his lonely introspectiveness, his raptures and the secretiveness and remorse so often involved with them were not a recipe for happiness. Ill-health and insomnia drove him to increasing use of chloral and whisky, and made his final decline a tragic one.

Christina Rossetti

As a personality and an influence, Dante Gabriel Rossetti has a status in literary history much greater than the quality of his poetry alone could justify. Since he was more gifted as painter than as poet, this is not remarkable. By contrast his sister Christina Rossetti (1830–94) has been too readily classified as a 'minor poet'. A little time spent reading her work, however, would be enough to convince a sensitive reader that she was a much better poet than her brother and that she was probably, in terms of the quantity and quality of her verse, the finest woman poet of her century, for Emily Brontë's output, excellent as it is, was very small by comparison with Christina Rossetti's. Christina fully entered into her mother's zeal as an Anglo-Catholic in the first flush of the Tractarian movement – the movement which, to a large extent, stimulated the so-called Anglican Revival of the mid-nineteenth century. (It is discussed in more detail in the section on Newman, see pp. 176–8 below.) So did her sister Maria who became a nun in one of the early religious houses that the movement established. Christina's piety did not relieve her of inner conflict. Indeed it was productive of severe tensions and was probably the decisive factor in her rejection of two proposals of marriage from men she loved. The first was James Collinson, the son of a Mansfield bookseller, an artist, and one of the Pre-Raphaelite Brotherhood. Christina was engaged to him at the age of seventeen, and she broke it off when he became a Roman Catholic three years later in 1850. There can be no doubt about what it cost her. When she happened to see him in the street several months after the break she dropped down in a faint. The second suitor was Charles Cayley, and her rejection of him was a more pondered one. Christina was now in her mid-thirties and could scarcely expect further offers of marriage. She loved Cayley, but he certainly did not share her religious devotion. Her brother, William Michael Rossetti, in his *Some Reminiscences* (1906), simply stated that 'she enquired into his creed, and found he was not a Christian'. C. M. Bowra (1898–1971), the scholar and critic, later observed of her that 'only in God could she find a finally satisfying object for the abounding love which was the mainspring of her life and character.'

Christina's poetry is not all piety, self-abnegation and gloom. One of her best known lyrics is the poem called 'A Birthday', beginning 'My heart is like a singing bird'. But there is an eloquent cartoon by Max Beerbohm showing Christina, looking like Jane Eyre in heavy mourning, facing a flamboyantly portly Dante Gabriel who is asking, 'What *is* the use, Christina, of having a heart like a singing-bird and a water-shoot and all the rest of it, if you insist on getting yourself up like a pew-opener?' The cartoon puts clearly the contrast between Christina and Dante Gabriel, but their relationship was a loving one and he was an active advocate of her poetry. She shows her interest in the Pre-Raphaelite Brotherhood and laments its decline in a sonnet beginning 'The P.R.B. is in its decadence'. The poem is particularly critical of Millais's pandering to popular taste:

> And he at last the champion great Millais,
> Attaining academic opulence,
> Winds up his signature with A.R.A.

The implication here is that by becoming an A.R.A. (Associate of the Royal Academy, London) Millais has capitulated to the uninspired art world 'establishment'.

Christina Rossetti's great gift was to handle a simple direct idiom, not casually conversational, but poised, neat and lucid, and to do so within conventional stanza forms, yet at the same time to allow herself a metrical flexibility that gives a winning piquancy and memorability to her best lines:

Does the road wind up-hill all the way?
  Yes, to the very end.
Will the day's journey take the whole long day?
  From morn to night, my friend.

('Up-Hill')

Ford Madox Ford (1873–1939), the twentieth-century novelist, who became acquainted with Christina Rossetti when her brother William Michael Rossetti married Lucy Madox Brown, the sister of Ford's mother, especially praised this metrical flexibility, 'this quality of the unexpected, the avoidance of the cliché in metre, the fact that here and there you cannot beat time.'

The poem in which the metrical flexibility is most extravagantly exploited is the narrative poem *Goblin Market* (1862), whose short lines trip and dance, roll and tumble along with an entrancing vivacity. It tells the tale of two sisters, Laura and Lizzie, who regularly hear the goblins offering their lusciously mouth-watering fruits for sale. Lizzie resists temptation but Laura succumbs and buys their fruit with one of her golden curls. Having eaten her fill and returned home, she pines for more of the magic fruit, but once having eaten of it you can never again hear the goblins crying out their wares. Lizzie, of course, can still hear them, and tries to get fruit for her sister. They will not give her any unless she tastes it herself first. She refuses and they turn upon her, lashing, clawing, mocking, tearing her dress and her hair, and squeezing their fruit against her mouth. Still she resists, and when they leave off she dashes home and calls her sister to hug her, kiss her, and suck the juices from her face:

  For your sake I have braved the glen
  And had to do with goblin merchant men.

The salvation of Laura by her sister's suffering and self-sacrifice has clear religious implications, but the allegory of sin and redemption is never intrusive. The fairy-tale flavour is sustained throughout.

Christina Rossetti's most distinctive themes are those of love and lost love, of sadness and death, themes which she voices with a keen intimacy and poignancy that eschew self-indulgence. Diction and cadence have a heart-felt limpidity:

  Remember me when I am gone away,
    Gone far away into the silent land;
    When you can no more hold me by the hand,
  Nor I half turn to go yet turning stay.

('Remember')

Such poems as this, and 'When I am dead, my dearest' and 'O

Earth, lie heavily upon her eyes' and the 'Last Prayer' ('Before the beginning Thou hast foreknown the end') have a grave dignity and a quiet intensity that only great poetry can achieve.

The same qualities emerge in the sonnet sequence, 'Monna Inno-minata', a record of love denied. Christina Rossetti purports to be speaking in the voice of a medieval lady loved by a troubadour but separated from him by a barrier which 'might be held sacred by both, yet not such as to render mutual love incompatible with mutual honour'. The personal self-revelation is evident:

> Come back to me, who wait and watch for you: –
> Or come not yet, for it is over then,
> And long it is before you come again,
> So far between my pleasures are and few.

She occasionally enriches her lines with a conceit in the Shakes-pearean tradition, but the prevailing mood remains one of earnest-ness and poignancy.

Emily Brontë

The only other woman poet in the Victorian age to produce work comparable in quality to Christina Rossetti's was Emily Brontë (1818–48). Her output was small in quantity, and the proportion of it which ranks her as a significant poet smaller still. But the handful of great poems are so great that critics tend to lose their sense of proportion in enthusiasm for them. It is not just that they are accomplished, memorable verse, but also that they seem to open up areas of experience not generally touched upon in Victorian litera-ture. There is a mystical strain which seems to hark back to the work of seventeenth-century poets such as Henry Vaughan (1621–96). In the celebrated fragment 'The Prisoner' the confined man rejects gloom and despair, for a 'messenger of Hope' visits him nightly offering 'eternal liberty' in exchange for short life. He comes with the dusk, visions rise, peace descends, and in climax the Invisible dawns, the Unseen reveals its truth, outward sense goes, the 'inward essence' bounds to freedom. The force and reality of the mystical experience is revealed in the anti-climax of its passing:

> O! dreadful is the check – intense the agony –
> When the ear begins to hear, and the eye begins to see;
> When the pulse begins to throb, the brain to think again;
> The soul to feel the flesh, and the flesh to feel the chain.

Emily Brontë divided her poetry by using separate notebooks for personal poems and for poems connected with the adventures in the

Gondal Saga which she began in her childhood. The devotion to freedom expressed in 'The Prisoner' is a constant theme in her work; so is passionate love, the other major interest in *Wuthering Heights*. In this respect the unquestioned lack of basis in her personal life for some of the moving love poems provides interesting evidence of her imaginative gifts, and a warning to those who, in the case of Christina Rossetti, a woman not dissimilarly gifted in this respect, would fabricate biographical dramas out of all her emotional lyrics. Emily Brontë's rhythmic patterns are more regular than Christina Rossetti's, but she can touch the same nerves with the same intensity of suffering or longing:

> If grief for grief can touch thee,
> If answering woe for woe,
> If any ruth can melt thee,
> Come to me now.

Two of her most memorable poems are concerned with death, the one the elegy 'Remembrance':

> Cold in the earth – and the deep snow piled above thee,
> Far, far removed, cold in the dreary grave!
> Have I forgot, my only Love, to love thee,
> Severed at last by Time's all-severing wave?

and the other, the more overtly personal verses 'No coward soul is mine', which were the last lines she wrote and which combine a confidence in 'Heaven's glories' with an unshakeable faith in the inner proof of immortality, the ever-present God within her.

William Morris

Returning to the Pre-Raphaelites, we find in William Morris (1834–96) a poet who was the exact antithesis of Emily Brontë in one respect. From Emily Brontë's small output a handful of rare gems leave unforgettable lines ringing in the mind. From William Morris's vast output it is difficult to recall half a dozen lines which sum up, in Pope's words, 'what oft was thought but ne'er so well expressed' and which pin a mood, an emotion or an insight permanently in the mind. He has to be judged by big works in all their totality of content and design. Morris, of course, was much more than just a poet, and his prose output will be considered later in this book. He was the son of an Essex broker who had made money in copper shares, and he was educated at Marlborough School and at Oxford. When Dante Gabriel Rossetti undertook to do the frescoes in the new Union building at Oxford, Morris chose to work on the subject of the hopeless love of Sir Palomydes for La Belle Iseult. This early interest in a rejected lover has its ironies. Both Morris and Rossetti fell in love with Jane Burden, daughter of an Oxford groom, whom Morris later married; he painted her as 'Queen Guinevere', the faithless wife, which is also ironic in view of her later liaison with Rossetti.

Disgust with contemporary civilisation inspired Morris to practical efforts as artist and craftsman. In 1861 he founded a firm that did fine art work in painting, carving, furniture and metals. Their products included wall-paper, stained-glass windows, textiles and furniture. Nearly thirty years later, in 1890, he founded the Kelmscott Press, being keenly interested in typography and book-production. The Press issued a Chaucer, printed in Gothic type, its borders decorated with floral designs, its initials fully ornamented. It also included wood-cuts by Edward Burne-Jones.

It would be difficult to calculate the long-term influence of Morris's work in his rejection of Victorian domestic knick-knackery, in his advocacy of high standards of design, and in the impetus he gave to disciplined individual craftsmanship. But the raising of standards of workmanship to a level which only the rich could afford created something of a conflict in Morris's own heart, for he shared Ruskin's disgust with what Victorian civilisation was doing to its working-classes, and he early embraced the socialist creed. How deeply he sensed the irony of his situation is revealed in a story told by Philip Henderson (in *William Morris*, 1952) that 'while at work on the interior decorations of Rounton Grange, Northallerton, in 1876, he was heard striding about one of its empty rooms and talking to himself excitedly. Asked if anything was the matter, he replied: "It is only that I spend my life in ministering to the swinish luxury of the rich".'

As a poet, however, Morris's escape from contemporary ugliness was to a past which became more and more idealised as time went on. In his first publication, *The Defence of Guenevere and Other Poems* (1858), it is notable that in the title poem Guenevere the Queen defends herself passionately with a bracing decisiveness which resembles more the conversational explosiveness of a Browning monologue than the smooth cadences of Tennyson's Arthurian blank verse. Though the sentences tend to be syntactically rather complex, the *terza rima* (a rhyme scheme in which lines one and three of each set of three lines rhyme, and the second line rhymes with lines one and three of the next set) binds them into shape:

'And in the Summer I grew white with flame,
And bowed my head down – Autumn, and the sick
Sure knowledge things would never be the same.'

So Guenevere describes the year of Launcelot's arrival at Arthur's court. She was 'bought', she says, 'by Arthur's great name and his little love' and has refused to deny herself what 'would ever round me move/Glorifying all things'. So in ethos as well as in style the work rebuts Tennysonian Arthurianism. The most celebrated poem in the same volume, 'The Haystack in the Floods', which tells how a tyrant and his henchmen catch up with two fleeing lovers and kill the young man Robert, includes a description of the butchery which conveys the brutality and savagery of unidealised medievalism.

But there is an increasing refinement in subsequent poems. The dramatic tension of the situation in 'The Haystack in the Floods' and the intimate intensity of Guenevere's outbursts in 'The Defence of Guenevere' give way to narratives disinfected of searing agony or passion. In *The Life and Death of Jason* (1867) Morris seems to shed an aura of enchantment over the adventures, rendering them nerveless and remote. An air of placidity pervades, too, the ambitious three volumes of *The Earthly Paradise* (1868–70). The poem tells how a band of Norsemen sail away from a plague to seek the Earthly Paradise 'where none grow old'. After wandering vainly afar for many years they come in old age to a city where the ancient Greek gods are still worshipped. Here they are welcomed, and hosts and guests alternate in telling stories. The device enables Morris to mix stories from Norse legends with those of classical origin. The former include 'The Lovers of Gudrun' and the latter include 'Atalanta's Race'. The twenty-four stories certainly display a magisterial ease in handling verse forms such as rhyme-royal, octosyllabic couplets and rhyming pentameters. 'Ease' is the word, for the fluency of the style seems to devitalise the tales. Dramatic energy gives place to decorative embellishment. The motive of the whole work is frankly escapist, a desire to forget the smoke and steam of industrial England:

Forget the spreading of the hideous town;
Think rather of the pack-horse on the down,
And dream of London, small, and white, and clean,
The clear Thames bordered by its gardens green.

So runs the Prologue. And in his personal 'Apology' Morris laments his inability to lift the burden of care weighing down contemporary bread-winners:

Dreamer of dreams, born out of my due time,
Why should I strive to set the crooked straight?
Let it suffice me that my murmuring rhyme
Beats with light wing against the ivory gate,

Telling a tale not too importunate
To those who in the sleepy region stay,
Lulled by the singer of an empty day.

The note of defeatism contrasts strongly with the freshness and vigour of Chaucer's (?1340–1400) *Canterbury Tales* (*c*. 1387) with which Morris made explicit comparison. 'Sad old men telling old stories to other sad old men', as one critic put it, is no recipe for rivalry with Chaucer. The pictorial quality of the work gives it static, tapestried grace. G. K. Chesterton observed that if Morris's 'poems were too like wall-paper, it was because he really could make wall-papers'.

Morris studied Icelandic and collaborated with Eiríkr Magnússon in a prose translation of the *Volsunga Saga* (1870). 'This is the Great Story of the North', he wrote, 'which would be to all our race what the Tale of Troy was to the Greeks'. This enthusiasm led him to write the epic *Sigurd the Volsung and the Fall of the Niblungs* (1876) in rolling anapaestic couplets (a verse form in which each foot consists of two short syllables followed by one long, so giving the verse a sense of momentum). One cannot but marvel at the massiveness of the undertaking and the achievement, and when the complaint is made, as it is by Ifor Evans (in *English Poetry in the Later Nineteenth Century*, 1933 and 1966) that Morris is here 'content to narrate without assaulting the imagination with phrases that conquer the mind and hold it in bewildered wonder', one queries whether some three hundred and forty pages of hexameters could ever be readably assimilated if the mind were constantly assaulted by what transfixes it with bewilderment and wonder. One has to accept such vast works for what they were when people still sat around the fire on dark evenings listening to prose or verse read aloud by the light of a single candle.

George Meredith

In 1862 Dante Gabriel Rossetti took a house in Cheyne Walk, Chelsea, and for a time he had Swinburne and George Meredith as sub-tenants. Rossetti's appreciation of *The Ordeal of Richard Feverel* had brought Meredith and himself together, and a striking impression of Meredith's handsomeness as a young man is preserved in the figure of Christ in Rossetti's 'Mary Magdalen at the Gate of Simon the Pharisee'. As early as November 1851 William Michael Rossetti had favourably reviewed Meredith's first volume, *Poems* (1851) in *The Critic*, noting especially the charm of 'Love in the Valley':

It is purely and unaffectedly sensuous, and in its utterance as genuine a thing as can be. We hear a clear voice of nature, with no falsetto notes at all, as spontaneous and intelligible as the wooing of a bird, and equally a matter of course.

Indeed it is a rapturous celebration of young love, throbbing with a joyous innocence:

> Under yonder beech-tree single on the green-sward,
>   Couch'd with her arms behind her golden head,
> Knees and tresses folded to slip and ripple idly,
>   Lies my young love sleeping in the shade.
> Had I the heart to slide an arm beneath her,
>   Press her parting lips as her waist I gather slow,
> Waking in amazement she could not but embrace me;
>   Then would she hold me and never let me go?

'It is something,' wrote Charles Kingsley, reviewing the same volume, 'to have written already some of the most delicious little love-poems which we have seen born in England in the last few years, reminding us by their richness and quaintness of tone of Herrick [Robert Herrick (1591–1674)], yet with a depth of thought and feeling which Herrick never reached'. Several of Meredith's poems from this and later collections have become favourites with anthologists, notably 'The Woods of Westermain', 'The Lark Ascending', 'Phoebus with Admetus' and 'Lucifer in Starlight'; but Meredith's most striking achievement as a poet is the sequence of fifty sixteen-lined sonnets, *Modern Love* (1862), which has something of the character of a novel in verse. It derived from the experience of his first, disastrous marriage to Mary Ellen Nicolls. The sonnets trace the development of suspicion and distrust between a married couple:

> By this he knew she wept with waking eyes:
> That, at his hand's light quiver by her head,
> The strange low sobs that shook their common bed,
> Were called into her with a sharp surprise,
> And strangled mute . . .

So the sequence begins. The husband awakes to find his wife sobbing and awake beside him. The fact that she suppresses her sobs on realising that he is listening makes this a moment of revelation for him. Nothing is said, but the seed of distrust is sown. What follows is not a straight record of jealousy. The wife's suffering arouses the husband's compassion, and the wife's unfaithfulness produces jealousy on her side too. There are moods of mutual consolation and attempts at reconciliation. Meredith will present a concrete situation and pull out the hidden agonies and ironies from it, as in the sonnet beginning 'At dinner she is hostess, I am host' in which the couple entertain guests with a deceptive cheerfulness, keeping conversation lively, hiding their true situation. Two ironies emerge: the one is that in playing the game of deception vigorously, husband and wife begin to admire each other's performance and to express the admiration in their mutual glances. The other irony is that their performance rouses their guests to 'envy of our happy lot'. But for the most part the sonnets analyse the ordeal of a disintegrating relationship with a sombre insight and a surgical fineness of perception. Nowhere could one find surer registration of the subtleties of pain produced by half-hearted attempted amendments that go awry:

> If I the death of love had deeply plann'd,
> I never could have made it half so sure,
> As by the unbless'd kisses which upbraid
> The full-waked sense; or, failing that, degrade.

The last sonnet, lamenting the lot of the ill-matched couple, lays the blame on their failure to feed 'on the advancing hours', the fatal cravings of their hearts for the buried past:

> Then each applied to each that fatal knife,
> Deep questioning, which probes to endless dole.

The effect of this work is totally unlike that of any other poetry of its period. It seems to bring a twentieth-century mentality to bear on a Victorian domestic tragedy.

Coventry Patmore

A poet who kept in touch with the Pre-Raphaelites was Coventry Patmore (1823–96). Indeed Patmore claimed that it was he who was approached by Millais, in great distress, after the *Times* made its furious attack on his picture 'Christ in the House of His Parents'. Millais begged Patmore to appeal to Ruskin to take up the matter. Patmore went to Ruskin at once and the famous letter of defence (quoted above on pp. 113–14) appeared the very next day. Patmore was employed in the Printed Book Department of the British Museum for eighteen years until his second wife's wealth made it unnecessary for him to earn his living. His first wife, Emily Andrews, daughter of a Nonconformist minister, died in 1862. It was in the happy years of this first marriage that Patmore managed to attract literary men to his home, including Carlyle, Ruskin, Browning and others. Patmore's second marriage in 1864 was to Marianne Byles.

She was a Roman Catholic convert and Patmore followed her into the Roman Church. A poem 'Departure' speaks movingly of his first wife's death, and 'Tired Memory' analyses, in religious terms, his decision to remarry. In fact Mary Patmore, as she was generally called, died in 1880, and Patmore then married a third time a year later.

Patmore is another very distinctive Victorian poet. His long poem, *The Angel in the House*, was published in two parts, *The Betrothal* (1854) and *The Espousals* (1856). It tells the story of the wooing of Honoria, daughter of Dean Churchill, by Felix Vaughan. In each part there are twelve episodes containing the narrative and each is prefaced by 'Preludes' reflecting and commenting on love in general. The episodes in Part I start with 'I, The Cathedral Close' in which Felix renews his contact with the family in Sarum Close after six years' absence. The stages of a Victorian courtship are decorously traced through to 'XII, The Abdication' in which the proposal is made and accepted. The twelve episodes of Part 2, *The Espousals*, conduct us from 'I, Accepted' to 'XII, Husband and Wife'. The work was followed by a sequel, *The Victories of Love*, also published in two parts, *Faithful for Ever* (1860) and *The Victories of Love* (1863).

The Angel in the House, like *Modern Love*, has been called a 'novel in verse', but even so, there could scarcely have been a greater contrast between the two poems. Meredith's is a packed, subtle, concise registration of emotional complexities. Patmore's poem ('a funny little story,' Ruskin called it) is a limpid, leisurely, common-place account of courtship and marriage within the familiar Victorian patterns of middle-class life. Thus Felix seeks an interview with papa to voice his honourable intentions. An after-dinner glass of wine braces him for the occasion:

A full glass prefaced my reply:
    I loved his daughter, Honor; I told
My estate and prospects; might I try
    To win her? At my words so bold
My sick heart sank. Then he: He gave
    His glad consent, if I could get
Her love . . .

The use of octosyllabic quatrains here, and of octosyllabic couplets in the sequel, gives the whole an air of ballad-like naivety, and inevitably Patmore lapsed into a kind of simplicity that cries out for parody:

'Mary, you'll make Papa his tea
    At eight exactly.'

Parody was, of course, forthcoming, from Swinburne, for instance. Nevertheless here and there throughout the work emerges a theme that was to be more fruitfully developed in Patmore's later work, the theme of a mystical significance in sexual love:

> This little germ of nuptial love,
>   Which springs so simply from the sod,
> The root is, as my song shall prove,
>   Of all our love from man to God.

Patmore's sense of a sacramental validity in earthly experiences as images of what is eternal and divine led him to explore in verse the traditional parallelism between man's love for woman and God's love for the human soul. Marriage is seen in the light of this parallel. Poems in *The Unknown Eros and Other Odes* (1877) explore this theme frankly, and do so in a free verse which has all the flexibility that the octosyllabics of the earlier poems lacked. 'Who is this Maiden fair?' he asks in 'Sponsa Dei', 'whom a man adores?' and answers:

> What if this Lady be thy Soul, and He
> Who claims to enjoy her sacred beauty be,
> Not thou, but God; and thy sick fire
> A female vanity,
> Such as a Bride, viewing her mirror'd charms,
> Feels when she sighs, 'All these are for his arms!'

Patmore presses the equation between the demure self-protectiveness which modest femininity is conventionally assumed to involve and the human soul's reluctance to surrender itself to God. Men and women alike are sought by the Divine Spouse and hold off in vanity or self-protectiveness. It follows that the consummation of marriage is parallel to a divine take-over of the human soul, also involving a 'surrender' and a 'dying' that new life may be born. It follows, too, that God's descent into human flesh in Christ is a comparable divine act of union. In his prose work, *The Rod, the Root, and the Flower* (1895), Patmore pushed the analogy to the point of seeing in the sacrifice of the Cross a consummation at which creation heaves a sigh like a woman taken.

In his odes Patmore's use of irregular line-lengths sometimes leads to a prosaic flatness, but at his best he seems to infuse the form with an inner rhythmic strength that defies analysis. 'Departure', written after his first wife's death, is a good example:

> It was not like your great and gracious ways!
> Do you, that have nought other to lament,

Never, my love, repent
Of how, that July afternoon,
You went,
With sudden, unintelligible phrase,
And frightened eye,
Upon your journey of so many days,
Without a single kiss, or a goodbye?

Francis Thompson

Among the friendships of Patmore's later years was that with the poet Francis Thompson (1859–1907). 'You are the only man with whom I can talk at all . . .' Thompson wrote to Patmore. 'Yours is the conversation of a man who has trodden before me the way which for years I trod alone, and often desperate, seeing no guiding parallel among modern poets to my aims and experience.' Thompson, the son of a Preston doctor, was first intended for the Roman Catholic priesthood but, after being turned down as unsuitable, was persuaded to study medicine at Owens College, Manchester. In fact he was physically repelled by the dissecting room and made little progress there, or at Glasgow University where his father next tried to launch him. Eventually he turned drop-out, drifted to London, lived like a tramp, and unfortunately became addicted to opium. He was rescued by the author and editor Wilfred Meynell (1852–1948) and his wife Alice Meynell (1847–1922) (a poet and also a Roman Catholic) who packed him off to hospital for treatment. His first volume, *Poems*, came out in 1893. It included 'The Hound of Heaven', much the most significant of his works, for though it is not free of the rhetorical artifices which disfigure some of his verse, it has an urgency of tone, a unity of design, and an earnestness of purpose that give it greatness.

Where Patmore's God is the divine Suitor wooing the human soul, the divine Husband taking possession of his earthly bride, Thompson's God is the awesome, terrifying Hound pursuing the human soul in its headlong flight from capture and commitment 'down the nights and down the days . . . down the arches of the years'. The connection between the beloved of Patmore's poetry who holds off the divine Wooer in self-protective vanity, and the quarry of Thompson's poem, who flees in desperation from the divine Pursuer, is not all that remote of course. Thompson's poem has a sensuous luxuriance in some of its imagery which has given rise to comparisons with the lush poetry of the Metaphysical poet Richard Crashaw (1612/13–49). And indeed there is a metaphysical quality in the concrete imagery in which the soul's flight from grace is expressed. There are so many worthy, loving relationships which the divine demand for total commitment seems to threaten:

> I pleaded, outlaw-wise,
> By many a hearted casement, curtained red,
>   Trellised with intertwining charities;
> (For, though I knew His love Who followed,
>   Yet was I sore adread
> Lest, having Him, I must have naught beside.)

But as the fleeing soul turns now to this long-valued consolation, now to that, the following feet pound after him, and the voice calls, reminding him that he will find full contentment in nothing except in Himself. The shattering of all delights in earthly consolations, and the realisation by the soul of its own utter worthlessness, ultimately induce the response of surrender. And in a fine image the soul at last realises that the great cloud of gloom which seemed to threaten all earthly happiness was but the shadow of the divine hand stretched out protectively over him.

The only other poem by Thompson to gain comparable attention has been 'The Kingdom of God' ('O world invisible, we view thee'), a mystical projection of the interrelationship between the natural and the supernatural worlds:

> But (when so sad thou canst not sadder)
>   Cry; – and upon thy so sore loss
> Shall shine the traffic of Jacob's ladder
>   Pitched betwixt Heaven and Charing Cross.

Gerard Manley Hopkins

Another friendship of Patmore's later life was that with Gerard Manley Hopkins (1844–89), a friendship based on their common faith as Roman Catholics, their common interest in mystical theology, and their common technical interest in metre. It was at Hopkins's prompting that Patmore destroyed the manuscript of his poem *Sponsa Dei*, a more adventurous exploration of the love between God and the human soul in terms of sexual equivalents. 'So mystical an interpretation of the significance of physical love in religion' was too intimate a matter for general publication. It became clear, however, that in substance what Patmore had to say in the lost poem was to be found in the odes and in *The Rod, the Root, and the Flower*.

On no poet does the label 'Victorian' sit so uncomfortably as on Gerard Manley Hopkins. The son of well-to-do parents who were devout High Anglicans, Hopkins came under the influence of the Anglo-Catholic movement at Oxford and eventually, under Newman's influence, was received into the Roman Church in 1886. What conversion cost in personal and family terms can be gauged from a letter he wrote to Newman: 'I have been up at Oxford long enough to have heard from my father and mother in return for my letter announcing my conversion. Their replies are terrible.' What conversion could cost in terms of public, social and cultural prospects was no doubt equally taxing. Hopkins joined the Jesuits in 1868. Thereafter his life was one of obedience and discipline. His devotion was never in question, but the anguish involved in deepening the spiritual life for a man with rich natural, literary and cultural sensitivities had sometimes a sombre and tumultuous intensity. He held various teaching appointments, and was finally Professor of Greek Literature at University College, Dublin.

Hopkins's poetry is so idiosyncratic in syntax and metre, and so intensely individual in the working out of his vision of life under God and in God, that on first acquaintance it can seem at best tortuous, at worst incomprehensible. It was not until 1918 that it was published – by Robert Bridges (1844–1930) who had been Hopkins's friend and had inherited the manuscripts. Even then, twenty-nine years after Hopkins's death, the strangeness of the poems stood in the way of sympathetic reception by any but a very few critics, and it was not until Charles Williams introduced a Second Edition in 1930 that enthusiastic appreciation began to grow. Before long, among the young especially, admiration for Hopkins's innovative virtuosity and imaginative intensity turned him into a cult figure.

Hopkins is essentially a religious poet in the tradition of Donne and Herbert (1593–1633), a wrestler with words, wrestling with the realities of the spiritual life. He practised what he called 'sprung rhythm', as opposed to 'running rhythm', the accepted metrical system based on two-syllable or three-syllable feet, in which each foot has a stressed syllable and one or two 'slack syllables'. 'Sprung rhythm' is measured by feet of from one to four syllables. Lines take their 'beat' from the number of stressed syllables round which the 'slack syllables' accumulate with little regularity. Hopkins invented two other expressions, 'inscape' and 'instress', which are philosophical rather than technical terms. The 'inscape' of a thing is its inner individuality, the structure and essence which make it what it is. The 'instress' is the divine force which endows the thing with its 'inscape', the unity and design which enable the human mind to recognise and respond to the Maker's touch.

When Hopkins joined the Society of Jesus he burned his previous poems, determined not to write poetry except at the request of his superiors. After seven years of near complete silence, the drowning of five Franciscan nuns on board the *Deutschland* and a hint from his rector provided the impulse for what proved to be his most ambitious poem, 'The Wreck of the Deutschland' in thirty-five stanzas of packed and powerful writing, alive with energy and thrust:

> Thou mastering me
> God! giver of breath and bread;
> World's strand, sway of the sea;
> Lord of living and dead;
> Thou hast bound bones and veins in me, fastened me flesh,
> And after it almost unmade, what with dread,
> Thy doing: and dost thou touch me afresh?
> Over again I feel thy finger and find thee.

There seems to be nothing in the way of stanzaic or metrical convention that is not brought into question by Hopkins's innovations. But this is the least of the shocks he gives to the reader. For the freedoms he takes with syntax (owing something no doubt to Browning) make a text which calls for disentanglement. He will telescope sentences elliptically, omit the relative pronoun, interrupt a statement with an apostrophe or a parenthesis, reverse word order, and devise compound adjectives such as 'sodden-with-its-sorrowing heart'. These devices serve the purpose of producing an intensely strained compression. The form seems to hold the utterance within such a strenuous grip that the whole rocks with a seemingly all but uncontrollable force of feeling:

> Ah, touched in your bower of bone,
> Are you! turned for an exquisite smart,
> Have you! make words break from me here all alone,
> Do you! – mother of being in me, heart.

This poetic technique perfectly matches Hopkins's understanding of life in sacramental terms. The world he surveys, its scenes and objects, beings and experiences, are alive with the impress of the divine touch. The created world of nature speaks God's praise and glory unconsciously. Man, with his gifts of reason and language, has the privilege of consciously joining in the utterance of worship and exultation. Thus man, Hopkins believes, was created to praise. The heavens declare the glory of God, not knowing what they do. The birds sing God's praise, not knowing what they do. It is man's especial privilege to turn creation's glory into a lively glory. 'Hurrahing in Harvest' is a paean of praise jubilant with the harvest of human senses gathered in Christ's acclamation:

I walk, I lift up, I lift up heart, eyes,
  Down all that glory in the heavens to glean our Saviour;
  And, eyes, heart, what looks, what lips yet gave you a
Rapturous love's greeting of realer, of rounder replies?

It will be clear from these quotations that form and substance are inseparably welded together in Hopkins's poems. The notion of 'inscape' – of the sheer unique, inimitable self-hood of the bird or the flower or the stream or the scene that confronts the poet – and of 'instress' – of the divine force upholding, defining its distinctiveness – requires of the poet an utterance to match the distinctiveness of the object or scene, and an utterance charged with the creative thrust that alone can define it. Among the celebrated poems which match up to experience with comparable rhythmic drive and verbal relish are 'The Windhover', 'Pied Beauty', 'Inversnaid', and two human portraits, 'Felix Randal' and 'Harry Ploughman'. In all the use of stress and alliteration, of percussive phrasing and vigorous rhyme, and of cunningly-placed monosyllables give an Anglo-Saxon sturdiness to the verse.

This sinewy quality characterises, too, what have been called the 'terrible sonnets' or the 'dark sonnets' in which Hopkins wrestles with the seeming contradiction between God's demand and the inclinations of his heart and his senses. Never have the strains of vocation accepted been so movingly recorded:

My own heart let me have pity on; let
Me live to my sad self hereafter kind,
Charitable; not live this tormented mind
With this tormented mind tormenting yet.

James Thomson

If Hopkins expressed superbly, and more powerfully than any other Victorian poet, both the agony and the exultation of faith, there was a contemporary at work who voiced both the agony and the anger of unbelief also more powerfully than any other Victorian poet. This was James Thomson (1834–82). His generosity as a critic led him in 1880 to make a review of Meredith's recently published novel *The Egoist* an opportunity for protesting against critical neglect of Meredith's 'magnificent genius and insight and energy' as both novelist and poet. His most celebrated poem, *The City of Dreadful Night* (1880, in book form), is a phenomenon so unutterably depressing that it needs to be accounted for, and certainly Thomson had his share of personal misfortunes. Born in Port Glasgow, he lost his mother when he was six, and his father, a sailor, was afflicted with paralysis. He was educated at the Royal Caledonian Asylum in London and then trained for work as an army schoolmaster. He held teaching posts in the army in Ireland and England until he was dismissed for some disciplinary reason in 1862. Meanwhile he had fallen in love with a girl, Matilda Weller, who died in 1853, and had become acquainted with one who was to influence his thinking a good deal, Charles Bradlaugh (1833–91). Bradlaugh was a free-thinking writer, lecturer and politician whose aggressive atheism aroused fierce opposition. He ran into legal trouble in 1876 when he collaborated with the American Annie Besant (1847–1933) in publishing a pamphlet on birth-control. When he was elected Member of Parliament for Northampton in 1880 he was rejected by the House of Commons for refusing to take the oath. He was to be re-elected four times in the next six years before he was finally allowed to sit after making an affirmation instead of taking a religious oath. Under Bradlaugh's influence Thomson began to write for rationalist journals. His enthusiasms are proclaimed in the pseudonym he adopted, 'B. V.' (Bysshe Vanolis) derived from Percy Bysshe Shelley and the German poet 'Novalis'. It was in Bradlaugh's paper, the *National Reformer*, that *The City of Dreadful Night* appeared first in March–May 1874.

Publication of Thomson's poetry in book form only began two years before his death, but much had appeared in periodicals, and the development of Thomson's thinking can be detected in it. There are cheerful early poems such as 'Let my voice ring out over the earth' whose three stanzas end 'Thank God for Life!', 'Thank God for Love!' and 'Thank God for you!'. There are poems from the 1850s in which the conflict between childhood faith (imbibed no doubt in the very earliest days from his evangelical mother) and scepticism is apparent. In 'A Recusant' the poet stands gazing 'yearningly' at a church spire:

> For ever when my heart feels most forlorn
>   It murmurs to me with a weary sigh,
> How sweet to enter in, to kneel and pray
>   With all the others whom we love so well.

But by 1870 Thomson had started to work on *The City of Dreadful Night* and he was already a victim of the alcoholism which destroyed him. In the 'Proem' to *The City of Dreadful Night* he answers the question why he should give voice to despair:

> Because a cold rage seizes one at whiles
>   To show the bitter old and wrinkled truth
> Stripped naked of all vesture that beguiles,
>   False dreams, false hopes, false masks and modes of youth.

The topography of the city is carefully described. It is a Venice of the Black Sea. Inside a great cathedral the poet hears a voice from the pulpit proclaiming 'Good tidings of great joy for you, for all'. It is that there is no God:

> I find no hint throughout the Universe
> Of good or ill, of blessing or of curse;
>   I find alone Necessity Supreme!

It is the atmosphere of gloom and desolation that Thomson evokes which gives the poem its strange power: the lamps burning in the silent streets, empty squares silvered in the moonlight, open spaces yawning with abysmal gloom, sombre mansions looming in dismal immensity, side-lanes 'black as subterranean lairs'. And a mighty river flows darkly through the City, known as the 'River of Suicides'. Some plunge into it as if in a 'blind and sudden frenzy', others wade in slowly and purposefully, and others drift down in it by boat to starve or drown out at sea. No one attempts to save them; everyone reflects that he may soon seek the same refuge of oblivion. A colossal female Image sits enthroned on granite, presiding as the symbol of despair over the living hell. A 'sense more tragic than defeat or blight' dawns 'in her tenebrous regard':

> The sense that every struggle brings defeat
>   Because Fate holds no prize to crown success;
> That all the oracles are dumb or cheat
>   Because they have no secret to express;
> That none can pierce the vast black veil uncertain
> Because there is no light beyond the curtain;
>   That all is vanity and nothingness.

Here is the ultimate contradiction to the philosophical optimism of Browning. If a reader is ever tempted to generalise about Victorian 'complacency' or 'confidence', Thomson will provide the corrective warning about the dangers of over-simplification. And twentieth-century poetry can scarcely provide a parallel to Thomson's wholesale and downright judgement on life itself. The quality of the work is uneven, though the seven-lined stanza form cited above is neatly handled. The secret of its power to disturb seems to lie in the fifth and sixth lines which break the metrical sequence of iambic pentameters as well as the sequence of alternate rhymes by a couplet of feminine rhymes, that is, lines which end with an extra, lightly stressed syllable. Matthew Arnold's melancholy over the ebbing of the tide of faith seems anaemic when put beside Thomson's angry nihilism. Even Swinburne's rebellious outbursts against the Christian God smack much of the study and the phrase-book by comparison. The concentration and will-power involved in fabric-ating a major work of such substance as *The City of Dreadful Night* bear testimony to the depth and force of Thomson's conviction, which can be compared perhaps only to the conviction which sustained Hardy in his sombre assaults upon the Power that governs the universe.

A. E. Housman

A vein of melancholy runs through the poetry of A. E. Housman (1859–1936). He, too, lost his mother in childhood when he was just twelve years old. Like Thomson's mother, she was a devout Chris-tian, though an Anglican whereas Thomson's mother was an Evan-gelical. Housman's career is apt to sound like an accumulation of oddities, his character even more so. At Oxford he failed his final examinations in Greats and thereafter took a post in the Civil Service. Then for ten years he studied so strenuously and single-mindedly, contributing abstruse papers to learned journals, that in 1892 he was chosen to be Professor of Latin at University College, London, where he stayed until he moved to a similar chair at Trinity College, Cambridge, in 1911. He went on devoting himself with fanatical assiduity to editing an out-of-the-way Latin poet, Manilius. Personally he was a remote, unsociable individual, a homosexual deeply wounded when his young Oxford friend and room-mate, Moses Jackson, married.

A Shropshire Lad (1896) gives Housman his place among Victorian poets. Brought up in the Midlands, he turned the Shropshire country-side into a pictorial Arcadia by emotive use of its place names. It is certainly not a native environment that he knew and loved as Hardy knew and loved his Wessex. Indeed Housman seems to have had little interest in the countryside. But Shropshire makes an ideal setting for sadly evoking the lost hopes and dreams of youth. Against its background lamentations are sustained against the transience of life, the ephemerality of happiness, the passing of youth, the fickle-ness of love, and the inescapability of death. Young men, in particular, go off to find bullets for their breasts if they do not find hangman's ropes for their necks. Housman made it clear that he regarded poetry as 'more physical than intellectual', intended to 'transfuse emotion' not to 'transmit thought'. The simplicity of his verses, the frankness of his conventionalism, the precision of his metrical control, and the directness of his emotional appeal give his poems a powerful attractiveness. Moods of melancholy nostalgia are captured and conveyed in a tone of homely incantation which only rarely seems false or vulgar:

The time you won your town the race
We chaired you through the market place;
Man and boy stood cheering by,
And home we brought you shoulder-high.

Today, the road all runners come
Shoulder-high we bring you home,
And set you at your threshold down,
Townsman of a stiller town,

('To an Athlete Dying Young')

It is ironic that the dominating passion of Housman's life should have been that of detailed application to the work of a Latin poet whose poetry is little regarded. Ironic because Housman seems to have been a Victorian version of the Grammarian buried in Browning's 'A Grammarian's Funeral'. Yet where Browning made such a career a basis for sturdy faith and abounding optimism, Housman's eccentric idealism as a scholar was balanced by angry resentment at the conditions of the human lot. There may have been beauty in Shropshire, he says; but what is lost is lost, and the recollection of it does not delight; it pains:

Into my heart an air that kills
    From yon far country blows:
What are those blue remembered hills,
    What spires, what farms are those?

That is the land of lost content,
    I see it shining plain,
The happy highways where I went
    And cannot come again.

Rudyard Kipling

Rudyard Kipling (1865–1936) is another poet with Housman's limpidity and accessibility, but with an incomparably vaster range in substance and technique. Walter Allen has observed that 'more lines and phrases from his verse have passed into the common mind and speech than those of any other English poet of the century.' On the other hand, in the immediate post-Victorian era no writer suffered more from revulsion against Victorian public values, and in so far as the twentieth-century Modernist movement in literature was suspicious of what appealed with sincerity and directness to standard emotional postures, Kipling became regarded as a symbol of philistinism and vulgarity. Yet major critics, including T. S. Eliot and C. S. Lewis (1898–1963), eloquently defended him. Eliot stressed his 'consummate gift of word, phrase and rhythm', and it is now accepted that he belongs to a poetic tradition going back through poets such as Burns (1759–96) and Dryden (1631–1700) to Chaucer himself, a tradition in which versification is clear and fluent rather than packed, subtle or demanding. Since the late 1950s readily assimilable verse with a ballad-like directness has made a comeback on the English literary scene. The work of Sir John Betjeman (1906–84) and his status as Poet Laureate have helped to establish a climate of opinion which no longer tends to downgrade poetry deficient in intellectual or verbal subtlety.

Kipling had been publishing poems in periodicals for over ten years when he gathered together his output to date in *Barrack-Room Ballads* (1892), and it was to become the world's best-selling book of verse for many years. Kipling continued to publish verse as long as he lived, but, though it may be claimed that his finest work in prose fiction belongs to the twentieth-century, there is no doubt that as a poet he can be most properly claimed for the Victorian age. Early poems which quickly seized the popular imagination include 'Danny Deever', a dramatic presentation of the mood in the barracks the day a soldier is to be executed, and 'Tommy', celebrating the typical English soldier, nicknamed 'Tommy Atkins' because the service manual issued to troops used the name 'Tommy Atkins' illustratively. Kipling's Tommy is pushed around by authority until war-time service is required of him:

> It's Tommy this, an' Tommy that, an' 'Chuck him out, the brute!'
> But it's 'Saviour of 'is country' when the guns begin to shoot.

Kipling's determination to win public compassion and respect for the ordinary soldier shows the breadth of his sympathies. Oscar Wilde mocked him as a 'man of talent who drops his aspirates' but there is no doubt that Kipling's flair for conjuring up vividly the persona of the so-called 'common man', warts and slang and all, paid rich dividends for him. His experience of the military world out East enabled him to spice many a poem with an exotic flavour and to associate the common soldier with the sustaining of imperial grandeur. The soldier in the celebrated poem 'Mandalay' pictures a Burmese girl remembering him, dreams that he hears the wind in the palm-trees, and the temple bells ringing and calling him back:

> Ship me somewheres east of Suez, where the best is like the worst,
> Where there aren't no Ten Commandments, an' a man can raise
>   a thirst;
> For the temple-bells are callin', an' it's there that I would be –
> By the old Moulmein Pagoda, looking lazy at the sea;

We must not over-simplify Kipling as a poet who waved the imperial flag and patronised natives. 'Gunga Din', after all, celebrates the virtues of a Hindu water-carrier serving a British Indian regiment:

An' for all 'is dirty 'ide
'E was white, clear white, inside
When 'e went to tend the wounded under fire!

The conclusion is 'You're a better man than I am, Gunga Din!' We can no longer tolerate the use of 'white' to praise the inner virtues of a coloured man by contrast with his outer skin, but we have to remember that Kipling is not speaking in his own voice. Rather, as so often, he is adopting the voice and attitude of a simple, uneducated, ignorant, prejudiced common man.

As for Kipling's glorification of the Empire, it is a glorification of something which makes demands on the rulers, and indeed subjects them to a law even more exacting than the rule they impose on others. The much-quoted poem, 'The White Man's Burden', speaks of sending 'sons to exile/To serve your captives' need', of accepting a great load of responsibility which puts the maximum strain on character and effort, and wins no thanks at all:

Take up the White Man's burden –
    And reap his old reward:
The blame of those ye better,
    The hate of those ye guard –
The cry of hosts ye humour
    (Ah, slowly!) toward the light: –
'Why brought ye us from bondage,
    Our loved Egyptian night?'

This most-quoted of poems at the expense of British imperialism was, in fact, addressed to the United States of America in 1899 in reference to the administration of the Philippine Islands.

Kipling's superb technical control of rhythm and cadence is sustained in a vast and varied range of forms. The stately sonorities of 'Recessional' ('God of our fathers, known of old'), the muscular chumminess of 'If', the pulsing declamation of 'The Glory of the Garden', and the rollicking, no-nonsense cockiness of 'The 'Eathen' are all effective by virtue of Kipling's unfaltering gift for putting the right word in the right place. He seems to set a pattern going and leave language to take its own natural course, dancing to its own tune.

Lewis Carroll, Edward Lear, W. S. Gilbert

It may be argued that the boundary line between some of Kipling's poetry and what is generally called 'light verse' is a very indistinct one. It is interesting, therefore, that some of the nonsense verse of Lewis Carroll (Charles Lutwidge Dodgson, 1832–98) depends upon a collision between the sheer naturalness of the shaped utterance that is the hallmark of Kipling's poetry and what it in fact means, if it means anything. The use of cliché, of clauses and phrases utterly pedestrian in shape and sound, is rendered absurd by the juxtapositions and the context:

> So, having no reply to give
>   To what the old man said,
> I cried, 'Come tell me how you live!'
>   And thumped him on the head.

There is not a remarkable expression in the four lines, but the sequence makes for absurdity. There is, of course, another kind of absurdity in Carroll where meaningless words posture as valid currency with an outrageous air of belonging where they are.

Edward Lear (1812–88) produced nonsense verse by making simple direct unambiguous statements in neatly poised sentences which together lack reason and logic:

> The Owl and the Pussy-cat went to sea
>   In a beautiful pea-green boat,
> They took some honey, and plenty of money,
>   Wrapped up in a five-pound note.

No study of Victorian literature can afford to ignore its light verse, for the legacy of it is still with us, and there is no comparable legacy of light verse from any previous age, still less from subsequent decades. Sir William Schwenck Gilbert (1836–1911) gathered comic verse together in *The Bab Ballads* (1869) and *More Bab Ballads* (1874), but he reached his immense public chiefly through the libretti of the comic operas which he wrote in collaboration with the composer Sir Arthur Sullivan. It can be argued, therefore, that it has been the quality of Sullivan's music that has preserved for our century the wit, the adroit metrical effects, and the vein of humorous satire in which Gilbert's verse is so rich.

Part 4

Victorian drama

THE VICTORIAN AGE was not a period productive of great drama. The modern reader has no difficulty in understanding what made *David Copperfield, Jane Eyre* or *The Mill on the Floss* highly successful with the contemporary reading public. It is less easy for us to understand what gave some of the most popular plays of the age their wide appeal. In considering Victorian fiction the reader is for the most part concerned with books which are still widely read, with authors abundantly represented on our library and bookshop shelves. In considering Victorian drama the reader will find little that is still alive. Two major writers only, Oscar Wilde and W. S. Gilbert, left works that are widely familiar to today's theatre-going public. Yet the Victorian theatre had to answer the need for public entertainment which television and the cinema have more recently helped to answer. When Victorian novelists, such as Trollope, take you to London and into society circles there is often talk of theatre-going. Yet very little is said of what people went to the theatre to see. When some of the highly popular plays are examined, it ceases to surprise us that contemporary novelists had little to say about them.

Edward Bulwer-Lytton

The Queen's reign had scarcely begun when Edward Bulwer-Lytton (1803–73) had a popular success with his extravagantly romantic drama, *The Lady of Lyons, or Love and Pride* (1838). Set in the period 1795–8, it centres on the daughter of a wealthy merchant, Pauline Deschappelles, who is sought in marriage by various eligible young men, including the former marquis, Beauseant. Pauline rejects them all. But Claude Melnotte, a gardener's son, a high-souled, self-educated poet, falls deeply in love with her, and when he woos her in the guise of a foreign prince, he wins her and marries her. Having taken her to his mother's humble home, he is overcome with remorse for his deception and indeed offers to obtain an annulment, but his genuine love and his honesty cement Pauline's love for him, and, after serving in Buonaparte's army and distinguishing himself, he comes back to Lyons just in time to save Pauline from a marriage to Beauseant made necessary by her father's bankruptcy. The melodramatic posturings enthralled Victorian audiences for so many decades that the sentimental young adolescent, Stephen Dedalus of James Joyce's *A Portrait of the Artist as a Young Man* (1914–15), was able to see the play performed in Dublin in the 1890s, and he mouthed the hero's 'soft speeches' to ease his romantic yearnings.

Two years after this play's first performance Lytton's comedy of contemporary life, *Money* (1840), was successfully produced. It was not to win the acclaim given to his plays of loftier romantic vein (which include the celebrated *Richelieu* (1839)) but it reads more convincingly than they do today and has a well-tailored plot. Alfred Evelyn, the poor, despised relation of a wealthy family, has learned the agony of dependence and the world's contempt for worth that lacks wealth. His noble spirit chafes at the indignities heaped upon him:

> 'And thus must I grind out my life for ever! – I am ambitious, and Poverty drags me down! – I have learning, and Poverty makes me the drudge of fools! – I love, and Poverty stands like a spectre before the altar!'

Evelyn finds himself unexpectedly the heir to a fortune which his scornful relations have expected to come their way, and his despisers become his fawning flatterers. Clara, his beloved cousin, also a dependant, has refused his offer of marriage because she cannot bear to think of prolonging his privations. This he misinterprets as unwillingness to marry poverty. On acceding to wealth he has the difficult task of distinguishing true love from mercenary love. The pretence that he has lost all his money by gambling and by the failure of a bank provides a real test of genuine friendship and love. The play makes a serious point about Victorian materialism and society's readiness to trade happiness and love in the marriage-market. Sometimes the dialogue seems to present in miniature the kind of situation explored at length in Trollope's novels, as can be seen in the following lines spoken by the worldly Sir John Vesey:

> My father got the title by services in the army, and died penniless. On the strength of his services I got a pension of £400 a year – on the strength of £400 a year, I took credit for £800; on the strength of £800 a year I married your mother with £10,000; on the strength of £10,000, I took credit for £40,000 . . . On the strength of my respectability I wheeled a constituency, changed my politics, resigned my seat to a minister, who to a man of such stake in the country could offer nothing less in return than a Patent Office of £2,000 a year. That's the way to succeed in life.

The love theme is heavily sentimentalised. The agonies Evelyn

suffers in not realising how generous Clara is, and the agony Clara
suffers through not realising how generous Evelyn is, are of a kind
that are familar to readers of Victorian novels. The dilemmas strike
the modern reader as essentially unnecessary, essentially avoidable.
The reticences seemingly imposed by Victorian etiquette on
communication between the sexes enabled novelists and dramatists
alike to stoke up misery and suspense in misunderstandings between
couples which ten minutes of uninhibited conversation together could
have cleared away. Without this etiquette of reticence many a plot
in Victorian fiction would have crumbled.

Douglas Jerrold

An interesting specimen of drama of lower-class life, *Black-Ey'd
Susan* (1829) by Douglas Jerrold (1803–57), achieved a popularity
which at first sight its text scarcely seems to justify. The play fastens
on the figure of the bold young sailor whose beautiful wife becomes
the object of persecution and sexual harassment while he is at sea.
The sailor is simply called 'William' and his wife 'Susan'. (At this
social level characters may have only a Christian name or – especially
if they are wicked – only a surname.) William is a descendant of the
salty tars of Smollett's novels, and his lingo and that of his
companions is plastered with racy nautical jargon and slang. At the
climax of the play William rescues his wife from ravishment by his
own superior, Captain Crosstrees, striking the man down and gravely
wounding him. The inevitable penalty is hanging, even though Crosstrees repents and admits that he is wholly to blame; but a *deus-ex-
machina* produces an eleventh-hour rescue. Plainly the court-martial
in the State Cabin of the ship and the scene in the ship's Gun-Room
of the last moments prior to the planned execution offered excellent
opportunities for theatrical tableaux, while the glamorisation of the
ingenuous, unselfish young tar and his loving wife plainly touched a
public nerve. Moreover the text notes that 'the Music throughout
this Piece is chiefly selections from Dibdin's Naval Airs'. Yet with
all these advantages the dialogue never catches fire and momentous
turns of events are crudely presented. Although he wrote a considerable number of plays, Jerrold's great achievement lay elsewhere in
the satirical articles which established the popularity of *Punch* in the
1840s, notably perhaps the series *Mrs Caudle's Curtain Lectures*, the
bed-time exhortations of a loquacious, domineering wife to a
husband who only wants to go to sleep.

Dion Boucicault

A dramatist of such stature that he bestrode the theatrical scene for fifty years was Dion Boucicault (1820–90). His prodigious output of over one hundred and twenty titles contains many translations and adaptations and several works written in collaboration. The adaptations from novels included plays based on Scott's *The Heart of Midlothian*, Richardson's (1689–1761) *Clarissa Harlowe* (1748–9), Dickens's *Nicholas Nickleby* and Thackeray's *Vanity Fair*. They also include *The Long Strike* (1866), an adaptation of Mrs Gaskell's *Mary Barton*. Boucicault's personality and career had an epic extravagance to match his theatrical productions. Born in Dublin, he was educated mostly in London and soon took to the stage as actor and writer, changing his original surname 'Boursiquot' to 'Boucicault'. His first wife, a French woman and a widow, died mysteriously. His second wife, Agnes Robertson, was a distinguished actress with whom he performed in many of his own plays. She bore him six children of whom the fifth, Nina Boucicault, was to become the first actress to play Barrie's Peter Pan. He married a twenty-one-year-old actress bigamously at the age of sixty-five – claiming that there was no legal marriage to Agnes Robertson. Massive successes on the London stage and in America enriched him more than once while his extravagances impoverished him in between. He benefited his profession by being the first playwright to insist on royalties instead of lump-sum payments for his plays.

Among Boucicault's London successes in the 1840s was the comedy *Old Heads and Young Hearts* (1844). The familiar Victorian theme of an impecunious young lawyer's need to marry for money is blended with the stock contrast (found, for instance, in Sheridan's (1751–1816) *The School for Scandal* (1777)) between a thriftless, wastrel brother and a solidly cautious one. The London lawyer Littleton Coke is the thriftless one; his brother Tom is his bucolic rural counterpart, looking after the family acres at home. At the same time Littleton's love affair is so entangled with that of his friend Lord Charles Roebuck, and so much pretence and disguise is seemingly needed to effect their plans for happiness, that in the upshot the two elope with partners exchanged by mistake. For this kind of material Boucicault is indebted to earlier dramatists, Congreve (1670–1729), Goldsmith and possibly Sheridan; and it is this tradition that he tries to revitalise. Though he lacks the sustained wit and polish of these predecessors, he handles situations adroitly in what, after all, never aspires to be a realistic account of contemporary life.

Boucicault had a tremendous success in a totally different genre when he adapted *The Corsican Brothers* (1852) from a French play based on a novel by Dumas (1802–70). This venture into cloak-and-dagger melodrama in an aristocratic French setting gave ample scope to Boucicault's theatrical flair as the scene moves from the hall of a chateau to a masked ball at the opera and to a glade in the Forest of Fontainebleau. The stage effects were so expertly managed that even G. H. Lewes (George Eliot's partner) praised the apparition of a spectre as 'a scenic effect more real and terrible than anything I remember'. In fact the spectacular effects made enormous demands on Victorian stagecraft. The two brothers of the title are identical twins, each telepathically aware of the moods and fortunes of the other. While Fabien is at home in the chateau with his mother, his brother Louis's spectre rises from the floor, and the tableau of his death after a duel at Fontainebleau is seen behind a transparent gauze as the interior wall of the room fades from view. Correspondingly in Act II, as Louis lies bleeding in the snowbound forest, he sees (and the audience sees) a vision of his brother and his mother at home. The play was one of the actor Charles Kean's great successes. He played the parts of both twins.

The grand melodramatic vein was tapped again to make the most of a stirring contemporary event in *Jessie Brown, or The Relief of Lucknow* (1858). Boucicault was quick to seize upon a press report of how forces under Sir Colin Campbell arrived in the nick of time to relieve Lucknow on 26 September 1857 during the Indian Mutiny. A graphic account was quoted by one of those rescued of how, when all seemed lost for the garrison amid the deafening roar of artillery and the wailing of women, Jessie Brown alone had detected the distant skirl of the bagpipes announcing the approach of their rescuers. Boucicault's play depicts the Indian as savages; in particular the Nana Sahib, played by Boucicault himself, is a blood-curdling villain. The extremes of posture and pathos could scarcely be taken seriously today. The play was first performed in New York. So, too, was *The Octoroon, or Life in Louisiana* (1859). In this play the near-bankrupt estate which could be rescued only by the young hero resorting to marriage to an heiress he does not love is transferred from the English or Irish countryside to the banks of the Mississippi. The hero's widowed mother could also salvage the estate by marrying the villainous landowner who has cunningly and dishonestly got his claws on the property. Shall she be allowed to sacrifice herself to save her son from sacrificing himself? He is in love with the illegitimate daughter of his father and a slave, Zoe, the octoroon (having one eighth of negro blood in her ancestry). In fact the crucial self-sacrifice is effected by Zoe herself who solves the problem by taking poison. When the play came to London the public would not have this at any price. So desperate was the clamour that Boucicault wrote a substitute happy ending. A crucial final attraction in the play remained, that of the explosion into flames of a river boat on the Mississippi.

Boucicault eventually turned to writing Irish plays, and in doing so produced his best work. *The Colleen Bawn, or The Brides of Garryowen* (1860) became a money-spinner. A domestic drama, its action moves with vivacity and naturalness. Boucicault took the story from *The Collegians* (1829), a novel by the Irish writer Gerald Griffin (1803–40). Griffin had based his tragic tale on the true story of a man who drowned his wife in order to marry a wealthy woman. Boucicault's adaptation, for its part, seems to transplant the framework of the plot of *The Octoroon* across the Atlantic, and for the banks of the Mississippi we have the banks of Killarney. Mrs Cregan's husband died leaving the estate deeply involved, and her son Hardress is expected to redeem the situation by marrying Anne Chute; but he has secretly married Eily O'Connor, the colleen bawn ('fair-haired girl'), a poor uneducated peasant girl who can embarrass him by her strong accent. A faithful hunchback servant, Danny Mann, devotedly tries to help by getting possession of Eily's marriage lines. Exasperated by her refusal, he pushes her off a rock into the lake. It is a spectacular scene – 'A Cave; through large opening at back is seen the lake and moon; rocks . . . gauze waters all over stage . . .'. Fortunately the rascally vagabond Myles-na-Coppaleen (played by Boucicault) arrives in time to dive in to the rescue. (Here, technicians ensured that the audience could see Myles underwater pulling up the drowning heroine.) Myles, who exudes stage Irishness, has the gift of the gab, a whiskey still in a cave accessible from the lake, and a heart of gold hopelessly devoted to Eily. By 1862 the play had been turned into an opera, *Lily of Killarney*, the music composed by Sir Julius Benedict (1804–85), and put on at Covent Garden. Its lilting tunes still charm.

The Shaughraun, first produced in New York in 1874 and in London in 1875, is perhaps the most interesting drama of all in that it concerns the Matter of Ireland. Boucicault's stage Irishmen are neither obtuse nor susceptible to patronisation. They are witty, resourceful, lovable, winning personalities. In their relationships with the English they give as good as they get. In the opening moments of the play the English officer, Captain Molineux, apologises for mispronouncing a place-name:

MOLINEUX: Beg pardon; your Irish names are so unpronounceable. You see I am an Englishman.

CLAIRE: I remarked your misfortune; poor crature, you couldn't help it.

Molineux and Claire fall in love. Yet Claire's brother, Robert Ffol-
liott, sentenced as a Fenian and transported to Australia, has secretly
landed near his home and the authorities are searching for him. The
English are not the villains, however, and Molineux is just doing his
duty as kindly as he can. The villains are the grasping local squireen
Kinchela, who would turn the heroine, Robert's beloved Arte
O'Neal out of her home, and the informer Harvey Duff, a police
agent in disguise. Boucicault's own part in the play was that of
Conan, the shaughraun ('wanderer'), 'the soul of every fair, the life
of every funeral, the first fiddle at all weddings and patterns'. He is
also the manipulator in the background who frustrates villainy and
aids the hero and heroine. His humorous, ironic commentary on
events enriches the imaginative texture of the play. Boucicault's
mingling of humour and melodrama, pathos and sensation, makes a
surprisingly palatable blend. His influence on George Bernard Shaw
(1856–1950) and on Sean O'Casey (1880–1964) was notable. O'Casey
went so far as to say: 'Shakespeare's good in bits, but for colour and
stir give me Boucicault.'

Tom Robertson

To turn from Boucicault to Tom Robertson (1829–71) is to turn to
a writer with his feet firmly on the ground. His parents were actors,
he appeared on stage as a child, and had early practical experience
as a stage-hand and performer. He was writing scripts in his teens,
but his great successes belong to the 1860s. They are plays of contemporary life, rooted in the actualities of smart drawing-rooms and
vulgar living rooms, of pianos and visiting cards and jugs of claret,
of kettles and tea-pots and parcels of ham from the grocer's. All this
is a far cry from Boucicault's exploding steamboats, blazing
tenements and underwater antics. Robertson's professionalism is
shown by the meticulously careful instructions for stage business, for
actors' positions, attitudes, gestures and the like. For him the conflict
between the call of true love and the need for money is still a central
issue, but there is a conflict which cuts even more deeply, and
that is the conflict which arises when class meets class. After all, a
gentleman or a lady may be impoverished; a crude member of the
working class may acquire wealth. In Robertson's *Society* (1865)
Sidney Daryl, younger son of a baronet, a barrister and writer, has
beggared himself by rescuing his elder brother and heir to the baron-
etcy from gambling the family fortune away, and, as a result of his
impoverishment, his love for Maud Hetherington is judged absurd
by her aristocratic guardian, Lady Ptarmigant. By contrast, self-
made John Chodd senior would purchase for his cloddish son John

junior all the education and gentlemanly acquisitions that unlimited money can purchase – and the acquisitions include a bride such as Maud. These crude upstarts, the Chodds, are cartoons of coarseness and insensitivity, but they can supply in plenty what Lady Ptarmigant seeks in a match for her ward. Love and gentlemanly impoverishment win the day, and Daryl's elder brother dies conveniently at the end of the last act to remedy the impoverishment.

In *Ours* (1866), whose title defines the brotherly togetherness of a common regiment, it is the young lady Mary Netley, a dependent companion, whose genteel impoverishment proves ultimately no obstacle to marriage, in this case to the wealthy Hugh Chalcot. A man embittered by an early disappointment in love, he takes some time to wake up to the solidly amiable qualities of Mary, for she exudes a superficial defensive shrewishness and rebelliousness ('I wish I hadn't been born a lady'). There is some psychological force here in the development of their relationship. But this plot is subordinate to the story of Blanche Haye, ward of Sir Alexander and Lady Shendryn. She is loved by the humble, faithful Angus MacAlister, but sought in marriage by an eminently eligible Russian Prince. The public world intrudes when the Crimean War breaks out, the male characters are whisked into uniform, and march off at the end of Act II to the singing of 'The Girl I left behind me' and 'God Save the Queen', and to the fluttering handkerchiefs of the womenfolk. Act III takes us to the war theatre in the Crimea whither the women manage to pursue their menfolk through the aid of a wealthy owner of a private yacht. Battle, of course, transforms the aspiring MacAlister into a brave hero who eminently deserves the fair.

Although Robertson's dialogue rarely sparkles, it has a constant freshness and fluency. He is capable of a telling satirical jibe, as when Hugh Chalcot ridicules the mercenary basis of society marriages by mocking the words of the marriage service:

> I, Brewhouse, Malt-kilns, Public houses and Premises, take thee, Landed Property, grass and arable, farm houses, tenements, and Salmon Fisheries, to my wedded wife, to have and to hold for dinners and evening parties, for carriage and horse-back, for balls and presentations, to bore and to tolerate, till mutual aversion do us part.

It is generally agreed that Robertson reached his apogee in the play *Caste* (1867). There is real seriousness in the study of the damage done by the class system when love defies its boundaries. George D'Alroy falls in love with a poor ballet dancer, Esther Eccles. His mother, the Marquise de St Maur, is a rigid stickler for aristocratic superiority. Moreover, though Esther has native charm and beauty,

Robertson has the wit to give her a thoroughly disreputable father, lazy, vain, mean and selfish, who is killing himself with drink. The playwright is thus in a position to earth events in a real social environment where marriage involves families as well as individual partners. D'Alroy's friend Captain Hawtree makes the point vividly:

> My dear Dal, all those marriages of people with common people are all very well in novels and plays on the stage, because the real people don't exist, and have no relatives who exist, and no connections, and so no harm's done, and it's rather interesting to look at; but in real life with real relations, and real mothers, and so forth, it's absolute bosh. It's worse – it's utter social and personal annihilation and damnation!

Although the working-class characters are somewhat idealised, the collision of attitudes, codes and values between them and the upper class is real enough, and Robertson vivifies it in semi-amusing, semi-sad altercations between Hawtree, the real swell, and plumber Sam Gerridge who is suitor to Esther's outspoken sister Polly. George defiantly marries Esther without telling his mother and a period of precarious happiness follows. Then, as in *Ours*, the public world intrudes. The regiment in which Hawtree and George serve is suddenly ordered to India. When the curtain rises on Act III George is no more than a portrait on the wall of the Eccles's home, for Esther has seemingly become a widow with a baby son. The pathos hovers on the edge of the tragic as the situation is unfolded. The money George left for his wife has been spent on drink by Esther's father. Esther herself refuses to apply for help to the mother-in-law who has despised her, but her unscrupulous father sends her a begging letter and the Marquise visits the Eccles's home, requesting to take away her grandson and give him the upbringing he is entitled to. Esther rebukes her with great dignity. The complex situation here fabricated is one of the great moments of Victorian drama: the total entanglement of emotional, social and financial motifs is powerfully conveyed. But a happy ending is contrived. George, who was last seen riding away in captivity with a band of sepoys notorious for their bloodthirstiness, ran into a former servant of his among them who contrived his escape, and he returns to claim his wife amid a welter of sentiment.

Robertson met with his share of criticism. There were those who thought his dialogue so realistic as to reproduce on stage what was too commonplace to be worth an audience's attention. There were also those who felt that he pandered too readily to the lowest common denominator of public taste; but, critical as he was of Robertson in some respects, Bernard Shaw defended him vigorously in other respects: 'After years of sham heroics and superhuman balderdash, *Caste* delighted everyone by its freshness, its nature, its humanity.'

Popular melodrama

Shaw's comment is understandable. *Caste* followed only a year after the production of one of the most notorious Victorian melodramas, *East Lynne* (1866), a dramatic adaptation (and not the first one) of the novel *East Lynne* (1861) by Mrs Henry Wood (1814–87). This book, which sold over half-a-million copies, tells the story of Lady Isabel Vane who leaves her husband for another man and then, after her husband has re-married, returns to him in the disguise of a nurse to look after her own children. The dramatic version, dubbed the most pathetic play of the era, includes an oft-quoted scene in which Madam Vane in the role of governess looks down on her own dying child:

> 'Look at me, William. I am your mother– (*Catches him in her arms. He says 'Mother' faintly, and falls back dead in her arms.*) – he is dead! Oh, William! wake and call me mother once again! My child is dead! . . .'

Even *East Lynne* could scarcely match the absurdities of *Lady Audley's Secret* (1863), adapted twice in the same year, and perhaps the more effectively by C. H. Hazelwood (1820–75), from the novel of the same name published in 1862 by Miss Braddon (1837–1915). Lady Audley having married for love, fabricates a report of her death to her husband when he is abroad, becomes a governess and marries the aged Sir Michael Audley for money. Accident brings the wronged husband to her home and she embarks on a series of attempted murders to protect her secret. The absurdity of the implausibilities and the crudity of the self-revelation to the audience in stage whispers *aside* are symptomatic of melodramatic sensationalism run riot, but the play had a huge box-office success. The audience which wept at the pathos of *East Lynne* hissed the villainies of Lady Audley with an equal lack of restraint.

Tom Taylor

The gap between Victorian melodrama proper and the contemporary social drama which Robertson established was a wide one, but nevertheless there were dramatists in whose work the conventions of melodrama existed alongside an element of social realism. Tom Taylor (1817–80) was one such. Robertson had a sadly short life, but

Taylor, like Boucicault, supplied successes for the London theatre over a long career. It was a busy career, too, for Taylor had a year as a tutor at Cambridge, practised law for three years, held Civil Service appointments for twenty years, and held the Chair of English at London University for two years meanwhile. After retiring from the Civil Service he became editor of *Punch*. There are some eighty titles in his list of plays, though many of them are adaptations or translations, and some were written in collaboration. There were early collaborations with the novelist, Charles Reade, including *Masks and Faces, or Before and Behind the Curtain* (1854). Reade had begun his career as a novelist with *Peg Woffington* (1852). Peg Woffington (1714–60) was a celebrated actress, the daughter of a Dublin bricklayer, who made her London debut in 1740, and became the mistress of the actor and play producer David Garrick (1717–79). A comedienne with a handsome figure, she excelled especially in 'breeches parts', that is, in acting male roles. She figures as the dominating character in *Masks and Faces*, playing the part of the 'good fairy' whose cunning machinations and acting skill get the troubled heroine out of her matrimonial difficulties. Ernest Vane, a gentleman of means, leaves his wife in the country and lingers in town in the hope of winning the great actress as his mistress. Mrs Vane (Mabel) comes up to town unexpectedly, innocently foreseeing a delighted welcome from her husband, at the very moment when he is entertaining the great actress. There is a good deal of 'masking' undertaken to save faces and reputations, but Peg the professional ultimately 'outmasks' them all to bring the erring husband back to his senses and his wife's arms. The playwright and poet laureate Colley Cibber (1671–1757) is another real character who appears in this play, and there is an interesting study of a struggling playwright, Triplet, laden down with a hungry family and a host of unwanted tragedies. There is no subtlety in the play; quite the reverse; nor is there any genuine evocation of an eighteenth-century period flavour; indeed Peg Woffington's espousal of Mabel Vane's cause reeks of Victorian sentimentality:

MABEL: Let me call you sister? I have no sister!
WOFFINGTON: Sister! oh, yes! call me sister! (*They embrace.*) You do not know what it is to me, whom the proud ones of this world pass by with averted looks, to hear that sacred name from lips as pure as yours.

One of the most successful, and justly successful, of Tom Taylor's plays was *The Ticket-of-Leave Man* (1863). It has many of the ingredients of tearful melodrama combined with a vivid contemporary realism that has deeper social implications. It concerns a young Lancashire lad, Robert Brierly, who has come up to London and is being seduced by its dissipations when he falls in love with a poor young woman, May Edwards. He becomes the prey of two villainous criminals, Moss and Dalton, who palm off a forged £20 note on him which he changes at a shop. The police arrest him and he is sent to gaol. Released early for good conduct on a 'ticket-of-leave', he plans to redeem himself by hard work, and determines to marry May. But whenever he gets a job the criminals reveal his record to his employers, who are compelled by the code of the time to sack him. In the end, of course, he is able to turn the tables on the criminals, but the passionate injured innocence of the young hero whose career is being blighted by the criminal world in the face of his most strenuous efforts to work faithfully and make good gives solid emotional substance to the play. Moreover, the urban settings in the Belle Vue Tea Gardens, a humble flat, a City Bill-Brokers Office, the Bridgewater Arms, a city street, and a city churchyard at night on which the back of the Bill Brokers Office abuts – all these offer possibilities of vivid and varied realism. It is a busy, vital play. Its frank use of such familiar ingredients of melodrama as the dyed-in-the-wool villains, the poor but honest hero and heroine, and the comic stereotypes (Green Jones and Emily St Evremond) is enlivened with delicious comic business and a fair ration of wit as well as by the vein of social awareness, and the detective, Hawkshaw, at large in disguise in the underworld is the fore-runner of many a stolid, resourceful stage detective. Revivals of the play have proved its staying-power.

Taylor was perhaps influenced by Tom Robertson when he turned to a straighter comedy of contemporary life in *New Men and Old Acres* (1869), for which he had collaborative assistance from Augustus William Dubourg (1830–1910). Although it lacks the sustained vitality of *The Ticket-of-Leave Man*, it is a discerning study of aristocratic life on which the growing wealth and influence of industrial manufacturers impinge uncomfortably. An altogether more restrained play in dialogue and in stage presentation, *New Men and Old Acres* explores the familiar Victorian theme of a country estate, Clive Abbey, the home of Marmaduke and Lady Matilda Vavasour, so heavily mortgaged that bankruptcy threatens unless some deal can be done at the eleventh hour. The deal that suggests itself is the marriage of daughter Lilian to a Liverpool merchant, Mr Brown, who has advanced the mortgage. It all begins to look a bit too easy when Mr Brown and Lilian fall in love. Then the blow falls: Brown's company fails, and he can rescue himself only by selling the deeds to vulgar new-rich neighbours, the Bunters, desperate to get their hands on the Clive Abbey estate. What complicates the issue – and what ultimately rescues the Vavasours – is the discovery that they are sitting on a fortune in the way of iron ore. The exchanges between the crude Bunters and the refined Vavasours are at times reminiscent of what John Galsworthy was to make of a similar conflict between a *nouveau-riche* factory owner and an old-fashioned landed gentleman in *The Skin Game* (1920). There are occasional witty exchanges, as when Fanny Bunter responds to the proposal of a penniless young man who says he expects to succeed to a title: 'Papa's a great radical; the title will go a long way with him.' And Lilian Vavasour is a lively study of a bright young thing of the 1860s, ready and apt with the latest trendy slang. But for the most part the play lacks the zest and sparkle of *The Ticket-of-Leave Man*.

James Alberry, Leopold Lewis

Surer signs of Robertson's influence than those traced in the work of Tom Taylor have been detected in the plays of James Alberry (1838–87), especially in *Two Roses* (1870) which, though it is commonplace in its plot and in its social commentary, bears the marks of theatrical professionalism and literary flair in its characterisation and dialogue. The story revolves around the impoverished gentleman, Digby Grant, who clings absurdly to his social pretensions, yet sponges humiliatingly on all and sundry. A plausible rogue, glib of tongue, vain and conscienceless, Grant provided the hugely successful actor Henry Irving (1838–1905) with a popular comic role. Grant's two daughters, Ida and Lotty, are high-spirited, irrepressible young things, and their marriage prospects become a central issue. Grant's attitude to this and other matters is transformed when he is suddenly discovered to be the nearest discoverable heir to a fortune, and just as suddenly modified again when a nearer heir is discovered. What gives the play life is the vitality of the dialogue, which is rich in banter, wisecracks, irony and word-play.

A year after launching *Two Roses* Irving played the lead role in a vastly different play, *The Bells* (1871), an adaptation from a French play made by Leopold Lewis (1828–90). It constituted Lewis's one and only success. Irving played the part of the Burgomaster Mathias who has for fifteen years concealed how he murdered a travelling Polish Jew. The Jew paused briefly at the Burgomaster's Inn in an Alsace village on a winter's night, and Mathias enriched himself by the crime. On the anniversary of the occasion the Burgomaster is busy arranging the marriage of his daughter to the Quartermaster of the local Gendarmerie, a marriage which he trusts will provide an additional safeguard from future detection. But Mathias has a troubled conscience. He hears (and the audience hears) the bells that rang on the Jew's horse on the fatal night. He is tortured by visionary recollections of striking down the Jew with an axe and disposing of the body in a lime-kiln. The paranormal evocations are projected behind gauze. Thus Mathias, in a nightmare, participates in a trial which unmasks his guilt. The opportunity for the melodramatic projection of guilt and remorse appears to have been seized upon by Irving with relish but the modern reader will find it difficult to take the extravagant agonies seriously.

William Schwenck Gilbert

It was in the later 1870s and the 1880s that the London theatre was dominated and the public enthralled by the operas of Sir Arthur Sullivan for which W. S. Gilbert (1836–1911) supplied the libretti. Gilbert's unique blend of whimsy and absurdity, of satire and topsy-turvydom, was combined with a musical fluency and inventiveness on Sullivan's part that have stood the test of time. It is worth recalling that while few of the plays named in this chapter so far are ever revived, the Gilbert and Sullivan operas are still being annually performed by enthusiastic amateur groups all over the country: *HMS Pinafore* (1878), *The Pirates of Penzance* (1880), *Patience* (1881), *Iolanthe* (1882), *Princess Ida* (1884), *The Mikado* (1885), *Ruddigore* (1887), *The Yeoman of the Guard* (1888) and *The Gondoliers* (1889). In all these Gilbert's skill at versification in a versatile range of metrical forms met with an inspired melodic and even contrapuntal agility in Sullivan that made the partnership fruitful. Gilbert's satirical shafts were directed at contemporary institutions and fashions – at the Navy in *HMS Pinafore*, at the police in *The Pirates of Penzance*, at the aesthetic movement in *Patience*, at the House of Lords in *Iolanthe*, at the Women's Rights movement in *Princess Ida*, and at the taste for *japonaiserie* in *The Mikado*. It may be argued that it is Sullivan's music that has kept these works alive on the modern stage, for Sullivan's melodic gift is matched only by the greatest melodists such as Verdi and Mozart. Nevertheless it was Gilbert's infectious rhythmic effects that brought this gift into play.

The outstanding charm of the Gilbert and Sullivan operas has tended to obscure the work of both artists which lay outside the partnership, but Gilbert had written burlesque and fantastic comedies with a 'fairy-tale' element before ever the partnership began. The last play he wrote before comic opera took over was *Engaged* (1877). It has the basic absurdity of the operas, but, in its own right, it is a cunningly shaped play rich in wit. The theme is the familiar competition between romantic love and financial interest pushed to a farcical extreme. It thus satirises dominant interests of contemporary society, but it satirises even more sharply and hilariously the representation of those interests in fiction and on the stage. The opening scene, a satire on idyllic ruralism, takes place in the garden of a humble cottage near Gretna Green on the Scottish Border. The cottager, Mrs Macfarlane, and her daughter Maggie are idealised rustics. So is Maggie's young lover Angus, who deflects stranded railway passengers to their cottage for hospitality after he has derailed their train by putting sleepers across the lines. The mixture of the criminal and bloodthirsty element with the Arcadian element is characteristic of Gilbert. So is the absurdity that arises after the young hero, Cheviot, has protected a strange young lady from desperate pursuit by the man she is fleeing. 'This lady is my wife,' he claims spontaneously in the face of the pursuer's pistols, and 'This gentleman is my husband,' the lady adds in inspired corroboration. Unfortunately, under Scottish law a simple declaration by both parties constitutes a legal marriage. The question whether the cottage is in Scotland or in England becomes a matter on which the future happiness of various couples hangs. The joy of discovering that the cottage is in England is later turned sour by the knowledge that the garden is in Scotland. Wit and irony give the play a sustained vitality. Michael R. Booth has said of it: 'It is surely the best nineteenth-century comedy before *The Importance of Being Earnest*, and Wilde's debt to it is very great.'

Sir Arthur Wing Pinero

To turn to the plays of Sir Arthur Wing Pinero (1855–1934) after reading the plays of the dramatists hitherto dealt with in this chapter is to experience a jolt. Of course, a jolt of a different kind would be experienced in turning to Pinero's plays fresh from reading those of his successors, Shaw or Granville-Barker (1877–1946), or even John Galsworthy. Pinero's Victorian values in putting society men and women under scrutiny set him at a distance from his successors. But in justice to Pinero, his work must be approached as his contemporaries approached it, fresh from encounter with the work of Boucicault and Robertson, and those churners-out of spine-chilling melodrama like *The Bells*, or of sentimental comedy of stickily moralistic sugariness like *A Pair of Spectacles* (1890) by Sydney Grundy (1848–1914). The latter, a highly popular play, is a specimen of how a plot composed of anaemic conventionalities could be re-minted by the rather trivial device of allowing a generous man's overpowering good-nature to lapse temporarily into querulous caution when his own glasses are broken and he has to see for a time through those of his mean-spirited brother. The play exudes the spirit of the high

Victorian theatrical noon; but within two years of its production London had had the chance to see Shaw's first play *Widowers' Houses* and Oscar Wilde's *Lady Windermere's Fan*, and within three years Pinero's *The Second Mrs Tanqueray* too. Certainly Pinero's work represents a turning-point. It is not just that in *The Second Mrs Tanqueray* (1893) he wrote what came to be called a serious 'problem play', for he did this only after justifiable success as a writer of farce. And again, it would be unjust to Pinero to judge his comic gift in the light of what Wilde and Shaw did after him. Rather it should be judged as his contemporaries must have judged it. There are shafts of wit in Boucicault and hilariously felicitous exchanges in Taylor and indeed in Alberry, but in the farces of Pinero there is a sustained fluency of humour in dialogue and situation which invites readers to cast their minds back to Sheridan and Goldsmith as well as foward to Wilde and Shaw.

These early farces, notably *The Magistrate* (1885), *The Schoolmistress* (1886) and *Dandy Dick* (1887), contain their fair share of implausibilities, but the slick theatrical craftsmanship makes the human encounters convincing and keeps the mirth bubbling. A good deal of the action of *Dandy Dick* takes place in the deanery of St Marvells, where the Dean, the Very Reverend Augustus Jedd, a stage cleric of impeccable respectability, has to deal as a widower with two high-spirited daughters, Salome and Sheba. The girls bounce with vitality, and have their eyes on two local army officers. They dramatise their own situations with comic relish. Their banter, their amusingly postured self-consciousness, and their unfailing sense of fun remind one of what Shaw was to do with a couple of hyperactive bright young things in the twins of *You Never Can Tell* (1899). Augustus Jedd's difficulties are not reduced when a long-estranged sister, Georgiana Tidman, turns up to care for the widower's daughters: for Georgiana, now ten years a widow, married into the horseracing fraternity and became an enthusiast for the turf. So she comes breezing into the dignitary's home, a boisterous, noisy woman in mannish clothes whose every idiom smacks of the stable or the racecourse. Dandy Dick is the race-horse in which she has a half-share. The logic of farce leads to a situation in which the Dean himself is held overnight in a police cell accused of administering a potion to the horse. Pinero's inventiveness does not fail him in the hilarious rescue of the cleric while handcuffed and in transit to the court; and the distinctiveness of the participants – village policemen, comic soldiery, racing buff and dedicated family retainers – gives the play its zest and sparkle.

The Second Mrs Tanqueray marks a theatrical advance in that it puts on the stage a study of a woman sketched with acute insight. For the first time it becomes possible to speak of a Victorian dramatist in the same breath as the major Victorian novelists. Indeed the critic William Archer (1856–1924) in an early review of the play wrote: 'It is the highest praise, then, that I can find for *Mrs Tanqueray* to say that its four scenes are like the crucial, the culminating chapters of a singularly powerful and original novel.' Certainly Pinero's Paula Tanqueray sets the mind wandering among studies of spirited and awkward women made by such novelists as Hardy and Trollope. She is the woman with a past, now seemingly trying to redeem herself, and failing because the past rises up against her. Aubrey Tanqueray is a gentleman of the class for whom an improper marriage could bring social ostracism, and, after years as a widower, he has chosen for his second wife a woman who is not of his own class and who has, moreover, cohabited with other men. Over-anxious that things may again go wrong in her life and produce more suffering, over-desperate to ensure that they shall not, Paula trembles on the edge of unhappiness. From her first appearance on stage she has lines which enable an actress to express a whole range of conflicting emotions. Defensive, over-sensitive, looking for slights, but eager to change, demanding and proud, she is tormented by her own longing for affection and by her incongruous gift for alienating those who might offer it. At times she behaves like a perverse child, 'so utterly incapable of self-restraint as to fly in the interests of her own ambitions and interests at every second word', William Archer noted. Mrs Patrick Campbell (1865–1940) played the part in the opening production and shot up overnight from being an unknown actress into a national celebrity. Tanqueray, by nature a generous, well-meaning fellow, is too ingenuous and too limited in imagination fully to understand or sympathise with her, let alone handle beneficially the volcanic temperament he has introduced into his home. The situation is complicated by the arrival of Aubrey's daughter Ellean, an innocent girl of nineteen who has been brought up in an Irish convent. Stepmother and stepdaughter lapse into a mutual antagonism almost inevitable when every tentativeness, restraint or reluctance by the younger can be interpreted as a personal rebuff by the elder. Pinero makes of their exchanges and of those between Paula and Aubrey a psychological mine-field, a conversational terrain charged with electric currents that at any moment an ambiguous word or response can fuse into a blinding flash of resentment. The crisis arises from the fact that Ellean meets and falls in love with a man who turns out to be one of Paula's former lovers. The tangle of agonies is resolved by Paula's suicide.

Pinero has been criticised in that Paula, spirited as she is, does not overtly challenge the moral code which makes self-justification impossible for her. A Shavian heroine might have done so. But it may be argued that in making his heroine the tragic victim of the accepted respectability-morality Pinero no less than Shaw passed judgement on his times.

Another of Pinero's lasting successes was *Trelawny of the 'Wells'* (1898). It centres on Rose Trelawny, a rising star of the Bagnigge Wells Theatre, with whom a wealthy, aristocratic young man falls in love. Rose thoroughly enjoys her work and her colleagues, but her own actress-mother impressed a lesson on her: 'If ever a good man comes along, and offers to marry you and take you off the stage, seize the chance – get out of it!' So when Arthur Gower proposes she accepts, and his grandfather and grand-aunt agree to take her into their home to acclimatise her to the leap across the social barrier. There, of course, she is bored to death, eventually realises that the alliance would be incompatible, and runs back to the theatre. Deeply hurt, Arthur himself turns actor, and an elaborately contrived happy ending brings the lovers face to face together on stage at a rehearsal of a new play. The aristocratic characters are gross cartoons, the theatrical characters a little more plausible; but certain themes give the play substance and depth. One is Pinero's exploration of the contrast between the real world and the play world. The barrier between the two is one which even old Sir William Gower crossed in his youth long years ago. When Rose returns from her chastening and saddening experience in the real world, she finds she can no longer act effectively at the conventionally extravagant level required in their standard melodrama. She has acquired a restraint which does not speak to the gallery. One of her colleagues, however, Tom Wrench, is a would-be playwright in a new naturalistic vein who is weary of the old 'rodomontade' (bragging). Wrench is, in fact, Pinero's study of the playwright Tom Robertson who had been so influential at the earliest stage of that development which was to lead from Boucicault to Bernard Shaw. Thus *Trelawny of the 'Wells'* made 'theatrical history' in two senses of the term. When Rose comes back to the company and the popular view is that she has lost her touch, Wrench is outraged: 'These fools at the "Wells"! Can't act, can't she! No she can no longer *spout*, she can no longer *ladle*, the vapid trash, the – the – the turgid rodomontade – .' But when Wrench writes a play to his own recipe, Telfer, the typical ham actor of the melodramatic school, has little time for it: 'Like it! there's not a speech in it, my dear – not a real *speech;* nothing to dig your teeth into – '. Pinero here was looking back thirty years and annotating a theatrical revolution.

Henry Arthur Jones

The dramatist Henry Arthur Jones (1851–1929) made more of a noise in the theatrical world of the 1890s than did Pinero himself, for Jones was indefatigable in writing and lecturing on the state of the drama, and, in particular, in insisting that the theatre had to deal with the serious issues of life. In practice, however, Jones's work as a playwright did not match up to Pinero's. His early melodramas, such as *Saints and Sinners* (1884) were undistinguished, though he tackled contemporary themes in *The Middleman* (1889), about an inventor who gets the better of an exploiting capitalist employer, in *Judah* (1890), which includes a satirical study of the 'new woman', and in *Michael and His Lost Angel* (1896), about a puritanical minister's own fall from grace. But the plays which have generally been regarded as his best focus on the marriage problems of society people, in particular the appalling social price paid by men and, more especially, women for settling down in extra-marital relationships, and the way the threat of having to pay this price operates to keep the tempted tottering on the brink of social calamity and to turn them back from the fatal precipice at the last moment. Thus in *The Liars* (1897) the flirtatiousness of Lady Jessica Nepean, who is encouraged rather than discouraged in her gaiety and coquetry in male company by the stolid and humourless heavy-handedness of her husband Gilbert, leads her to a private dinner-party with the adoring Edward Falkner. Falkner is captivated by her charm and beauty, and is desperate to whisk her away with him. But she is only enjoying herself irresponsibly with him, and when her brother-in-law stumbles upon the guilty couple in their assignation, instead of eloping with her lover she plots with her friends an elaborate network of falsification to pull the wool over her husband's eyes. The upshot is that the play ends with the chastened Falkner, who already has a record of colonial heroism, embarking for Africa to tidy up a little matter of warring chieftains. The action is neatly managed, but the characters are a collection of stereotypes, and the various couples seem to be so ill-matched and so little satisfied with their partners that the assumed motive for costly reinforcement of the married condition is elusive.

Jones's most celebrated play, *Mrs Dane's Defence* (1900), takes up the same issue as that of *The Second Mrs Tanqueray* but does so without either Pinero's psychological penetration or his power to touch the emotional nerves. Mrs Dane turns up in an English village to play her part in its social life. She is really Felicia Hindemarsh, a former governess whose relationship with her employer caused the suicide of his wife and his own subsequent insanity. All this happened in faraway Vienna, but a rumour of past scandal and suspicion about her identity bring into question not only her fitness to marry Lionel Carteret but also her fitness to have a stall at the parish bazaar. (The local Duchess is threatening to refuse to open it if she does.) Lionel's father Sir Daniel Carteret, now Mr Justice Carteret, brings all his forensic skill to bear on an extensive cross-examination of the poor woman in Act III. Her carefully constructed camouflage is torn apart. But to non-Victorian eyes the degree of sexual frailty is so disproportionate to the crushing dialectical apparatus employed to unveil it, let alone to the question whether Mrs Dane is fit to have a stall at the village bazaar, that what was at the time regarded as a scene of powerful dramatic climax will scarcely move a modern reader.

Reading any number of the domestic dramas of the 1890s is apt to produce an impression of an obsession with marital unhappiness. A year before *Mrs Dane's Defence* and two years after *The Liars*, Charles Haddon Chambers (1860–1921), an Australian of Irish stock, had considerable success with *The Tyranny of Tears* (1899), another tightly-constructed domestic drama, with only six characters, which focuses with force and economy on the situation of a celebrated writer, Mr Parbury, whose wife's possessiveness and recourse to the emotional blackmail of tears is gradually isolating him from his male friends, depriving him of interests outside the home, and interfering with his work. His devoted secretary becomes the object of his wife's jealousy and produces a climactic row so nearly final in its effects on the marriage that chastening remorse and penitence on the wife's part make a happy ending possible. The contrast between the hearty freedoms of bachelordom and the crippling demands made by the need to restrain a wife's fractiousness and ensure her docility form a background to the commentary on marriage made forcibly both here and in Pinero's *The Second Mrs Tanqueray*.

Oscar Wilde

It was Oscar Wilde (1854–1900) who rang down the curtain on the Victorian theatre and at the same time on many Victorian proprieties. He was born in Dublin, the son of distinguished and notorious parents, for his mother Lady Wilde had written patriotic articles and verse under the pseudonym 'Speranza', and his father Sir William Wilde, a notable eye and ear surgeon, had also written travel and topographical books and biography. Lady Wilde was a vast, flamboyant hostess to all and sundry. Sir William's career went gravely adrift when a patient claimed that he had seduced her under chloroform. After brilliant academic achievements at Trinity

College, Dublin and at Oxford, Wilde went to London, married in 1884, and began to write. He had already established a reputation as an aesthetic eccentric, dressed in velvet, knee-breeches and silk stockings, and fashioning his own persona into a compelling work of art. The compulsion derived chiefly from his Irish charm and wit. His gift for epigrammatic declamation and riposte was perhaps the most startling manifestation of conversational genius to have struck London since Dr Johnson (1709–84) died. As a public speaker he entranced audiences in America; he shocked and fascinated society at home. The story of his fatal transference of verbal outrageousness into a public challenge to Victorian morality is well known. When the Marquis of Queensberry, angered by the homosexual liaison between Wilde and his son Lord Alfred Douglas, left a card at his club for Wilde the 'sodomite', Wilde foolishly brought a libel action and provoked the counter-charge of homosexual practices which resulted in his being sentenced to two years in Reading gaol.

Wilde's inspired conversational brilliance gave him a head start as a dramatist, and there is no doubt that his plays abound in dialogue that sparkles with wit. Not since the plays of Sheridan had the English stage presented anything to match the scintillating shafts and hilarious paradoxes. In some respects the plays exploit standard Victorian formulas. In *Lady Windermere's Fan* (1892) Mrs Erlynne is the woman with a past, like Pinero's Mrs Tanqueray and H. A. Jones's Mrs Dane, and she is attempting to make a place for herself in London society against the resistance of the highly virtuous Lady Windermere. (The play's subtitle is 'A Play about a Good Woman'.) Lord Windermere seems to have been drawn to Mrs Erlynne like a bee to a honey-pot, and Lady Windermere is tempted to yield to infidelity on the rebound. The irony of it all is that Mrs Erlynne, the 'wicked woman', proves ready to sacrifice herself in order to protect the 'good woman' who is in fact misjudging her. Wilde's dialogue at its best has an element of pure humour that is alive with personality. In this respect the conversation of the women is often a delight. When the Duchess of Berwick meets the Australian Mr Hopper she does her best to respond appropriately:

> DUCHESS: Do you know, Mr Hopper, dear Agatha and I are so much interested in Australia. It must be so pretty with all the dear little kangaroos flying about. Agatha has found it on the map. What a curious shape it is! Just like a large packing case. However, it is a very young country, isn't it?
>
> HOPPER: Wasn't it made at the same time as the others, Duchess?

But the amoral juggling with values in paradoxical epigrams is the more familiar vein – 'A man who moralises is usually a hypocrite, and a woman who moralises is invariably plain', and, 'It is absurd to divide people into good and bad. People are either charming or tedious.'

What is most remarkable about Wilde's plays prior to the pure comedy of *The Importance of Being Earnest* is the mixture of pathos and wit. Indeed in *A Woman of No Importance* (1893) the archetypal Wildean persona, Lord Illingworth, whose talk abounds throughout with Wildean witticisms, has converted his own life into a performance of which he is the ever amused and delighted spectator. Yet he has left a trail of misery in the life of a good woman who trusted him, the 'woman of no importance' who long ago bore his son and whom he refused to marry. Illingworth is flippant, cynical, armour-plated in total selfishness and vanity. Yet there is a gravity of moral judgement in the dignity of the tortured woman he has played with. Her last line rightly declares him a 'man of no importance'. He has made himself that. It is difficult not to read into the play a penetrating self-judgement by its author.

In *An Ideal Husband* (1895) there is a more sustained seriousness in studying the crisis in the career of Sir Robert Chiltern, a politician on the edge of public achievements, whose past rises up against him. His wealth was founded many years ago when as a young secretary to a Cabinet minister he gave away secret State information about the forthcoming purchase of shares in the Suez Canal. Since then he has tried to atone by giving lavishly to charity and has been a model of rectitude, idolised by none more devotedly than by his wife. Once more a woman from the past intrudes. She is in possession of the fatal revelatory letter he wrote, and is bent on blackmailing him. Public reputation and domestic happiness are under threat. The play acquires tragic dimensions as Chiltern writhes in his dilemma. The one character with a touch of the Wildean persona, Lord Goring, is an altogether mellower, less cynical and much less selfish trader in epigrams than his predecessors. Nevertheless there are moments in the play when his witticisms strike a discordant note.

If humour thus intrudes inappropriately at certain points in *The Ideal Husband* it is certain that seriousness never intrudes for a moment into *The Importance of Being Earnest* (1895) to spoil the most dazzling display of wit and humour the age had seen. Only a handful of post-Elizabethan English comedies (and they are mostly written by Irishmen, such as those by Sheridan, Goldsmith, Synge (1871–1909) and Shaw) can stand comparison with *The Importance of Being Earnest*. It concerns the intrigues of two young men, Jack Worthing and Algernon Moncrieff. Jack, having succeeded to the care of a ward, the attractive young Cecily Cardew who lives at his country home, calls himself Ernest to his friends in town so that his

innocent ward shall hear nothing to the discredit of her guardian.
As a further safeguard, he pretends that he has a rather wild brother,
Ernest. Algernon, having made this discovery, goes down to Jack's
country home to pass himself off on Cecily as the wicked cousin
Ernest. This neat tangle is superimposed on Jack's suit for the hand
of Gwendolen Fairfax, Algernon's cousin, whose mother Lady
Bracknell is one of the most comically formidable society ladies in
English literature. Naturally she enquires into the antecedents of her
would-be son-in-law, and is horrified to learn that Jack can say
nothing of his parents, because his guardian, Mr Cardew, found him
as a baby in a hand-bag in the cloak-room at Victoria Station. Lady
Bracknell is outraged:

> You can hardly imagine that I and Lord Bracknell would dream
> of allowing our only daughter – a girl brought up with the utmost
> care – to marry into a cloak-room and form an alliance with a
> parcel!

George Bernard Shaw

While Oscar Wilde was thus ringing down the curtain on the
Victorian theatre in a riot of laughter, another Irishman, George
Bernard Shaw (1856–1950), was ringing up the curtain on the post-
Victorian theatre. From the start he forsook the formulas of the
well-made play, the codes of Victorian social relationships, and the
constraints of established stage themes and concerns. In *Widowers'
Houses* (1892), his first play, Shaw pushes a very Shavian young
English doctor, Harry Trench, into the company of a wealthy
gentleman, Sartorius, with whose daugher Blanche he falls in love.
Making the terrible discovery that Sartorius's wealth is derived from
slum-landlordism, brutal and mean in its effects, Trench decides that
he can marry Blanche only on the condition that the two of them
live on his own small income alone and not on the tainted family
money. Neither Blanche nor her father will accept these conditions.
A characteristic Shavian irony establishes that Trench's own income
is derived from a mortgage on some of the slum property in question.
The reader will notice how distant is this moral issue and the personal
perplexities it provokes from the familiar concerns of Victorian
drama. A similar revolution in taste was effected in Shaw's *Arms
and the Man* (1894), in which a professional mercenary Swiss soldier,
Captain Bluntschli, an anti-hero serving in the Serbian army, arrives
by chance to shatter the dreams and eventually dominate the heart
of the romantic idealistic young lady, Raina Petkoff, hitherto captivated by the glamour of her more conventional idol, Sergius. The

anti-romantic logic here subjects the glorification of battle and heroism to searching scrutiny. In *The Devil's Disciple* (1897) it is applied to another brand of conventionalism. Shaw's setting is a little New Hampshire town during the American War of Independence. The minister Anthony Anderson is sought by British soldiers, but in fact they arrest by mistake the local reprobate, Richard Dudgeon, self-confessed 'Devil's disciple'. In the upshot the reprobate decides to live out – or rather, to die out – the role, and the minister's wife is gratefully touched by his heroism. But when her husband learns what is happening, then preacher turns man of action as decisively as the reprobate turned martyr, and he rides off to obtain a reprieve in the nick of time.

It is quite apparent that the world of drama was immeasurably broadened by the issues Shaw raised and by his persistence in subjecting accepted attitudes to scrutiny. His most popular nineteenth-century comedy, *You Never Can Tell* (1899), exploits stock comic characters and situations with verve and wit which match those of Wilde in *The Importance of Being Earnest*, but even here the comedy is enriched by attention to a pressing new issue, that of Women's Rights and the so-called 'New Woman'. Yet there is no question of propaganda marring the comedy. Even emancipated womanhood proves no match for the ability of a clever but impecunious young dentist to manipulate the female heart.

Shaw's nineteenth-century plays represent only a magnificent opening to twentieth-century literary career of astonishing productiveness. It was a career that was to include such comedies as *Candida* (1904), *John Bull's Other Island* (1904), *The Doctor's Dilemma* (1906) and *Pygmalion* (1914), all rich in wit and vital in analysis of public issues and private problems; while on the more serious side *Heartbreak House* (1920) pictured Europe, 'cultured leisured Europe', drifting towards the First World War. The comic gift, however, remained Shaw's surest talent, and it was still sparkling as late as 1936 in *The Millionairess*.

Part 5

Victorian prose

Thomas Carlyle

It is not possible to read much about Victorian life and thought without coming across the name of Thomas Carlyle (1795–1881). He achieved a reputation and a position in his own day which gave him the status of a Victorian Dr Johnson. For one thing he was a great talker; he was also a great moralist and sage. But the comparison with Dr Johnson stops there. In place of Johnson's wit, poise and logic, Carlyle exudes urgency, compulsiveness and passion. Born in Ecclefechan, Dumfriesshire, a few miles north of the Border, Carlyle was the son of a self-made builder, a stern, devout Presbyterian who instilled into his children the gospel that work and duty over-ride all personal inclinations. He recognised his son's intellectual promise, and it was assumed that Thomas would become a minister in the Church. Although Thomas's studies then led him in a different direction and out of the Presbyterian fold, and he experienced a deep inner crisis, faith in God survived, along with a sense of the exacting demands of obedience to transcendental moral authority. Carlyle's story was one of persistent struggle. Aware of his own genius and of his vocation as a writer, he was impatient with all that interfered with his pursuit of this calling. Fortunately he found in Jane Welsh a wife devoted to his well-being, often sorely tempted by his temper, but in sheer wit and literary vitality a fit match for him. The married life of the Carlyles, at whose home in Chelsea many Victorian notabilities were entertained, is a theme touched upon by many contemporaries. The mixture of tenderness and tragedy moves all who read the story. Carlyle became aware in Jane's later years of what his eventually obsessive mania for work had cost her, and he was devastated by her death in 1866.

Carlyle gradually made a name for himself by his articles. His translation of Goethe's *William Meister's Apprenticeship* (1824) won praise from Goethe himself. But he was a long time in discovering his true *métier* as a historian. His little-regarded book, *Sartor Resartus* (1836), first appeared in *Fraser's Magazine* in 1833–4. 'Sartor Resartus' means 'The Tailor Re-clothed'. Supposedly a record of the life and opinions of an imaginary Professor

Teufelsdröckh, it suggests that just as clothes are but temporary veils and disguises, so are human institutions. A memorable section of the work contrasts the 'Everlasting NO' which despairs of a universe void of meaning and purpose and the 'Everlasting YEA', the positive impulse of faith and hope.

It was Carlyle's massive *History of the French Revolution* (1837) which fully established him. It covers the period from the death of Louis XV in 1774 to Napoleon's suppression of the rising in Paris in 1795. On its publication Carlyle suddenly found himself a national celebrity. This is not surprising, for he managed to bring history to life by vivid portraiture and by bringing a transforming poetic imagination to bear on the stirring events. He believed that 'Reality, if rightly interpreted is grander than Fiction', that 'History . . . is the true Poetry'. And thus, in re-creating the past, in making it live again, he found a new use for an elaborate rhetorical style, rich in metaphor, in biblical and Shakespearean echoes, in pulpit declamation, in irony and humour, in probing appeals to the heart and spectacular presentations to the imagination. Carlyle's dogged obduracy in vast undertakings had been severely tested by his work on *The French Revolution*, for after completing the first volume in six months and embarking on the second, he was visited one day by the political philosopher John Stuart Mill (1806–73) in great distress. Carlyle had lent the manuscript of the first volume of the work to Mill, a friend of Mill's had begged to look at it, and her servant lit the fire with it. Carlyle had to start again from scratch, and he achieved the re-writing in three months.

The success of *The French Revolution* created a demand for Carlyle as a public speaker, and to great acclaim he delivered the lectures later published as *On Heroes and Hero-Worship* (1841), in which history is seen as the history of Great Men. He considers the Hero as Divinity, the Hero as Prophet, the Hero as Poet, as Priest, as Man of Letters, and as King, and among those celebrated are Shakespeare, Luther, John Knox, Dr Johnson, Burns and Cromwell. But a work of very different character succeeded this when Carlyle turned his attention to the social miseries of his own time in *Past and Present* (1843). The work contrasts a picture of English life in the twelfth century based on an old monkish chronicle with a scathing account of the contemporary condition of the supposed 'free' working classes and the oppressed poor brought about by *laissez-faire* economics. The passionate fervour and the rhetorical force which Carlyle brought to bear on his critique of contemporary materialism have an egalitarian impulse which perhaps sits uncomfortably alongside his praise of the mighty heroic forerunners of history, and certainly in his later years Carlyle's dread of revol-

ution and anarchy pushed him towards authoritarianism. His great-
ness remains that of an inspirer: it is characteristic of his role that
The French Revolution inspired Dickens to write *A Tale of Two
Cities*.

Thomas Babington Macaulay

Another Victorian historian who earned himself a distinguished place
among men of letters was Thomas Babington Macaulay (1800–59),
whose *History of England from the Accession of James II* came out
in four volumes between 1849 and 1855. Whereas Carlyle had but a
poor opinion of his compatriot Sir Walter Scott, Macaulay learned
a lot from him, actively determining to show the social and economic
causes of political events as vividly as Scott had done in the *Waverley
Novels*. The twentieth-century historian, G. M. Trevelyan, reviewing
the achievements of Scott and the eighteenth-century historian
Gibbon (1737–94), has observed that Gibbon 'conceived of mankind
as essentially the same in all ages and countries', but 'to Scott each
age, each profession, each country, each province, had its own
manners, dress, ways of thinking, talking, and fighting'. This was
what Macaulay learned from Scott. 'The difference between Gibbon
and Macaulay is a measure of the influence of Scott', Trevelyan
declares. In contrast to Carlyle who exudes prophetic evangelism,
Macaulay has a winning narrative fluency and descriptive power.
He is a patient celebrant of the ordinary, content to delight in the
moderating influence of the English constitution established under
William of Orange. His opinionated and simplistic *Essays Critical
and Historical* (1834) are no longer much read, but his *Lays of
Ancient Rome* (1842), celebrating stirring events from Roman
history, and especially 'Horatius', about the heroic holding of the
bridge across the Tiber against invading forces, have a persuasive if
sometimes over-mechanical rhythmic vitality.

John Ruskin

The Victorian prophet who perhaps had most in common with
Carlyle was John Ruskin (1819–1900). Like Carlyle he was master
of a richly rhetorical prose style of compulsive splendour. Like
Carlyle he became a legend in his own day. Like Carlyle's his
prophetic message influenced the makers of opinion throughout his
own lifetime. Yet like Carlyle's his work is now little read if we
compare it with the work of the great contemporary novelists and
poets. Beyond these kinships lies a strange and deeper kinship in
personality and in private destiny. For Ruskin's marriage to Effie

Gray was to be annulled by her evidence of non-consummation, though any charge of impotence is certainly open to question. What is not open to question is that Ruskin's prosecution of his own work had obsessive priority for him that made married life all but impossible for his wife. After their divorce she married the painter Sir John Everett Millais. Ruskin's emotional instability led him later to a doomed love for a young girl, Rose La Touche, to whom he eventually proposed marriage when she was eighteen and he was forty-seven, but the fulfilment of this feverish and protracted dream was denied him. Rose herself became mentally incapacitated and died in 1875. Four years later, Ruskin, now in his sixties, suffered a series of mental breakdowns, and for the last ten years of his life was mentally disabled.

Ruskin was the son of a well-to-do wine-merchant. His father and mother brought him up in isolation from youthful companions but in contact with literature, art and scenic beauty. His publications as an art critic began with the five volumes of *Modern Painting* (1843–60) in which he championed especially the work of the land-scape painter J. M. W. Turner (1775–1851), a master in capturing fleeting effects of light. Ruskin became an enthusiast for Gothic architecture, contrasting the static, poised quality of the Classical style with the restless dynamic, unsatisfied spirit manifested in Gothic niches, pinnacles and the 'labyrinthine knots and shadows along wall and roof'. This is the style, he argued, that matches the skies, the forests and the ravines of northern Europe. Ruskin's architectural pursuits represented in *The Seven Lamps of Architecture* (1848), which he fully illustrated, led him to grave dissatisfaction with the values of contemporary culture, and thence to an interest in econ-omics and in social reform. His *Unto This Last* (1860) takes its title from Christ's parable of the householder who rewarded equally the men who had laboured in his vineyard whether from dawn or from late in the day, thereby strictly fulfilling his promise, 'I will give unto this last, even as unto thee' (Matthew 20: 14). The book protests against regarding human beings as units in an economic machine. A labourer is not a component in a vast national engineering project; he is a living individual endowed with a soul, and must be recognised by his employer as a fellow human being. This attack on the class system was regarded by many as virtual incitement to revolution and called forth angry condemnation. But Carlyle wrote in praise of Ruskin's logic and 'the pincer-grip (red-hot pincers) you take of certain bloated cheeks and blown-up bellies. More power to your elbow . . .'. *Unto This Last*, in fact, became an influential text for the movement that produced the British Labour Party.

The social passion emerges again in lectures he delivered in

Manchester in 1864, published as *Sesame and Lilies* (1865). The first lecture attacks the money-ethic and declares under five heads: 'We have despised literature', 'We have despised science', 'You have despised Art', 'You have despised Nature', and 'You despise compassion'. In evidence of the last charge Ruskin quotes verbatim a contemporary item from the *Daily Telegraph*, a pathetic account of a coroner's hearing after the death of a poor 'translator' (reconditioner) of old boots from lack of sustenance and warmth: 'The deceased had had no bedclothes. For four months he had had nothing but bread to eat. There was not a particle of fat in the body. There was no disease . . .'. So ran the medical report. Ruskin pours scorn on the complaint that the deceased's widow and son had refused to go into the workhouse: 'Well, the poor seem to have a prejudice against the workhouse which the rich have not; for of course every one who takes a pension from the government goes into the workhouse on a grand scale: only the workhouses of the rich do not involve the idea of work, and should be called playhouses.'

It is plain from such outbursts that Ruskin's judgement on his age had much in common with Dickens's. He took up the campaign against capitalist society in *Fors Clavigera: Letters to the Workmen and Labourers of Great Britain* which appeared between 1871 and 1884. His method is to set forth contemporary conditions and to contrast them with the idealistic human aspirations represented in art and literature. It was in one of them in 1877 that Ruskin rashly attacked the *Nocturnes* painted by the artist J. A. M. Whistler (1834–1903) and on display in London. Whistler's delicate, misty landscapes were arrangements of form and colour only vaguely representational. Ruskin deplored his 'Cockney impudence' in asking 'two hundred guineas for flinging a pot of paint in the public's face'. Whistler brought an action for libel, and Ruskin managed to call on the artists Burne-Jones and W. P. Frith (1819–1909) and the dramatist Tom Taylor in his defence. The jury found for the plaintiff, but awarded only a farthing damages. Ruskin, much hurt, thereupon resigned the Slade Professorship of Fine Art which he held at Oxford, saying bitterly, 'I cannot hold a Chair from which I have no power of expressing judgement without being taxed for it by British Law.'

Whereas Ruskin's earlier works were written in a lavish rhetorical style consonant in its structure and cadences with the multifarious grandeurs of Gothic architecture, his *Unto This Last* was appropriately written in a plain, straightforward style free of decorative effects. And by the time he came to work in the 1880s on his (unfinished) autobiography *Praeterita* (1886–9) he unfolded the story of his early days with a graceful, limpid eloquence. Ruskin has been charged with inconsistency. Certainly his thinking represents a mixture which the twentieth-century mind finds remarkable. Highly sensitive to the evils of capitalist exploitation of labour and to all the ills of a profit-oriented economic system, he was yet a staunch imperialist, suspicious of universal suffrage, who praised the aristocratic ideal and valued the hierarchical social order.

Matthew Arnold

Superficially, the life of Matthew Arnold (1822–88) was marked by few of the personal strains and stresses experienced by Carlyle and Ruskin. The son of Dr Thomas Arnold, Headmaster of Rugby School, he was a contemporary of his fellow-poet Arthur Hugh Clough at Oxford. The desire to marry Frances Lucy Wightman impelled him to seek a secure post as Inspector of Schools, and he served as such from 1851 to 1883. The work was arduous, much of it monotonous, and exacting in the demands it made on home life by the constant need to travel. Nevertheless Arnold found the work interesting, recognised its importance, and was stimulated by it to reflect on the state of contemporary culture. It is interesting to compare the impulse to reflection stirred in Ruskin by architecture and by natural beauty with the impulse which arose in the mind of Matthew Arnold in the midst of daily drudgery which inevitably became something of a bondage.

His poetry apart, Arnold can claim to stand among a cluster of English writers who achieved a status as critics that has outlasted their lifetimes: Dryden, Dr Johnson and Coleridge come to mind in this context. Inevitably, the output of the critic includes work scattered in periodicals and lectures. Crucial publications in the Arnold canon are *Essays in Criticism*, eventually issued in three volumes (1865–1910), *Culture and Anarchy* (1869) and *Literature and Dogma* (1873).

In Arnold there is none of Carlyle's blazing rhetoric and none of the luxuriance of Ruskin's early prose. He writes a measured, lucid prose in keeping with the detachment of mind he cultivated. This is not to say that Arnold carries no prophetic message. Rather it indicates that his cultural roots are distinct from those of Carlyle and Ruskin. Carlyle's volcanic, apocalyptic grandeur and Ruskin's variegated Gothic abundance were both alien to his classical taste. Indeed Arnold contrasted the 'Hebraic' and the 'Hellenic' strains in our culture in an endeavour to establish that there was a disastrous neglect of the latter. The Hebraic tradition is that of prophetic certainty, the crude puritanical, anti-intellectual inheritance sharply evident in Victorian Nonconformity. The Hellenic tradition is that which encourages the free play of the intellect in rational openness.

But Arnold was the last man to devalue the moral emphasis so strong in the Hebraic tradition. Indeed his concept of culture has a moral and even a religious basis:

> The moment . . . culture is considered not merely as the endeavour to *see* and *learn* this (i.e. the will of God), but as the endeavour, also, to make it *prevail*, the moral, social, and beneficent character of culture becomes manifest.

The evangelical propagation of culture was the fruit of Arnold's worried resignation to the prevailing criticism of biblical fundamentalism, of Christian dogma and of ecclesiastical institutionalism. He sought a faith in God divested of what had given body to the faith through history. As a result he was the first of a long line of thinkers who endowed culture, and literature especially, with a quasi-religious function if not a quasi-religious status. 'In determining generally in what human perfection consists, religion comes to a conclusion identical with that which culture . . . likewise reaches.' 'Culture lays on us the same obligation as religion which says . . . that "to promote the kingdom of God is to increase and hasten one's own happiness".'

Thus Arnold's attack on Victorian philistinism and materialism has much in common with Ruskin's. Culture provides a salutary restraint on material greed, an effective brake on the worship of wealth, a concept of spiritual health to which popular ideals of physical health ought to be subordinate. In this respect Arnold praised the Greek fusion of aesthetic and moral ideals, lamenting the neglect of the former and the gross over-estimate of the latter in English Protestantism. Men have been taught to value themselves not by what they *are* but on the number of railways they have built, and this is training in philistinism. By contrast Arnold takes up an expression from Swift's (1667–1745) *The Battle of the Books* (1704) – 'the two noblest things, sweetness and light' – and makes of sweetness and light characters of perfection fit to provide a new social ideal, a new apostolate of equality:

> He who works for sweetness and light, works to make reason and the will of God prevail. He who works for machinery, he who works for hatred, works only for confusion. Culture looks beyond machinery, culture hates hatred; culture has one great passion, the passion for sweetness and light.

We have seen that Arnold was not alone in experiencing the loss of traditional Christian faith, but he seems to have been consciously and profoundly worried by the gap this loss created for man attempting to find his feet in a seemingly alien and indifferent universe and grappling with the malaise of an increasingly philistine and materialistic age. For him the Romantic poets, Shelley, Byron and Wordsworth, though they had plenty of creative force, simply 'did not know enough' to provide an interpretation of the world. The French Revolution, 'the most animating event in history', derived from the affirmation of Reason, yet took a political, practical character fatal to culture, so that English Romantic poetry had its source 'in a great movement of feeling, not in a great movement of mind'. 'Literature is the criticism of life,' Arnold insisted. In an age animated by a lively current of ideas the creative power of writers draws animation and nourishment from their mental environment. Even in the absence of this stimulus 'books and reading may enable a man to construct a kind of semblance of it in his own mind, a world of knowledge and intelligence in which he may live and work'. This power of thought to shape the conditions of existence through reading is summed up in the sentence 'Literature is the criticism of life.' Thus the function of criticism is to exercise curiosity in seeking familiarity with 'the best that is known and thought in the world', irrespective of practical considerations, 'and to value knowledge and thought as they approach this best.'

William Morris

In some respects William Morris (1834–96) stands apart from these prophetic figures who shared his disgust with the materialism and philistinism of the Victorian age. For Morris was never tormented by the conflict between traditional Christianity and contemporary doubt. When the question of belief in God or unbelief was raised in his presence, he said, 'It's so unimportant.' C. S. Lewis, an admirer and defender of Morris's work, including his prose romances, said of him, 'He is the most irreligious of all our poets – *anima naturaliter pagana*'. Morris's judgement upon his age was that of a socialist who was prepared not only to project in literature his vision of what the ideal society might be, but also to go about addressing groups of uncouth, ill-educated labourers whose motivation for revolution was very different from his own. Morris's prose is so little read today that it is necessary to re-emphasise how powerful his influence was. W. B. Yeats (1865–1939) said of the prose romances, *The Sundering Flood* (1898) and *News from Nowhere* (1891), that they were 'the only books I ever read slowly so that I might not come quickly to the end', and once, when he was charged with being anti-English, Yeats replied, 'How could I hate England; owing what I do to Shakespeare, Blake, and Morris?'

Morris's socialistic dreams were earthed in his liking for well-made handicrafts and for the life of the agricultural community. We must love the earth, we must work for our families, we must follow our adventurous aspirations; however, we must not expect their fulfilment in happiness. When the Lord of *The Story of the Glittering Plain* (1891) comes to the land of the undying, he senses a falseness in its unchanging charm and easy merriment, and begins to long for what he has left behind, 'the house of his fathers and the men of the spear and the plough'. For Morris the problem of death so overpoweringly an issue for Carlyle is resolved in the realisation that desire for immortality is delusive. In *The Well at the World's End* (1896) his Innocent Folk know that 'the gods have given us the gift of death lest we weary of life'.

The most celebrated of Morris's prose romances are *A Dream of John Ball* (1888) and *News From Nowhere* (1891). They differ from the excursions into wholly imaginary realms in that they are rooted in English history. In *A Dream of John Ball* the narrator is taken back in his dream to the days of the Peasants' Revolt in 1381. John Ball, the rebel priest, preaches from a village cross on the fellowship that belongs to heaven and the lack of fellowship which pertains to hell. 'Therefore, I tell you that the proud, despiteous rich man, though he knoweth it not, is in hell already, because he hath no fellow . . .'. The medieval scene is recaptured with great vividness. The narrator has a long discussion with the priest through the night. John Ball senses that this elderly personage who resembles Chaucer in appearance is really a visitant from another age, and he questions him about what is to come. The subsequent survey of developments culminating in the condition of nineteenth-century society is heavily satirical, but the narrator offers hope for a future in which workers will have thrown off the shackles of exploitation. Finally the narrator wakes in his Hammersmith bedroom to hear the factory hooters calling workers to their daily toil.

News from Nowhere; or, An Epoch of Rest, Being Some Chapters from a Utopian Romance is another dream-allegory, this time taking the narrator into the future. He has been to a meeting of the Socialist League and spent the evening in eventually acrimonious discussion of what will happen on the Morrow of the Revolution. He goes to bed in his suburban home and wakes next morning to find himself in the twenty-first century. The revolution occurred some one hundred and fifty years back and Londoners are now living in an ideal communist environment. The squalor of industrialism has been cleaned up. Money has been abolished and so has formal education. Legislation is unnecessary. Everybody lives in freedom and equality. In place of the shoddy artifacts of the industrial era there is everywhere evidence of beautiful craftsmanship. Piccadilly is an arcaded Italianate shopping street and Trafalgar Square is an orchard. The

Houses of Parliament have been put to a useful purpose and function for the storage of manure. The narrator encounters an old historian, Hammond, who describes how revolution and civil war broke out in 1952. Corrupt capitalism could not be painlessly destroyed, but the world had to be brought to its second birth, and tragedy was inevitable in the process. In Morris's Utopia there is no place for 'art' in isolation because it has been subsumed into workmanship. People work at what interests them. There is no enforced drudgery. The urban horrors of commercial capitalism have given place to simple rural communities. When the narrator returns to wake up again in Hammersmith he brings back the message that 'there is yet a time of rest in store for the world, when mastery has changed into fellowship – but not before'. The prophetic vision has given him hope in the wearing struggle and the motive to go on striving for the cause.

Charles Darwin

The intellectual unease experienced by so many Victorian writers in the climate of failing attachment to traditional Christianity was fuelled by the work of seminal thinkers such as Charles Darwin (1809–92), the naturalist. Darwin sailed to South America and the Pacific on *HMS Beagle* in 1831–6 and reported his findings on the natural history and geology of the countries visited in his *Journal* (1839) and in later books. As a prose writer Darwin has been praised for his precision and his lucidity. His style is unobtrusively direct, yet when occasion demands it can sound a note of grandeur or tap a vein of caustic wit. His celebrated work *On the Origin of Species* (1859) presents his case for the natural development of species. It regards all species, including mankind, as descending from their predecessors by a process of 'natural selection' whereby organic beings possessing the most advantageous mutations and having therefore the most favourable chances of survival, succeed in the struggle for existence. This theory of evolution by the 'survival of the fittest' was based on a conception of world history extending over millennia and was therefore irreconcilable with a literal interpretation of the Old Testament account of Creation. Similarly the philosophy of evolution seemed to bring into question the notion of the natural world in its known form as a direct product of God's workmanship. Darwin's later work *The Descent of Man* (1871) directly applied the principles explored in *The Origin of Species* to the human race in particular, showing human beings to have evolved from the higher primates. A question mark was thus placed over traditional assumptions about man's unique status in the universe as made in the image of God. Controversy between orthodox theologians and scientists ensued. By 1881 the cry is heard in Gilbert and Sullivan's *Patience* that:

> man however well behaved
> At best is only a monkey shaved.

Harriet Martineau

Christian orthodoxy had, of course, been under fire before the Darwinian theory of evolution came into the field of controversy. George Eliot, after a period of firm evangelical piety, had shocked her family by renouncing her faith. Another woman writer, Harriet Martineau (1802–76), a friend of Charlotte Brontë, after upbringing as a devout Unitarian, turned freethinker and wrote polemically as such in her *Letters on the Laws of Man's Nature and Development* (1851). Miss Martineau, a woman of fiercely independent spirit, had a prodigious literary output. Her *Illustrations of Political Economy* (1832–4), a series of instructive stories, made her a celebrity. Like George Eliot she was conscious of the constraints laid by contemporary society on educated women who sought a field of useful work. Her novel *Deerbrook* (1839) presents a full-scale picture of the impact of two sisters on a village community and the overpowering effect of love on these two sensitive women at a time when society imposed rigid restraints on their ability to clarify emotional problems by speaking openly. It is a moving book, yet heavily overburdened by the weight of moralising.

Samuel Butler

One must not oversimplify the battle-lines of Victorian controversy. It was not only Christians who attacked the Darwinian theory of natural selection. In books and articles Samuel Butler (1835–1902) criticised the notion of purposeless 'mechanical evolution' in favour of the doctrine of so-called 'creative evolution' which was to be taken up by George Bernard Shaw. Butler was eventually to produce a most devastating attack on the Victorian family ideal in his posthumous autobiographical novel *The Way of All Flesh* (1903) where the hero Ernest Pontifex has for father a clergyman presented as a hypocritical bully. The bitter satire of Victorian middle-class family life gave the book status when conscious rejection of Victorian respectability and supposed prudery ran high in the early decades of our own century. Butler's name as a novelist in his own lifetime rested on his satirical Utopian fantasy *Erewhon* (1872), a visit to an imaginary country where disease is treated as criminality and criminality as disease, and where churches are ridiculed as 'Musical Banks'. It had a sequel, *Erewhon Revisited* (1901). ('Erewhon' is 'Nowhere' reversed.)

John Henry Newman

Of all the Victorian writers who entered the field of religious controversy none was more gifted nor more distinguished than John Henry Newman (1801–90). He was a key figure in the early days of the Oxford Movement, the High Church movement in the Church of England which was to transform and revitalise the worship and teaching of the Church in the course of the next hundred years. The movement has been seen as, in some respects, the historical corollary and perhaps even the consequence of the movement for political reform which culminated in the 1832 Reform Act. Readers of Victorian novels cannot but be aware that the Church of England was in need of reform. Higher clergy often held their offices as little more than sinecures. Livings were dispensed as tickets to respectability and a comfortable income. Patronage might be exercised by those who held the gift of incumbencies to provide a fit status for a patron's would-be son-in-law. Ordination, as in the case of Tennyson's father, might be a last desperate recourse for a young gentleman deprived of expectations. Such corruptions were not the only things that disturbed the pioneers of the Oxford Movement. They reacted, too, against reformers who tackled the problem of Church organisation as though the Church were just one more human institution in need of adjustments to its mechanisms. The leaders of the Oxford Movement, John Keble (1792–1866), Edward Bouverie Pusey (1800–82) and Newman himself took the High Church view that the Church was not a mere human society but a divinely established institution, bearing forward through the centuries in its episcopal and sacerdotal hierarchy the Apostolic authority bestowed upon it at Pentecost. The Church of England was not something inaugurated by Henry VIII: it was the ancient Catholic Church in this country, cleansed in the sixteenth century of medieval corruptions and of the alien authority of the Pope in Rome.

Alongside this sense of the Church's supranatural origin and status there existed an awareness of the unfittedness of secular power as such to determine matters ecclesiastical and theological. This critique of secular authority led to an acute sense of the injustices to which the State's management of human interests could lead in the absence of any mollifying awareness of man's status as a child of God and of the claims the Gospel made on behalf of the poor and the sick. Thus the Oxford Movement produced on the one hand a new spirituality in the Church, a new feeling for ritual, an enhanced notion of the significance of the sacraments as vehicles of spiritual nourishment, and a status for bishops and priests which was spiritual and sacerdotal rather than social or political. On the other hand, the movement produced a number of heroic parish priests who devoted themselves to the cause of the poor and the afflicted in the slums of inner cities, and it produced the revival of religious communities, for women and also for men, which gave priority to a life of self-sacrifice, prayer and worship, and in many cases also undertook good works on behalf of the poor, the disabled and the supposedly disreputable.

The pioneers of the Oxford Movement were labelled 'Tractarians' because Keble, Pusey and Newman contributed to a series of challenging statements of their position, *Tracts for the Times*, published between 1833 and 1845. Keble, who was Professor of Poetry at Oxford from 1831 to 1841, had published a volume of sacred verse, *The Christian Year* (1827), which became extremely popular in the Victorian age. He became Vicar of Hursley in Hampshire, where he exercised great influence on Charlotte Mary Yonge (1823–1901), a novelist of family life who won praise from many distinguished contemporaries. Although these novels are richly observant of contemporary middle-class life, only *The Heir of Redclyffe* (1853) is much read today. It is a study in moral contrasts between a rash, generous-hearted hero and his only seemingly virtuous cousin.

When defence of the Church of England's catholic and apostolic status met with opposition or ridicule from the very men, the bishops, who were themselves by their office the supposed upholders of that status, it was scarcely surprising that some of the key figures of the Tractarian movement should have turned from the Church of England in despair and joined the Church of Rome. Of those who did so by far the most distinguished was Newman. He had been Vicar of St Mary's, the University church at Oxford, from 1828 until 1843, and he was received into the Church of Rome in 1845. He was an eloquent preacher who made an unforgettable impression on his generation. J. A. Froude (1818–94), the historian, spoke of his 'force of character' which was to become 'a power in the world'. He had 'a clearness of intellectual perception, a disdain for conventionalities; a temper imperious and wilful, but along with it a most attaching gentleness, sweetness, singleness of heart and purpose . . . I had then never seen so impressive a person.'

Newman's pre-conversion works include his contributions to the *Tracts for the Times* and *An Essay on the Development of Christian Doctrine* (1845) in which he reconciled the notion of a given primitive deposit of faith with the evolutionary principle of development and change in all human ideas, systems and institutions. After his conversion Newman's most startling and influential work was his *Apologia pro Vita Sua* (1864). It was a 'History of My Religious Opinions' that marked the culmination of a controversy sparked off by a rash accusation made against him by Charles Kingsley in *Macmillan's Magazine*: 'Truth for its own sake has never been a virtue with the Roman clergy. Father Newman informs us that it need not be, and on the whole ought not to be . . .'. The injustice of the charge brought a riposte from Newman and an exchange of public correspondence in which Kingsley wriggled unworthily out of direct apology or recantation. He was trapped by Newman's remorseless logic, devastating irony and unfailing refusal to lose his temper or his head. Newman has indeed been called the most brilliant polemicist in our literature. The *Apologia* is also a work of winning charm and grace, a moving personal document. Other influential books include *The Grammar of Assent* (1870), perhaps his most important philosophical work, and *The Idea of a University* (1873), the product of his years as first Rector of the Catholic University of Ireland (1854–8). This was the university to be attended decades later by James Joyce, and it is interesting that Joyce's *alter ego*, the young Stephen Dedalus of *A Portrait of the Artist as a Young Man* proclaims Newman the greatest writer of prose. Sentences from Newman's works, even from *The Grammar of Assent*, run through Stephen Dedalus's mind, their mellifluous phrases and haunting cadences exercising their charm.

Walter Pater

If one were to seek comparable distinction in Victorian prose one might well turn to Walter Pater (1839–94). His subtly woven sentences, whose modulations seem too carefully contrived ever to perturb or excite, flow with the hypnotic compulsiveness of plainsong. George Moore pin-pointed the strangely devitalised dignity of Pater's prose when he said, 'In the pages of Pater the English language lies in state.' An Oxford don, Pater spent most of his life moving between Oxford and London. His early work, *Studies in the History of the Renaissance* (1873), shows him as the apostle of aestheticism. Like Arnold he defines the critic's first duty as 'to see the object as in itself it really is', but he parts from Arnold's moral emphasis on building the good life on 'the best that has been thought and said' in literature. For Pater stresses man's isolation, an isolation fractured only by the experience of the senses which all men share. Thus the enrichment of the personality through contemplation of a work of art is a matter of analysing the pleasurable sensations produced by the 'fairer forms of nature and human life'. This doctrine is not quite so devoid of a moral element as it might seem, in that Pater recognises the 'artistic and accomplished forms of human life' as among the objects with which the critic must deal.

Pater's most celebrated work is the 'novel', *Marius the Epicurean* (1885). It tells the story of the youth and development of Marius against the background of the Rome of Marcus Aurelius in the second century. Marius, early orphaned, loses his faith in the Roman religion of the household gods and encounters a handsome young aesthete, Flavian, whose moral corruption exemplifies pagan decadence and whose death moves Marius to an emotional and intellectual crisis in the face of mortality. He becomes secretary to Marcus Aurelius in Rome and is lured in turn by epicureanism and by the Emperor's stoicism, but can find no answer to the disillusionment produced by the riddle of death until he meets a community of Christians. By contact with Christian martyrdom he learns that death can be joyful, and ultimately he sacrifices his own life to save his friend Cornelius. But the conclusion has its ironic overtones. Marius is not so much a believer saved by grace as an artist adding the final role to his explorations.

Pater emptied Ruskinism as well as Arnoldism of its ethical content, and then tried to subsume the religious as an adjunct of aesthetic self-nourishment. The autobiographical element in *Marius the Epicurean* is persistent, and the civilisational condition of Antonine Rome mirrors that of Victorian England. As the prophet of aestheticism Pater was naturally associated with Rossetti, Swinburne and Burne-Jones. The Pre-Raphaelite movement impinged on the Anglo-Catholic movement: indeed Pater, too, went through an Anglo-Catholic phase in his youth. The connections between such seemingly diverse tendencies can be gleaned from Newman's novel, *Loss and Gain* (1848). It presents a young Oxford freshman who 'having been spoilt at home, and having plenty of money, professed to be an *aesthetic*, and kept his college authorities in a perpetual fidget lest he should some morning wake up a Papist!'

Oscar Wilde

In pursuing the ideal of the hero who is renewed through an aesthetic synthesis of sensuous response to things, Pater had a seriousness of purpose evidenced by his determination that his ideal should subsume and transcend all kinds of human excellence, moral and spiritual. But when Oscar Wilde (1854–1900) cottoned on to Pater's thinking, it was to empty it of all seriousness and indeed to parody it in word and deed. The contrast between the two personalities is significant. Pater was a reticent, isolated, quiet-voiced figure whose persona remains mysteriously elusive. Wilde was a garrulous, flamboyant entertainer playing the Irishman to the admiring English. He prefaces his most substantial prose work, *The Picture of Dorian Gray* (1891), with a collection of aphorisms seemingly calculated to infuriate the conventionally minded public:

> There is no such thing as a moral or an immoral book. Books are well written, or badly written. That is all . . . No artist has ethical sympathies. An ethical sympathy in an artist is an unpardonable mannerism of style . . . We can forgive a man for making a useful thing as long as he does not admire it . . . All art is quite useless.

The story that follows, however, is a parable showing how too high an evaluation of physical beauty can be morally corrupting. Dorian Gray turns evil into a mere mode for realising the beautiful and in the process is destroyed. He is a handsome young man who has his portrait painted by Basil Hallwood. Gray falls in love with his own beauty and prays that 'the portrait should bear the burden of his days and he keep the unsullied splendour of eternal youth'. The prayer is granted. Gray, corrupted by the amoral Lord Henry Wotton, watches the portrait reveal his growing cruelty and viciousness as well as his advancing years, while he personally retains his youth and beauty. When he finally stabs the painting it is restored to its original form and he himself is found with the knife through his heart, bearing all the marks of his age and degeneracy.

Wilde's critical works, 'The Decay of Lying' and 'The Critic as Artist' which both appeared in the collection of essays, *Intentions* (1891), played their part in making him suspect to his contemporaries. It was not that Wilde was fundamentally a mere slave to paradox and flippancy, but that his artistic ideals and his way of challenging the public in expressing them made him suspect as such, and then he tended to play up to the role ascribed to him. He denied that art was an imitation of life: rather it offered delights which life itself could not provide. It was the artist's business to exercise his imagination in the creation of beauty, untrammelled by canons of naturalism or morality. All he could fruitfully discuss in relation to his art would be matters of technique. For Wilde the validity of an artistic standpoint was that of an attitude which could never be permanent, let alone absolute. Thus he could logically write of his own work: 'Not that I agree with everything in this essay. There is much with which I entirely disagree.' Such assertions, like the Preface to *Dorian Gray*, suggested at best a flippant evasiveness, at worst sheer verbal clowning, and it is significant in this respect that his major critical works, 'The Decay of Lying' and 'The Critic as Artist', both took the form of dialogue between dandified young men ever ready with cheerful digression and clever witticisms. Thus both Wilde's persona and his method tended to put obstacles in the way of attempts to take his critical theory seriously.

A. W. Kinglake, George Borrow, Richard Jefferies

Among minor classics of the Victorian age are a handful of travel books. They include those of the novelist Robert Louis Stevenson (1850–94), his *Travels with a Donkey in the Cévennes* (1879) and *An Inland Voyage* (1878), the record of a canoe tour in Belgium and France. A lesser-known writer, Alexander William Kinglake (1809–91), gave an account of his travels in the Middle East in his *Eothen, or Traces of Travel Brought Home from the East* (1844) ('Eothen' means 'dawn-wards'). He sought successfully to avoid any display of pedantry and to achieve a chatty, personal relationship with his reader. The contrast between the accepted rational conventions of the West and the 'splendour and havoc of the East' gives Kinglake the opportunity for quiet satire of what he has left behind. At the same time he records the real perils encountered and discomforts endured with an engagingly deflationary air. Among the memorable episodes is an encounter with Lady Hester Stanhope (1776–1839), who had been housekeeper to her uncle, William Pitt the Younger, and who left England for good in 1810 and set up a somewhat despotic establishment in a ruined convent in the Lebanon. A legendary eccentric, she naturally became a tourist attraction for European travellers.

Kinglake's subtly modulated escapism made an appeal to the sophisticated reader far different from the appeal of George Borrow (1803–81), a much-travelled writer who roamed Europe for several years, attaching himself to gypsies, and later went to Russia, Spain and Portugal as agent for the British and Foreign Bible Society. He published a record of adventures in *The Bible in Spain* (1843), and then in the semi-fictional *Lavengro, The Scholar – The Gypsy – The Priest* (1851) told the story of his own life and how he became acquainted with gypsies, tinkers and a range of criminal types. The story is continued in the sequel, *The Romany Rye* (1857). A writer who could speak about the world's outcasts and drop-outs with sympathy and enthusiasm naturally gained the public's ear. Borrow had much to reveal of gypsy lore, of low life seen from the inside, and of the world as viewed by its weird personalities.

Richard Jefferies (1848–87) tried his hand unsuccessfully at novels of social life before making his name as journalist and essayist of country life. His exact descriptions of the detail of the rural scene and his intense physical awareness were balanced by scorn of the contemporary literary world and of book-learning in general. *Bevis: The Story of a Boy* (1882) is a story of country childhood and boyhood based largely on Jefferies's own youth on his father's farm in Wiltshire. *The Story of My Heart* (1883) is an autobiographical novel tracing his emotional and spiritual development from the age of eighteen. Jefferies's pantheistic sense of kinship with 'the visible universe' made him scornful of Christianity. He speaks of a 'soul-life' sensed within the natural order and tells how through the touch of earth and grass, air and flower, he made contact with 'the unutterable existence infinitely higher than deity'. Thus he lost his sense of separateness, felt himself 'a part of the whole', and likewise found his awareness of time submerged in a present eternity. Like Kinglake's spirited truancy from the conventional rationalities of European civilisation and Borrow's heady plunge into the company of outrageous characters on the periphery of the social order, Jefferies's vaguely mystical embrace of the natural world reflects that same mood of unease with the massive civilisational achievements of the Victorian age which possessed so many of the great prose-writers reviewed in this study.

Part 6

Suggestions for further reading

NOVELS BY Victorian writers surveyed here are for the most part readily available, many of them in editions with introductions especially designed for students. Similarly, in the case of Victorian poets and prose writers, selections from their works with introductions and notes are widely available. The following lists of books on the Victorian novel and Victorian poetry draw attention to biographical and critical studies which will deepen the student's understanding of the writers and their works. The bibliographical section on Victorian drama, however, also lists specific texts in the case of those playwrights whose work is not widely available. The bibliographical section on Victorian prose includes alongside books about the influential thinkers of the period a number of studies concerned with the age's literature as a whole or with specific aspects of it. Finally, under the heading 'General historical background', some books are recommended which will enrich understanding of the Victorian social scene and the historical developments of the age.

The Victorian novel

CAREY, JOHN: *Thackeray, Prodigal Genius*, Faber and Faber, London, 1977.

COHEN, NORTON: *Rider Haggard: His Life and Work*, Macmillan, London, 1968.

COLLINS, BRENDA: *Charles Kingsley, The Lion of Eversley*, Constable, London, 1975.

DRABBLE, MARGARET (ED.): *The Genius of Thomas Hardy*, Weidenfeld and Nicolson, London, 1976.

DUNLEAVY, JANET E.: *George Moore in Perspective*, Colin Smythe, Gerrards Cross, Bucks, 1983.

DYSON, A. E.: *The Inimitable Dickens*, Macmillan, London, 1970.

GERIN, WINIFRED: *Emily Brontë: A Biography*, Oxford University Press, Oxford, 1972.

GERIN, WINIFRED: *Elizabeth Gaskell, A Biography*, Oxford University Press, Oxford, 1972.

GITTINGS, ROBERT: *Young Thomas Hardy*, Heinemann, London, 1975.

GITTINGS, ROBERT: *The Older Hardy*, Heinemann, London, 1978.

GROSS, JOHN (ED.): *Rudyard Kipling, The Man, His Work, and His World*, Weidenfeld and Nicolson, London, 1972.

HAIGHT, GORDON S.: *George Eliot, A Biography*, Clarendon Press, Oxford, 1968.

HARDWICK, MICHAEL: *The Osprey Guide to Anthony Trollope*, Osprey, London, 1974.

HARVEY, JOHN: *Victorian Novels and their Illustrators*, Sidgwick and Jackson, London, 1970.

HENNESSY, JAMES POPE: *Anthony Trollope*, Jonathan Cape, London, 1971.

LASKI, MARGHANITA: *George Eliot and Her World*, Thames and Hudson, London, 1973.

LEE, BRIAN: *The Novels of Henry James*, Edward Arnold, London, 1978.

LLOYD EVANS, BARBARA and GARETH: *Everyman's Companion to the Brontës*, Dent, London, 1985.

LUCAS, JOHN: *The Melancholy Man: A Study of Dickens's Novels*, Methuen, London, 1970.

MONSARRAT, ANN: *An Uneasy Victorian: Thackeray the Man*, Cassell, London, 1980.

MOORE, HARRY T.: *Henry James and His World*, Thames and Hudson, London, 1974.

PETERS, MARGOT: *The Unquiet Soul: A Biography of Charlotte Brontë*, Hodder and Stoughton, London, 1975.

SNOW, C. P.: *Trollope*, Macmillan, London, 1975.

STERN, G. B.: *Robert Louis Stevenson*, Longman, Harlow, rev. 1971.

TINDALL, GILLIAN: *The Born Exile: George Gissing*, Temple Smith, London, 1974.

WILLIAMS, DAVID: *George Meredith: His Life and Lost Love*, Hamish Hamilton, London, 1977.

WILSON, ANGUS: *The World of Charles Dickens*, Martin Secker and Warburg, London, 1970.

Victorian poetry

ARMSTRONG, ISOBEL: *Arthur Hugh Clough*, Longmans Green, London, 1962.

BATTISCOMBE, GEORGINA: *Christina Rossetti: A Divided Life*, Constable, London, 1949.

BERGONZI, BERNARD: *Gerard Manley Hopkins* (Masters of World Literature), Macmillan, London, 1977.

DOBBS, BRIAN and JUDY: *Dantë Gabriel Rossetti: An Alien Victorian*, Macdonald and Jane's, London, 1977.

EVANS, IFOR: *English Poetry in the Later Nineteenth Century*, Methuen, London, rev. 1966.

FLOWERS, BETTY S.: *Browning and the Modern Tradition*, Macmillan, London, 1976.

FULLER, JEAN OVERTON: *Swinburne: A Critical Biography*, Chatto and Windus, London, 1968.

GRAVES, R. P.: *A. E. Housman, The Scholar Poet*, Routledge and Kegan Paul, London, 1979.

HAYTER, ALETHEA: *Elizabeth Barrett Browning*, Longmans, Green, Harlow, 1965.

HENDERSON, PHILIP: *Swinburne, the Portrait of a Poet*, Routledge and Kegan Paul, London, 1974.

HENDERSON, PHILIP: *William Morris*, Longmans, Green, London, 1952.

HENDERSON, PHILIP: *Tennyson, Poet and Prophet*, Routledge and Kegan Paul, London, 1978.

JUMP, J. D.: *Matthew Arnold*, Longmans, Green, London, 1955.

LINDSAY, JACK: *William Morris*, Constable, London, 1975.

MACKENZIE, NORMAN: *Gerard Manley Hopkins* (Reader's Guide Series), Thames and Hudson, London, 1981.

MARTIN, ROBERT BERNARD: *Tennyson: The Unquiet Heart, A Biography*, Faber and Faber, London, 1980.

REID, J. C.: *The Mind and Art of Coventry Patmore*, Greenwood Press, London, 1978.

RICHARDSON, JOANNA (ED.): *Fitzgerald: Selected Works*, Rupert Hart-Davis, London, 1962.

RICHARDSON, JOANNA: *Edward Fitzgerald*, Longmans, Green, London, 1960.

ROWSE, A. L.: *Matthew Arnold, Poet and Prophet*, Thames and Hudson, London, 1976.

Victorian drama

BAILY, LESLIE: *Gilbert and Sullivan and their World*, Thames and Hudson, London, 1973.

BOOTH, MICHAEL R. (ED.): *English Plays of the Nineteenth Century* (5 vols): I, *Dramas 1800–1850*; II, *Dramas 1850–1900*; III, *Comedies*; IV, *Farces*; V, *Pantomimes, Extravanganzas, & Burlesques*, Clarendon Press, Oxford, 1969, 1973, 1976.

*BANHAM, MARTIN (ED.): *Plays by Tom Taylor*, Cambridge University Press, Cambridge, 1984.

DUNKEL, W. B.: *Sir Arthur Pinero: A Critical Biography with Letters*, Kennikat Press, New York, 1941.

FAWKES, RICHARD: *Dion Boucicault: A Biography*, Quartet Books, London, 1979.

HARDWICKE, MICHAEL and MOLLIE: *The Bernard Shaw Companion*, John Murray, London, 1973.

*JACKSON, RUSSELL (ED.): *Plays by Henry Arthur Jones*, Cambridge University Press, Cambridge, 1982.

PINE, RICHARD: *Oscar Wilde*, Gill and Macmillan, Dublin, 1983.

PURDOM, C. B.: *A Guide to the Plays of Bernard Shaw*, Methuen, London, 1963.

ROWELL, GEORGE: *The Victorian Stage, A Survey*, Cambridge University Press, Cambridge, 1978.

ROWELL, GEORGE: *Theatre in the Age of Irving*, Basil Blackwell, Oxford, 1981.

ROWELL, GEORGE (ED.): *Nineteenth-Century Plays*, Oxford University Press, Oxford, 1972.

*ROWELL, GEORGE (ED.): *Plays by Sir Arthur Wing Pinero*, Cambridge University Press, Cambridge, 1986.

SMITH, JAMES L. (ED.): *Victorian Melodramas*, Dent, London, 1976.

SOUTHERN, RICHARD: *The Victorian Theatre: A Pictorial Survey*, David and Charles, Newton Abbot, 1970.

*THOMSON, PETER (ED,): *Plays by Dion Boucicault*, Cambridge University Press, Cambridge, 1984.

*TYDEMAN, WILLIAM: *Plays by Tom Robertson*, Cambridge University Press, Cambridge, 1982.

Victorian thinkers and the Victorian literary scene

BELL, QUENTIN: *Ruskin*, Hogarth Press, London, new edition 1978.

CAMERON, J.M.: *John Henry Newman*, Longmans, Green, London, 1956.

CAMPBELL, IAN: *Thomas Carlyle*, Hamish Hamilton, London, 1974.

CHAPMAN, RAYMOND: *The Victorian Debate: English Literature and Society, 1832–1901*, Weidenfeld and Nicolson, London, 1968.

COLLIS, JOHN STEWART: *The Carlyles*, Sidgwick and Jackson, London, 1971.

GAUNT, WILLIAM: *The Aesthetic Adventure*, Jonathan Cape, London, 1945.

HILTON, TIMOTHY: *The Pre-Raphaelites*, Thames and Hudson, London, 1970.

HUNT, JOHN DIXON: *The Wider Sea: A Life of John Ruskin*, Dent, London, 1982.

HUXLEY, JULIAN and KETTLEWELL, H. B. D.: *Charles Darwin and His World*, Thames and Hudson, London, 1965.

KEATING, P. J.: *The Working Classes in Victorian Fiction*, Routledge and Kegan Paul, London, 1971.

*These volumes in the 'British and American Playwrights' series contain substantial critical and biographical introductions.

LEVEY, MICHAEL: *The Case of Walter Pater*, Thames and Hudson, London, 1978.

MORRISON, N. BRYSSON: *True Minds: The Marriage of Thomas and Jane Carlyle*, Dent, London, 1974.

STONYK, MARGARET: *Nineteenth-Century English Literature* (The Macmillan History of Literature), Macmillan, London, 1983.

TILLOTSON, GEOFFREY: *A View of Victorian Literature*, Clarendon Press, Oxford, 1978.

TREVOR, MERIOL: *Newman: Light in Winter*, Macmillan, London, 1962.

General historical background

AVERY, GILLIAN: *Victorian People*, Collins, London, 1970.

BENSON, E. F.: *As We Were: A Victorian Peep-Show*, The Hogarth Press, London, new edition 1985.

BRIGGS, ASA (ED.): *The Nineteenth Century: The Contradictions of Progress*, Thames and Hudson, London, 1970.

BRIGGS, ASA: *Victorian People; A Re-assessment of Persons and Themes*, Penguin, Harmondsworth, 1954.

CHESNEY, KELLOW: *The Victorian Underworld*, Penguin, Harmondsworth, 1970.

CLARK, G. KITSON: *An Expanding Society: Britain 1830–1900*, Cambridge University Press, Cambridge, 1967.

DRABBLE, MARGARET: *For Queen and Country: Britain in the Victorian Age*, Andre Deutsch, London, 1978.

EVANS, JOAN: *The Victorians*, Cambridge University Press, Cambridge, 1966.

HUGGETT, FRANK E.: *Carriages at Eight: Horsedrawn Society in Victorian and Edwardian Times*, Lutterworth Press, London, 1979.

PEARL, CYRIL: *Victorian Patchwork*, Heinemann, London, 1972.

PETRIE, SIR CHARLES: *Great Beginnings in the Age of Queen Victoria*, Macmillan, London, 1967.

PRIESTLEY, J. B.: *Victoria's Heyday*, Penguin, Harmondsworth, 1974.

SEAMAN, L. C. B.: *Victorian England: Aspects of English and Imperial History 1837–1901*, Methuen, London, 1973.

STRACHEY, LYTTON: *Queen Victoria*, Chatto and Windus, London, 1921.

WOODHAM-SMITH, CECIL: *Queen Victoria, Her Life and Times*, Hamish Hamilton, London, 1972; Sphere Books, 1975.

Index

The index lists authors and selected works.

The author of this Handbook

HARRY BLAMIRES is a graduate of the University of Oxford, where he studied English Language and Literature. He spent a large part of his teaching life as Head of the English department at King Alfred's College, Winchester, but retired early to turn to full-time writing in 1976. His publications include works of fiction and theology as well as literary history and critical books. He has contributed *Studying James Joyce* (1986), an introduction to Joyce's work as a whole, to the York Handbooks series, and his earlier work, *The Bloomsday Book* (Methuen, 1966), has become the standard page-by-page guide to Joyce's *Ulysses*. His *Short History of English Literature* (Methuen, 1974, revised edition 1984) established his reputation as a literary historian. His more recent books include *Twentieth-Century English Literature* (Macmillan, 1982), a volume in the Macmillan History of Literature (ed. A. N. Jeffares), and *A Guide to Twentieth-Century Literature in English* (Methuen, 1983), which he edited and to which he contributed the articles on the writers of the United Kingdom and Ireland.